Advance Praise for

The Afternoon of Christianity

"Tomáš Halík is one of the most important public intellectuals of our time, heroic in his engagement with the most challenging questions for church and society." —Janet Soskice, author of *The Sisters of Sinai*

"Tomáš Halík is remarkable, always, for his intellectual balance and his pastoral insight. He sees modernity as an opportunity for a recovery of a genuine biblical vision, deeply traditional, in a way that can enliven even this 'afternoon' of Christianity, which, he reminds us, is neither an evening nor a night." —John C. Cavadini, co-editor of *Pope Francis and the Event of Encounter*

"*The Afternoon of Christianity* serves to shine a light on the hope that is in the Church and the world. Halík's ecclesiology is one that is badly needed in today's Church, and one from which we must all learn if we are to be the community that we are called to be." —Daniel Cosacchi, vice president for mission and ministry at the University of Scranton

"When one happens upon a work like Tomáš Halík's *The Afternoon of Christianity*, one experiences a most refreshing and capacious reflection on Christian faith's necessary maturation through the crucible of doubt. A Christianity and a Church attentive to the Spirit, less concerned with power, more devoted to the spiritual passion that afflicted the heart of the great mystics, unanxious over discovering God in all things, more humble and able to forgive as we have been forgiven—such are the hues in Halík's vision of Christianity's next form. A welcome reminder that love alone is credible." —Jordan Daniel Wood, author of *The Whole Mystery of Christ*

"This book is key to understanding Pope Francis's effort to lead Catholicism and religion in general in a period not primarily of structural or institutional reform, but of spiritual deepening in light of the global crisis. Halík describes the present suffering not as agony but as pangs of labor." —Massimo Faggioli, author of *The Liminal Papacy of Pope Francis*

"Clearly and engagingly written, this book is a visionary product of a major thinker whose work cannot be pigeonholed as religious or spiritual but rather, by interweaving philosophy, theology, sociology, and psychology, seeks to address the human condition in toto." —William A. Barbieri Jr., editor of *At the Limits of the Secular*

The Afternoon of Christianity

The Afternoon of Christianity

THE COURAGE TO CHANGE

TOMÁŠ HALÍK

Translated by
GERALD TURNER

UNIVERSITY OF NOTRE DAME PRESS
Notre Dame, Indiana

University of Notre Dame Press
Notre Dame, Indiana 46556
undpress.nd.edu

Published in the United States of America

This publication was produced with the support of the project
"Creativity and Adaptability as a prerequisite for Europe's success in
an interconnected world," reg. no.: CZ.02.1.01/0.0/0.0/16_019/0000734,
financed by the European Regional Development Fund.

Library of Congress Control Number: 2023946550

ISBN: 978-0-268-20747-2 (Hardback)
ISBN: 978-0-268-20749-6 (WebPDF)
ISBN: 978-0-268-20746-5 (Epub3)

Dedicated to Pope Francis with reverence and gratitude.

Look, I am doing something new, now it emerges; can you not see it? Yes, I am making a road in the desert and rivers in wastelands.

—Isaiah 43:19

God is everywhere and we have to know how to find Him in all things. . . . Yes, in this quest to seek and find God in all things there is still an area of uncertainty. There must be. If a person says that he met God with total certainty and is not touched by a margin of uncertainty, then this is not good. For me, this is an important key. If one has the answers to all the questions— that is the proof that God is not with him. It means that he is a false prophet using religion for himself. The great leaders of the people of God, like Moses, have always left room for doubt. You must leave room for the Lord, not for our certainties; we must be humble. . . .

Abraham leaves his home without knowing where he was going, by faith. . . . Our life is not given to us like an opera libretto, in which all is written down; but it means going, walking, doing, searching, seeing. . . . We must enter into the adventure of the quest for meeting God; we must let God search and encounter us. . . . I have a dogmatic certainty: God is in every person's life.

—Pope Francis, *My Door Is Always Open*

CONTENTS

PREFACE

"We are not living an epoch of change so much as an epochal change," Pope Francis says.[1] The forms of religions and their roles in different societies and cultures are also changing. Secularization has not brought about the end of religion but rather its transformation. While some forms of religion are experiencing major upheavals, others are so vibrant that they have transcended their former boundaries. Traditional religious institutions have lost their monopoly on religion. The culminating process of globalization is encountering resistance: manifestations of populism, nationalism, and fundamentalism are on the rise. The world community of Christians is not united—today the greatest differences are not between churches but within them. Differences in doctrine, and in religious and political attitudes, often have roots hidden in the deeper layers of people's intellectual and spiritual lives. Sometimes people reciting the same creed in the same church pew have very different ideas about God. Among the transformations of today's spiritual scene is the collapse of the wall between "believers" and "nonbelievers"; noisy minorities of dogmatic believers and militant atheists are being marginalized, while there is a growing number of those in whose minds and hearts faith (in the sense of "proto-faith") and unbelief (in the sense of doubting skepticism) are intertwined. I am finishing this book in the midst of a coronavirus pandemic; around me many sick people die daily in overcrowded hospitals, and many of the living and healthy are slipping into existential insecurity. The certitudes of our world are also shaken by this experience. In addition to the long-standing crisis of traditional religious certitudes, there is also a crisis of traditional secular certitudes, especially the belief in humans' dominion over nature and their own destiny. The state of the Catholic Church today in many ways resembles the situation just before the Reformation. When an unsuspected number of cases of sexual and psychological abuse were exposed, it shook the credibility of the Church and raised many questions about the whole system of the Church. I regarded the closed and empty churches during the coronavirus pandemic as a prophetic warning sign: this may soon be the state of the Church if it does not undergo a transformation. Certain inspiration can be found in the Catholic Reformation, which was carried on by courageous mystics such as John of the Cross, Teresa of Avila, Ignatius of Loyola, and many others who, through their original spiritual experience, enriched both the theological reflection on faith and the visible form and practice of the Church. The current reform efforts cannot remain limited to changes in some institutional structures and a few paragraphs in the catechism, the code of canon law, and the moral textbooks. The fruitfulness of the reform and the future vibrancy of the Church depend on a reconnection with the deep spiritual and existential dimension of faith. I regard the present crisis as a crossroads where the possibility of moving into a new "afternoon" epoch in the history of Christianity presents itself. Also, through its painful experiences, a shaken Christianity can—like a wounded physician—unleash the therapeutic potential of faith. If the churches manage to resist the temptations of self-centeredness as well as collective narcissism, clericalism, isolationism, and provincialism, they can make a significant contribution to a new, wider, and deeper ecumenism. The new ecumenism is about more than the unity of Christians; the renewal of faith can be a step toward the "universal fraternity" that is the great theme of Pope Francis's pontificate. It can help the human family move not toward a clash of civilizations but toward the formation of a *civitas oecumenica*—a culture of communication, sharing, and respect for diversity.

In history, God is revealed in the faith, love, and hope of people, even people on the margins of the churches and beyond their visible boundaries. The search for God "in all things" and in all historical situations frees our life from monological self-absorption and transforms it into dialogical openness. Here I see a sign of the times and a light of hope even in difficult times. This is the hope that this book aims to serve.

ACKNOWLEDGEMENTS

I would like to thank in particular the University of Notre Dame and the Templeton Foundation for providing me with the opportunity for an intensive exchange of ideas with a number of American theologians, sociologists, and philosophers during my two academic stays at the Institute for Advanced Study in 2015 and 2017. I would also like to thank the University of Oxford for inviting me to actively participate in a stimulating conference on religion in public life in 2017. I thank the Jesuit university of Boston College, where I served as a visiting professor in early 2020, and Harvard University professors for inspiring conversations in 2018 and 2020. I am also grateful to other theologians, philosophers, and church leaders who have helped me to broaden my perspective during study and lecture tours in Europe, Australia, the USA, Asia, and Africa over the past few years.

For critical comments, I thank friends who kindly read my manuscript and the responsible editor, Barbora Čiháková, for her help in the final editing of the text.

ONE

Faith in Motion

"We have empty hands and empty nets, we worked all night and caught nothing," said the tired and frustrated Galilean fishermen to the wandering preacher standing on the shore of the new day.

Many Christians in a large part of our Western world have similar feelings at this time. Churches, monasteries, and seminaries are being emptied, and tens of thousands are leaving the Church. The dark shadows of the recent past are depriving the churches of credibility. Christians are divided—today the differences are not primarily between churches but within them. The Christian faith no longer confronts militant atheism or harsh persecution, which might awaken and mobilize believers, but instead there is a far greater danger—indifference.

The prophet from Nazareth chose such a moment of weariness and frustration to address his future disciples for the first time. Disappointed fishermen after a sleepless night were not the best-disposed audience for his sermon on the coming kingdom. Yet they manifested what constitutes the antechamber and portal of faith: the courage to trust. "Try again," ran his first sermon, "go to the deeps and spread your nets!"[1]

Even at this time of weariness and frustration, we need to give Christianity another try. Trying again does not mean doing the same thing over again, including repeating old mistakes. It means going deeper, waiting attentively, and being ready to act.

This book is a book about the transformations of faith in human lives and in history. I ask what transformations are taking place today, and what possible future forms of Christianity are already being signaled in many of the present crises. As at every period of significant historical change, the position and role of faith in society and the forms of its self-expression in culture are changing. In the face of these many changes, we must always question anew the identity of our faith. What does it consist in and what reveals its *Christian* character? This is a book about faith as a journey in search of God in the midst of a changing world, about lived faith, the act of faith, how we believe (*fides qua*) rather than what we believe (*fides quae*), what is the "object" of faith. By faith, I mean a certain attitude of life, an orientation, a way of being in the world and how we understand it, rather than mere "religious beliefs" and opinions; I am interested in *faith* rather than *beliefs*.

We encounter the *concept* of faith (with the Hebrew verb *heemin*) in the Jewish prophets of the Axial Age (around the fifth century BC);[2] the *phenomenon* of faith itself is older, however. I will leave aside the debate about whether faith in the sense of an act of trust, a personal relationship to the transcendent, is a completely original biblical contribution to the spiritual history of humanity; or whether and to what extent faith in this sense—or corresponding phenomena— is already part of prebiblical religions and spiritualities; or whether faith can be regarded as an anthropological constant, an essential part of humanity as such. My focus is on that strand of the history of faith that has its roots in Judaism and continues in Christianity, while at the same time transcending Christianity in its traditional ecclesiastical form.[3]

As faith made its way through history, the Hebrew Bible imprinted two essential features on it: the experience of the Exodus, the journey from slavery to freedom (faith has a *pilgrim nature*); and the incarnation of faith in the practice of justice and solidarity—the manifestation of true faith, according to the prophets, is to "take in the orphan and stand up for the widow."[4] The archetype of the believer is Abraham, the "father of believers," who is said to have set out on a journey without knowing where he was going.[5] Faith, especially the faith of the prophets, is in tension not only with magic but also with the temple religion of priests and sacrificial rituals. Jesus draws on this prophetic lineage: at the heart of his preaching is a call for transformation, conversion (*metanoia*).

Martin Buber distinguished between two types of faith: the faith denoted by the Hebrew word *emunah* (faith as trust) and the faith expressed by the Greek word *pistis* ("faith in," "faith with an object"). The former type was associated with Judaism and the latter with Christianity, especially Paul the apostle's faith in Christ.[6] This distinction between two types of faith is a kind of analogy with the Latin distinction between *fides qua* and *fides quae*. Unlike Buber, I am convinced that in Christianity faith does not lose its *emunah* nature, that faith in Christ does not have to mean its objectification. Christian faith is not primarily a cultlike worship of the person of Jesus but is the path of following Christ. Following Christ does not mean imitating Jesus of Nazareth as a historical person from the distant past (as the original Latin title of Thomas à Kempis's famous devotional manual *The Imitation of Christ* might be understood). Rather, it is a journey toward and with Jesus, the one who declared of himself "I am the way" and promised the disciples that they would do even greater deeds than he did. Faith in Christ is a journey of trust and courage, of love and faithfulness; it is a movement toward the future that Christ inaugurated and to which he extends an invitation.

This dynamic understanding of Christianity presupposes a certain type of Christology: namely, a conception of Christ as the alpha and omega of the development of all creation.[7]

Paul accomplished the first radical reform of early Christianity: he transformed it from a Jewish sect by transplanting it into the *oecumene*—the sphere of Roman civilization. I consider this to be Christianity's radical contribution to the history of faith: namely, its emphasis on its universal mission. Christianity, in Paul's terms, transcends the previously unbridgeable boundaries between religions and cultures (it made no difference if one was a Jew or a Greek—a pagan), the boundaries of social stratification (it didn't matter if one was free or a slave—a "speaking tool" without rights in the Roman world), and the boundaries of clearly defined gender roles (it didn't matter whether one was male or female).[8]

I see this Pauline universalism as the Church's ongoing mission in history. Christianity must always cherish and extend this radical openness. The present-day form of this universalism is ecumenism, the opposite of arrogant ideological imperialism. If Christianity is to overcome the crisis of its many previous manifestations and become an inspiring response to the challenges of this time of great civilizational change, it must boldly transcend its previous mental and institutional boundaries. The time has come for Christianity to transcend itself. We will return to this idea repeatedly in this book.

If we want to learn something essential about other people's faith, we should disregard whether or not they believe in God, what their views on God's existence are, or what their church or religious affiliation is. What should interest us is what role God plays in their lives, *how* they believe, how they live out their faith (in their inner world and in their relationships), how their faith is transformed during their lives and how it transforms their lives—and whether, how, and to what extent their faith transforms the world in which they live. It is only the practice of faith—involving both believers' inner spiritual life and their life in society—that tells us what kind of God they do and do not believe in. Faith as *emunah*, as "ontological proto-faith," is not a mere emotional fideism, a vague pious feeling. It would be wrong, of course, to underestimate the content of faith (*fides quae*) and to divorce it from the act of faith. However, the existential element of faith, the act of faith embodied in life practice, takes precedence in several respects over its content and the cognitive aspect.

The object of faith is in a sense implicit in the act of faith, in the life of believers. Therefore, people's life experience alone can provide the hermeneutical key to knowing what they really believe, what they base their lives on, and not just what they profess verbally.

This understanding of faith also allows us to speak of the "faith of unbelievers" (those who claim not to believe) and the "unbelief of believers" (those who claim to believe). The concept of implicit faith is already to be found in the New Testament—in the Gospel of Matthew and in the Letter of James: faith contained even "anonymously" in the way one lives one's life. One can show one's faith through one's works, as we read in the Letter of James.[9] Sometimes one can be surprised by the faith implicit in one's own actions: according to Matthew's Gospel, those who took care of the needy encountered Christ without knowing it.[10] The ancient author Theophilus of Antioch writes: "If you say, 'Show me your God,' I would reply, 'Show me yourself, and I will show you my God.'"[11]

A person's way of being human is the most authentic expression of their belief or unbelief. A person's life speaks more about their faith than what they think or say about God. But when we talk about the way people live, let us beware of reducing the totality of life to the realm of morality, virtues, and sins; the way people live, the way they are, also includes their emotional richness, their imagination and creativity, their sense of beauty and sense of humor, their capacity for empathy, and a host of other qualities. How one fulfills the task of being human speaks volumes about the kind of person one is and the kind of faith that inspires and informs one's life.

TWO

Faith as Experience of Mystery

Both faith and lack of faith reside in a much deeper dimension of the human person than the conscious and rational realm; they reside in the preconscious and unconscious structures of people's mental lives, which are the focus of depth psychology. The idea that faith is something we can readily understand and soon be done with, something we can easily categorize and measure empirically, has caused a lot of misunderstandings and misconceptions. People's responses to magazine polls and opinion surveys, or census data, do not tell us much about their faith. To answer the question of whether or not they believe in God, many people today feel the need to add a "but"; I also answer that question by saying, "I do—but perhaps not in the God you have in mind."

Faith, as I understand it in this book, is found not only in the lives of people who identify themselves as religious believers but also in an implicit, anonymous form, in the spiritual search of men and women beyond the visible boundaries of religious doctrines and institutions. Secular spirituality also belongs to the history of faith.[1]

However, I do not intend for this broad understanding of faith to blur the concept of faith and render it vague by the banal assertion that "everyone believes in something" and that even a nonbeliever is in some sense a believer. I am talking about "the unbelief of believers" and "the belief of nonbelievers"; however, by claiming the faith of non-believers, I do not intend to arrogantly colonize the world of non-believers, to disrespect their own self-understanding, to impose on them something that is alien to them. I only want to show the broader context of the phenomenon of faith; what faith is and what it is not must be explored again and again through a careful study of the various forms of belief and unbelief.

Belief and unbelief are not "objective realities" existing independently of the observer. They are different interpretations of the world, and they too are interpreted differently. These interpretations are primarily dependent on the observer, on their "pre-understandings," determined by their culture, language, experience, point of view, and (mostly unconsidered) intentions. The current spiritual situation can be variously described as a decline of religion, a crisis of faith or of the Church, a religious and spiritual renaissance, a "return of religion," a transformation of religion into spirituality or ideologies of political identity, a pluralization of religion or individualization of faith, or an opportunity for a new evangelization. For all these interpretations we can find many arguments and support in empirical research. These interpretations become serious when they motivate the attitudes and practical actions of those who adopt them. That there is a legitimate conflict between them on a theoretical level does not mean that all interpretations are of equal value; their value is only fully revealed when they are embodied in human action. Here the biblical principle applies: You shall know them by their fruits.

Belief and unbelief cannot be clearly differentiated and treated separately—particularly nowadays, in the culture of a globalized world, where different spiritual currents and attitudes constantly interact—because they are intertwined in the minds of many people. Nowadays, the dialogue between belief and unbelief does not take place between two strictly separate groups but *within* the minds and hearts of individual people.

In the light of faith's transformations, it is clearly necessary to reassess many traditional categories of the sociology and psychology of religion. The categories of belief and unbelief, of believers and non-believers, as understood by previous generations, are no longer able to encompass and reflect the diversity and dynamism of the spiritual life of our time; the impenetrable walls between believers and non-believers, and between faith and skepticism, have fallen, in common with some seemingly unshakeable walls on the political and cultural scene. If we want to understand our multifaceted and rapidly changing world, we must discard many unduly static categories. The spiritual life of the individual and society is a dynamic energy field that is constantly changing.

In terms of theology, the first source (the "subject") of faith is God. Humans were created by God in God's image and the desire for God was implanted in the structure of our humanity: the gravitation of the image toward its model. Some schools of theology draw a fairly strict distinction between the "natural" human desire for the absolute and God's "supernatural" response, the gift of grace. Others maintain that within human beings this longing itself acts as "grace," as divine energy that renders humans receptive and susceptible to the greatest gift of all: God's self-giving.

This thirst for the absolute awakens in individuals with varying degrees of intensity, at different ages, in diverse circumstances; it comes to them in a variety of ways and in various different forms. It may manifest itself as an inner urge for spiritual seeking or as a search for meaning; it may be prompted by upbringing and culture. Spiritual seeking sometimes manifests itself in seemingly nonreligious forms, such as the desire for goodness, truth, and beauty (which are, of course, traditional attributes of God), or for love and meaning. Sometimes it is quietly at work for a long time in the depths of the unconscious before bursting forth at moments described as enlightenment, awakening, or conversion. In their desire for depth, for life's deeper meaning, people can hear a voice calling and summoning them—and they listen to it or not; they understand and interpret it in different ways, they respond to it in different ways. But this call and the search for meaning can also be relegated to the unconscious or go unheeded by the people in question or by those around them. I am convinced that God speaks to everyone, but to everyone in a different way, in a manner appropriate to their capacity to listen and understand. However, this ability is given to us only in embryonic form. It is necessary for us to nurture it. The culture in which we live may or may not facilitate this. Some cultures have regarded *care for the soul* as their main task and purpose, others seem indifferent to this dimension of humanity.

According to traditional Christian doctrine, God comes through the Word, through the Word of the biblical message and through the Word incarnate in history—through Christ and through the Church, which mediates the Word to man in many ways. But God's response can also come quietly and from within, even anonymously. In the act of faith—especially in the event of faith in the life of a particular person—one can only theoretically separate transcendence and immanence, God as the one who is "wholly other" and all-transcending, and the God who is deeper within us than our own self, the "self of our self." The human free response to God's call is the culmination of the dialogical character of faith. Our response is our personal faith—both its existential aspect, the act of faith (*fides qua*), and the substance of our personal faith, its articulation in the form of our belief (*fides quae*).

Fides qua and *fides quae*, the act of faith and the substance of faith, belong together, but while the "object of faith" may be implicitly and latently present in the act of faith as "ontological proto-faith," the reverse is not the case. Mere "religious belief" without faith as an existential orientation, an outlook on life, cannot be considered faith in the biblical and Christian sense.

Fides quae, "conviction," gives faith in the sense of *fides qua* the words, the possibility of verbal and intellectual self-expression and communication with others. *Fides qua* (faith) without *fides quae* (belief) may be "mute," but this "muteness" need not indicate lack of substance; it can be an awestricken and humble silence in the face of mystery. Mystics have always been aware that blank emptiness is just another aspect of fullness, perhaps even its most authentic aspect.

As Søren Kierkegaard wrote, the act of faith can also take the form of a leap into paradox.[2] It can take the form of mystical entry into the *cloud of unknowing*[3] or Abraham's venturing forth into the unknown.[4] Such faith is not objectified (reified), but it is not without substance. In the Bible and in the traditions growing out of the Bible, we find both the phrase "I know in whom I have believed"[5] and very articulate professions of faith, but we also find a strict prohibition against speaking God's name and a mystical silence about God. The mystical traditions in particular know that God is "nothing" (no "thing" in the world of beings, things, objects) and that the word *nothing* is perhaps the most appropriate expression of God's mode of being. God's uniqueness must not be lost in a world of different "things," for the God of biblical faith does not dwell among idols, nor must God become part of the world of human religious notions, wishes, and fantasies. At the Athenian Areopagus, St. Paul passed by all the altars of the known gods, and only at the altar to the unknown god did he discern the presence of the God of his and our faith.[6]

The act of faith usually takes the form of an intentional relationship with a specific counterpart (one believes in something, trusts someone or something)—this is then *fides quae*. Thus, there is a certain degree of specificity in the act of faith, it is focused on something, it has an object. The original source, the subject of faith, becomes the object, the object of faith. But if the object of faith is an all-embracing mystery, then by its very nature it cannot become an object in the sense of "one thing among other things"; mystery cannot be "objectified." Absolute mystery, even in its self-revelation, remains a mystery: what is evident and comprehensible about it alludes to what is nonevident and incomprehensible.

It is impossible to confine the absolute mystery within the world of our imaginings and our words, a world limited by our subjectivity and the limitations of the time and culture in which we live and think.

Therefore, whereas the *fides qua*, the existential submission to God, relates to God as such, our *fides quae*, the attempt to articulate and therefore to some extent objectify this mystery, comes up against the limits of human rational knowledge and presents us only with an *image* of God limited by our language and culture. As a symbol, it may be a path to God, but it cannot be mistaken for the mystery of the absolute itself. This mystery is given to us in a way that is fully sufficient for our salvation (if we open our lives to it), but it remains a mystery and thus leaves room for our further seeking and maturing in faith.[7]

Perceiving God as a person does not mean accepting primitively anthropomorphic notions of God and treating God with a superficial familiarity and ceasing to perceive God as a mystery. By attributing a "personal" character to the absolute mystery, Christianity emphasizes that our relationship with it is dialogical: it is not merely an act of knowledge and understanding on our part but an encounter in which God receives us. This mutual reception between God and humankind is not a one-off act; it is a story, a story that is unfolding.

The Spirit of God leads the Church ever deeper into the fullness of truth; we must let ourselves be led by it. But this journey is not to be confused with progress as understood by secular eschatology and ideology; it is not a one-way journey and does not end in any ideal situation in the middle of history but only in the fullness of time in the arms of God. As St. Augustine watched a boy playing with a shell on the seashore, he realized that all our theology, catechisms, and dogmatic textbooks are but a small shell compared to the fullness of the mystery of God. Let us gratefully use all the instruments of knowledge that have been given us, but let us not cease to marvel at the immensity and depth of that which infinitely transcends them.

The existential understanding of faith that I espouse in this book is probably closest to the notion of *spirituality* in religious and theological parlance, provided we do not view it too narrowly as simply the inner life or subjective aspect of faith. Spirituality is "the lifestyle of faith"; it fills virtually the entire space of the *fides qua*. It is the sap of the tree of faith, it nourishes and animates both dimensions of faith: the spiritual life, the inner religious experience, the way in which faith is lived and reflected upon; and the outward practice of faith, manifested in the actions of believers in society, in communal celebration, in the embodiment of faith in culture. I consider this dimension of faith to be crucial, especially in the time ahead, so I will devote a separate chapter to it later.

Another concept inseparable from this understanding of faith is *tradition*—a living stream of creative transmission and witness. Tradition is a movement of constant recontextualization and reinterpretation; to study tradition is to seek continuity in discontinuity, to seek identity in the plurality of ever-new phenomena that emerge in the process of development. In this process of transmission, faith emerges as a dynamic, changing phenomenon that cannot be squeezed into the confines of a narrow definition.

When we study the forms of faith in history and in the present, we encounter many surprising phenomena that challenge existing definitions and go beyond our too-narrow ideas and theoretical concepts. Just as evolutionary biology has shown the unsustainability of a static understanding of nature, the study of cultural anthropology challenges naive ahistorical conceptions of an unchanging nature— human existence is a dynamic part of an ongoing historical process. Questions about God and the "essence of man" repeatedly demand plausible, meaningful, and intelligible answers in the context of a particular culture and historical situation. Here, hermeneutics and the phenomenology of faith are more helpful than classical metaphysics.

Faith, as I refer to it in this book, is something more substantial than the assent of reason to articles of faith presented by ecclesiastical authority. The *metanoia* demanded by the Gospel—conversion, acceptance of the faith—is not just a change of worldview but an existential turnaround and a resulting change of perspective: a new way of seeing and perceiving, it is more like waking up and embarking on a journey of new life. Such an awakening may mark the beginning of a journey of faith, or it may be a repeated experience, opening a new stage on the journey.

The apostles on Mount Tabor probably had a similar experience.[8] Jesus's disciples had already followed their master: they believed in him when he told them where to cast their nets, when they heard his sermons, when they saw his signs, when they left their homes and joined him on his journeys. But the vision on the mountain was the next step in the journey of faith. There they experienced something that later theology would incorporate into dogmatic articles about the nature of Jesus and his place in salvation history (alongside Moses and Elijah). There they glimpsed something they had not yet been able to grasp in words; besides, their gaze was obscured by a cloud. They did not become wise and discerning, an enlightened elite (Gnostics). They had to abandon their longing to dwell in that experience of intimacy and luminosity far and high above the valley of the everyday ("to make three tents on the mountain"); after this *peak experience,*[9] they would face a downward path and, in time, the darkness of Gethsemane. The "light from Mount Tabor" does not eliminate the nature of the mystery, thereby rendering it a solved problem, nor does it exempt the believer from the task of continuing on the path of seeking God, "seeking in all things."

Faith, as I understand it, is by its nature a pilgrimage and it has an eschatological goal. Even if we recognize the right of the ecclesiastical authority to declare certain expressions of faith authentic and mandatory, this does not mean that we can close the mouth of God and no longer perceive the ongoing flow of the Spirit. No single religious experience, no single understanding and expression of faith in the course of history can exhaust the fullness of God's mystery. The word "mystery" is not a warning "stop sign" on our path in search of God through thought, prayer, and meditation but rather an encouragement to have trust in these journeys to inexhaustible depths.

God remains an impenetrable mystery, and God's action in the depths of the human heart (in the unconscious) is also hidden. The inner life of God is a mystery, which our senses, reason, and imagination cannot understand or grasp, and which is beyond the perception of our concepts. Perhaps it is not because God is alien and distant but precisely because God is so incredibly close to us: God is closer to us than our own hearts, St. Augustine maintained. Precisely because of this proximity, because we are not at a distance from him, we cannot make him into an object or thing, and every attempt to objectify him turns God into an idol. We cannot see God—just as we cannot see our own face; we can only see the reflection of our face in the mirror. Similarly, as the apostle Paul teaches, we see God only as in a mirror, in hints, in riddles.[10] God is *non-aliud* ("not-other"), as Nicholas of Cusa argued.[11]

The question of "where God is in himself" is as unanswerable as the question of where our self resides; neither God nor the human self can be fixed and located—objectified. Mystics claim that God's self and our human self are intrinsically interconnected. Hence, also, the encounter with God and the existential transformation of our self—the discovery of God as the Self of our self—are two essentially interconnected realities. In faith, in this existential encounter with the all-pervading mystery, the true nature of human existence is revealed: its *openness*. Theological anthropology, based on mystical experience, sees in this openness the very essence of human existence: *homo est capax Dei* (man has the capacity to receive God).

Christian theology identifies the point where mutual human and divine openness meet as the person of Jesus Christ. But Jesus—as we read in the earliest texts of the New Testament—did not appropriate this divine dignity for himself;[12] through him and with him and in him, all humanity—every human being—is invited and drawn into the Christmas mystery of the Incarnation, the union of the human and the divine. This fulfillment of the meaning of our humanity happens not only where people say "Lord, Lord" to Jesus but also wherever they live in a manner that fulfills God's will.[13]

I repeat: If we are seeking some measure of the authenticity of faith, let us not look for it in what people profess in words but in the degree to which faith has penetrated and changed their existence, their hearts. Let us look for it in the way they understand themselves, in their lived relationship with the world, with nature and people, with life and death. Belief in the Creator is not affirmed by what one *thinks* about the origin of the world but by how one *treats* nature; belief in a common Father is affirmed by accepting other people as brothers and sisters; belief in eternal life is affirmed by how one accepts one's own finiteness. When Church officials judged the faith of others by what those people said or wrote about their understanding of faith (often burning them to death, or until recently persecuting or admonishing them in various ways), they tragically failed to recognize that it is God who will judge people's faith—even the faith of those inquisitors!—according to how it was manifested in their behavior and relationships, what their life experience said about their faith, about its authenticity or perversity, about their real belief or unbelief. We can and should share our different experiences of faith in fraternal dialogue, we can help, inspire, complement, correct, and deepen each other's statements of faith, but over the door to the hall of such a meeting Jesus's words should be distinctly engraved: Judge not! (In my friendly visit to a colleague working in the Vatican Palace of the Congregation for the Doctrine of the Faith, I did not find this inscription above any door of this former seat of the Holy Inquisition.)

Faith and unbelief concern the whole person, and therefore only God alone can judge its authenticity in the lives of particular people. One thing we can say for sure, however: militant fanaticism tends to be a favorite mask for unbelief.

I do not subscribe to the deistic idea of a God who dwells somewhere outside the reality of the world of nature and history, who is separate from it and intervenes in it at most from the outside as a deus ex machina. I believe in a God who is the depth of all reality, of all creation, who encompasses it and at the same time infinitely transcends it; I believe in the God of whom the apostle Paul says that "in him we live, move, and have our being."[14]

The God in whom I believe is present in our world primarily through prayer and the work of human beings (remember the Benedictine *ora et labora*), through human responses to God's impulses (traditionally speaking, the action of grace), and through a life of faith, hope, and love. Theologically speaking, faith, hope, and love are not merely human attitudes but a place of encounter and essential connection (*perichoresis*) between the divine and the human, between grace and freedom, between heaven and earth. In them, God and his life are open to our investigation. The theology to which I subscribe is a phenomenology of divine self-revelation in acts of faith, accompanied by love and hope.

THREE

Reading the Signs of the Times

I devote this chapter mainly to methodological issues; among other things, the relationship of faith to history and culture. I call the theological approach taken in this book *kairology*. I use this word to denote a theological hermeneutic of the experience of faith in history, especially at moments of crisis in social and cultural paradigm shifts.[1]

I consider crisis a time of opportunity, an opportune moment (*kairos*). Two Greek words refer to two different understandings of time. *Chronos* refers to the quantum of time, the sequence of hours, days, and years, the flow of time measurable by our clocks and calendars. The word *kairos* points to the quality of time; *kairos* is a time of opportunity, a time to do something, a time of coming, a time of visitation; it is the coming (advent) of unique and unrepeatable moments whose meaning must be understood, whose challenges must be risen to and fulfilled; it is a time to decide, a decisive moment not to be missed or wasted. "There is a season for everything, a time for every occupation under heaven: A time for giving birth, a time for dying; a time for planting, a time for uprooting what has been planted. A time for killing, a time for healing; a time for knocking down, a time for building. A time for tears, a time for laughter," we read in the Bible in the book of Ecclesiastes.[2] Jesus begins his public ministry with the words: "The time has come!" He reproaches his contemporaries for being able to predict the next day's weather but not understanding and not wanting to understand the signs of the times.[3]

Discerning and interpreting the signs of the times (*ta semeia tón kairón*) was the role of prophets in the Bible and in the Christian tradition. The biblical prophets were not oracles, futurologists, fore-tellers of the future: they were primarily interpreters of present events as God's pedagogy. Kairology espouses this prophetic task that Jesus bequeathed to the Church. It undertakes it using the methods available to theology from contemporary philosophy—especially phenomenology and hermeneutics.

I am convinced that theology that operates within the framework of traditional metaphysics is incapable of fulfilling this task. Kairology differs fundamentally from ontotheology, from the metaphysical "science of God" that confuses the biblical God of history with the Greek immovable prime mover. I am totally avoiding ("bracketing") speculations about the existence, nature, and attributes of God or evidence for God's existence. I have always found theological tracts entitled "God and His Life" to be implausible unless they dealt with God's life in us, in our lives, and in our history.

In Christianity, worship cannot be separated from human ministry, nor the knowledge of God from the knowledge of people and the world. If theology is to be taken seriously as a necessary part of serving people, it must be a contextual theology, reflecting the experience of faith and its presence in people's lives and in society. It must reflect on faith in the context of culture and historical change, and thus also in dialogue with the sciences that concern themselves with human beings, culture, society, and history. Kairology could be described as socio-theology (the intersection of sociology and theology) rather than "pure" theology. My experience of interdisciplinary academic collaboration on international research assignments on religion involving theologians, philosophers, and sociologists of religion has convinced me that responsible intellectual work by contemporary theology must be accompanied by both a contemplative approach to reality and an honest dialogue with contemporary philosophy and the social sciences. The complex and changing phenomenon of religion cannot be understood if the perspectives of theology and sociology remain separate and one-sided. It is necessary to overcome the mutual prejudices between theologians and sociologists, to learn to understand each other's language, and thus to broaden our perspective and experience with a complementary perspective from the other side. In the past, the blind spots in both disciplines' perspectives on religion have spawned a number of superficial and ideologically distorted theories of religion.[4]

We need to continue our efforts to bring together the perspectives of theology and the social sciences; kairology still needs to draw stimulus and inspiration from related disciplines such as political theology, liberation theology, Catholic social teaching, and Protestant social theology. Theology is at the service of faith, but Christian faith is embedded in culture and society, and if we want to understand and serve it, we must see it in context and study that context as well.

I subscribe to the theology of Michel de Certeau, who argued that human experience—and thus historical experience—is where God is revealed.[5] Kairology supplements the analyses of sociologists, historians, political scientists, cultural anthropologists, and social psychologists with a spiritual diagnosis of the times. It asks how faith, hope, and love are present in the cultural and moral climate of the time—even in very unconventional forms.

It is necessary to realize that traditional ecclesial Christianity no longer has a monopoly on these "divine virtues." After all, the Christian Church itself has taught and still teaches that God's gifts are given freely and unrestrictedly. Faith, hope, and love have a life of their own beyond the institutional boundaries of the churches, but in a non-church context they change a lot and are given new names. Should the Church see this expansion and emancipation of its most cherished treasure as something positive—or should it view this loss of control with concern, fear, and frustration? Perhaps the emergence of transformed "Christian values" in secular culture can inspire theology to a new ecclesiology, a broader and deeper self-understanding of the Church.

The theological conception of the Church must be broader than the sociological description of the form of the Church already established in the past. From a theological point of view, the Church is more than just one social institution or interest group; it is a sacrament—that is, a symbol and effective sign (*signum efficiens*) of the unity of all humanity in Christ. It should effectively point to what is not yet there and what cannot be expected in fullness in the course of history. The Church conceives that promised consummation of history and fulfillment of the meaning of its existence as an eschatological goal (that is, transcending the horizon of history). The vision of a "Church without borders" (a truly Catholic and universal Church) is therefore *utopian*, historically speaking, in the sense that it has no place (*topos*) within history. However, this "utopia" can be important and effective insofar as it becomes the inspiration and motive for Christian action, which, within the historical process, will already be heading toward this omega point.

This vision, however, must be accompanied by a warning and a critique of ideologies that declare a certain form of the Church and its knowledge (a certain state and form of theology) to be perfect, thus preventing the possibility of development and reform. Throughout history there have been many unfortunate attempts to "ideologize utopias," various chiliastic attempts to build heaven on earth—whether in heretical forms of Christianity or in the secular ideology of communism, which—in this sense—was also one of the Christian heresies. Equally unfortunate were the aforementioned attempts of Christian triumphalism to declare a certain state of the Church and theology as definitive. In my previous books I have warned how the omission of the eschatological distinction between the earthly Church militant (*ecclesia militans*) and the celestial Church triumphant (*ecclesia triumphans*) can lead to triumphalism and militant religion.[6] Later in this book I will try to offer another way of gradually achieving the "catholicity of Christianity"—namely, a way of broadening and intensifying its ecumenical openness.

I consider kairology to be part of *public theology*. It therefore has to express itself in language that is comprehensible beyond the boundaries of theological academia and the Church. Public theology regards public space as both the object of investigation and the addressee of its utterances; there are many cases of public theologians being directly involved in social activities, civic initiatives, and resistance movements.[7] Their social involvement is motivated by their faith and reflects it theologically. Public theologians strive to comment competently, intelligibly, and credibly on events in public life, society, and culture. Inspired by the biblical prophets, they perceive the changes in the world as God's self-expression in history.

The emphasis on history and historicity is absolutely essential for contemporary theology. The old theology referred to two books of divine revelation, the Bible and Nature (Creation): if you want to find God, read about God in the Bible and in the book of Nature. Whereas for prebiblical mythologies and pagan religions, the theophany— the place where the sacred is revealed—is primarily nature and its cyclical character: the perpetual return of the same, in the Bible, the theophany is primarily history. But is history a "third book" alongside the Bible and Nature (Creation)?

The God of the Bible is the Creator of the world and the Lord of history. Nature (creation) and history cannot be separated; nature is a process of constant evolution and human history is a specific part of this process. Creation, this ongoing "preaching" of God, is the world, and, in the biblical perception, the historical world, the evolving and changing world. Creation is an ongoing process, *creatio continua*, and human society and culture are integral elements of it. The biblical poem of creation at the beginning of the book of Genesis already depicts creation as a story, as an event in time, although the mythopoetic language of the biblical text attributes to this event a specific understanding of time, justifying the institution of a holy day of rest.

To Darwin we owe the creative idea—inspired probably by Hegel—to make history out of biology, to project history into biology. Thanks to evolutionary theories, we have come to understand nature as a dramatic development that feeds into human history. Teilhard de Chardin and process theology offered a theological interpretation of evolutionary theory, showing its inspirational significance for Christian theology and spirituality.

Just as nature and history cannot be separated, nor can the Bible be separated from history; history is not something parallel to the Bible. The Bible is both the narrative of history and the fruit of history. It is both witness to history and co-creator of history. The Bible's stories live through cultural memory in history, offering a key to understanding history and thus co-creating it. They also co-create the life stories of individuals, the "personal history" of the believer. Faith is the openness through which biblical stories enter and transform a person's life.

The Council of Trent identified scripture and tradition as the two sources of divine revelation. But the Bible is part of tradition, and it includes not only the history of its origin but in a sense the ongoing history of its interpretation, its life in the Church and in culture. Only in this context is the Bible the living Word of God for us.

The God of the Bible is revealed primarily in the unique events of history—*and in the stories that are told about those events and that interpret them.* YHWH, the God of Israel, *happens* in history and becomes audible in the events that are God's word to God's people—and also in the narratives, the stories that articulate and convey that word. History first becomes *human* history in the narratives that interpret it, that turn events and the transmitting of experience—tradition—into culture; history without interpretive narratives is mute.

The God of the Bible is not "behind history," moving people around like puppets from backstage, as it were. The Creator is present in the work of creation, in nature and in history, incorporated and embedded in the body of history in various ways—God is also present in human history and human culture. Christianity identifies as the ultimate form of God's presence in history (not only in human history but in the whole process of creation) the incarnation—that is, the person and story of Jesus of Nazareth, "in whom all the fullness of the Godhead dwells,"[8] who is God's "yes and amen" to humans and the world and who accomplished the work of redemption, liberation, and healing of the human race and human history. Jesus Christ is referred to in scripture as "the leader and perfecter of faith."[9]

Faith, as people's free "yes" to the Creator and his action, is an expression of the *partnership* between God and humankind, a covenant relationship; therefore, we can see in it the ultimate realization of human freedom and human dignity. It makes possible a conscious and reflective dialogical relationship with God, who is the totality and depth of all reality. God as a whole, an all-encompassing and all-pervading whole, is the *context* that gives meaning to nature and to history: through faith, people discover this context and, within it, they come to a new understanding of the meaning of their existence.

The theology of the past few centuries has drawn primarily on the defined articles of faith; today, theology has other rich sources available: the living experience of faith, spirituality, mysticism, the theological interpretation of art, which is developing as an important expression of spiritual life. We have said that an essential part of human history is culture—in other words, people's search for meaning and their effort to understand themselves and history.[10] It is culture that makes history human history and makes society a truly human society. That is why culture is where we must above all look for the signs of the times. If culture is the medium of the search for meaning, including the Ultimate Concern,[11] then it can be considered a *locus theologicus*, a legitimate subject of theological research.

People are the co-creators of history and the environment, not only when they fulfill God's command to transform the earth, but also through their entire specific way of being within nature and history; their spiritual life is intrinsically part of it. Through their search for meaning and their understanding of their being (that is, through their culture), they transcend themselves, discovering and fulfilling the opportunities that gradually open up to them. Through their creativity, people fulfill the mission assigned to them by the Creator and give concrete expression to their likeness to God.

Art and the interpretation of works of art can be as supportive and inspiring to depth theology[12] as dream interpretation is to depth psychology. For it is particularly in art that we encounter great dreams, and in and through them the significant (sometimes unconscious and unacknowledged) desires and aspirations not only of individuals but of entire generations. These great dreams—such as, for example, Nietzsche's account of the madman heralding the killing of God, or Freud's retelling of the myth of Oedipus—acted as a latent moving force in culture; they were powerful images that expressed the forces that impelled people's thought and action. Can we ignore them if we want to understand, for example, the roots of modern atheism? And can we ignore the testimony of the Bible (and other religions) that through dreams God speaks to people?

There is an intrinsic affinity between faith, love, and artistic creation: in them we can encounter *passio* (passion), the energy that animates the world. Romanticism rightly sensed the sacred character of the *eros* present in religious, amorous, and artistic passion, the *mysterium tremendum et fascinans*. In creation, as in love and faith, one gives, but at the same time one receives and accepts. Both the giving and the discerning acceptance of a gift—that is, of something *new*—is a means of transcendence, of self-opening.

Insofar as culture, and especially art (as opposed to superficial consumer kitsch, including the religious kind), is an expression of the human search for meaning, then it is in this longing, openness, and restlessness of the heart (*inquietas cordis*) that God is present, even here on earth, even before this divinely aroused restlessness reaches (in Augustine's words) its ultimate eschatological goal. I believe that God, fully manifested in Jesus's *kenosis* (self-emptying), is humble enough to be present anonymously in expressions of human openness, desire, and hope, even where God is not recognized and named—that is, even in secular culture, if it is humanly authentic.

With regard to the relationship between God and human culture, one can also paraphrase Master Eckhart: the eye through which we look at God and the eye through which God looks at us are one and the same. We encounter a similar idea in Orthodox icon theology and in the practice of meditation using icons. When we "write icons" or when we meditate before icons, we are looking at God through our creation and through its fruit, the image, and we can feel at the same time that God is looking at us. This experience—standing in front of an image and having the impression that it is looking at us—is the basis for Nicholas of Cusa's theology of prayer: in prayer and contemplation we experience the kindly gaze of God, which rests on all creatures, but especially on the questioning and contemplating human being. In the light of God's gaze, one gives oneself to God and becomes more oneself. God says, "Be your own and I will be yours."[13] Thus is fulfilled the mystery of God's acceptance of human existence and humans' acceptance of God's existence "without confusion . . . without division."[14]

Human beings are joint creators of history and of their environment, of nature, not only by their activity and their power, which is amplified by the fascinating possibilities of science and technology, but also by their contemplative approach to life and their openness to the mystery of the absolute. Similarly, the reader, the viewer, and the listener are joint creators of a work of art—literary, visual, or musical. A work of art is not only the product of its creator; it is an *event of encounter*, to which, in addition to the author, these other participants— readers, viewers, listeners—inherently belong. A work of art lives and becomes complete through the perception of those who are affected by it, thereby also helping to create and complete it. Just as the process of creation continues and completes itself in human history, in the freedom of human lives, so the work of art lives, happens, and completes itself in those who experience it; art demands the art of communication and is itself interpretation and invitation to interpretation.

As has already been said, the contemplative approach to life changes human life from a monologue into a dialogue—it is about something other than human self-assertion, the technical transformation of nature, or the manipulation of society by power, something other than an engineering approach to the world and to history. It is about being silent, listening, trying to understand, persevering in the search for an authentic answer. When the technical and manipulative approach to the world is not tempered by a contemplative one, the world of humans is under threat.

In the human world, it is culture that embodies faith, hope, and love; they are the setting for *perichoresis*, the interpenetration of the divine and the human. Through them, God is present in human culture. However, the theological interpretation of culture, especially contemporary art, should not forget that God can also be present in our world *sub contrario*, in God's opposite, if I may borrow a term from Luther's theology of the cross. Both absurd drama and some seemingly blasphemous artifacts of contemporary art that chiefly provoke and offend Christian fundamentalists and puritans merit a perceptive theological interpretation. At certain moments, it is the experience of God's absence, the incomprehensibility of the world and the tragedy of human destiny that become the motif of waiting for God and thirsting for God.

God awakens this desire and in a certain way is already present in it; God comes to us not only as an answer but also as a question. God comes in the desire to understand, a desire that transcends every partial answer and constantly revisits it with new questions, instigating a fresh search; God imparts a pilgrim character to our existence. The one who alone was permitted to say: I am the truth, also said that he is the way and the life. Truth that ceases to be a way is dead. By faith one journeys eternally toward God, in whom the way and the goal are not separate.

If we are looking for the meaning of historical events (the signs of the times), we can look for it in a deeper dimension of culture, especially in the prophetic dreams in art through which these events are heralded or reverberate. Dreams have their own language and their own logic, and call for an appropriate hermeneutical approach; we cannot enter the world of this language of God by adopting the methods of classical metaphysical theology. What we learn when we contemplate images and koans in the world of art can be applied when we contemplate everyday paradoxes and riddles; it can help us make a spiritual diagnosis of the times. Theological aesthetics and the theology of culture, especially the theology of art (including a meditative approach to contemporary fiction and film), is an important part of contemporary Western theology.

As I repeatedly contemplated the aforementioned chapter about the madman in Nietzsche's *The Gay Science* (the scene in which the famous statement about the death of God is voiced), I recalled Jung's comment that archaic tribes made a distinction between small, private dreams and large dreams of significance to the whole tribe. Nietzsche's story about the collective killing of God, consigned to oblivion, was undeniably a great dream message for our entire tribe! Nietzsche was well aware that in his time he had not yet "grown ears" for it; however, the events of the twentieth and twenty-first centuries allow us to understand and reinterpret it again and again.

Art is a treasure trove of prophetic dreams with sometimes explicit, sometimes latent religious content, inviting theological interpretation. This is how I perceive, for example, the Legend of the Inquisitor from Dostoevsky's *The Brothers Karamazov*, or Kafka's *The Trial*, or Orwell's vision of the totalitarian state in the novel *1984*—as well as many other works of literature, film, and art that can become the subject of theological analysis.

Northrop Frye, a leading twentieth-century literary scholar (who for a time served as a clergyman), wrote that a major shift in human consciousness occurred when drama was born out of the Dionysian rituals in Greece. "The great evolution of what we now call literature out of mythology took a decisive turn."[15] Perhaps a contemplative approach to symbols in literature and in art in general, together with a theological hermeneutic of works of art, can bring about a significant shift in our relationship to religion, opening up to the children of a secularized world a new (postsecular) approach to understanding religious experience.

How can we awaken the therapeutic power of faith and turn a torpid and internally divided Church into the field hospital of which Pope Francis often speaks, and make it the light of the nations? How can we resist the temptation to turn the Church and religion into a ghetto, a locked and fortified bunker, a mausoleum of yesterday's certitudes or a private garden for consumers of soothing and soporific drugs? Can Christianity, which is discredited by fundamentalists and flatly rejected and written off by the liberal left, inspire the formation of a political culture capable of transforming a chaotic polyphony into a moral climate of mutual respect, communication, and shared values?

It is my wish that kairology should not remain confined to non-evaluative analysis and diagnosis. As someone who spends most of my time teaching and pastoring university students, I would like to help answer the aforementioned question regarding the *type of faith* (not religion) that can best assist the rising generation to cope with the challenges presented by the emerging new age, and what type of transformation the Church, theology, and spirituality must undergo in order to embrace the current crisis as an opportunity to be a support for people in what I call in this book the afternoon of Christianity.

FOUR

A Thousand Years Like a Day

I have called this book *The Afternoon of Christianity*. I was inspired to use the word "afternoon" by the metaphor chosen by C. G. Jung, the founder of analytical psychology, to describe the dynamics of an individual human life. I have tried to apply this metaphor to the history of Christianity.

Jung compared the human lifetime to the course of a day. According to Jung, the morning of life is youth and early adulthood, the time when people are developing the basic features of their personality, building the outer walls and pillars of their life's home, arranging their household, taking their place in society, choosing their career, starting their professional career, getting married and creating a family environment. They create an *image* of themselves—an idea they want others to have of them, a mask (a *persona* in Jung's terminology)[1] that is their "outer face"—lending them an identity and at the same time protecting them externally from the hurtful intrusions of others into the intimate sphere of their self. Jung argues that those who want to embark on a journey of spiritual maturing, a journey into the deeps, without first putting down roots in this world recklessly run the risk of damaging their soul.

Then comes the noonday crisis. It is a time of fatigue, of sleepiness; people cease to enjoy all the things that used to satisfy them. Even the ancient hermits knew about the snares of the "noonday demon," the "arrow that flies by day."[2] They warned against the vice of acedia. The word means more than sloth, though it is commonly translated as such. Rather, it is a loss of energy and zest for life, a spiritual malaise, a dullness—today we might even reach for terms like depression or burnout syndrome. A crisis can affect our health, our careers, our marital and family relationships, our faith and spiritual life.

But this crisis—like every crisis according to Jung—is also an opportunity. It is a chance to address a part of our being that we have not developed enough, that we have neglected or even subconsciously or consciously suppressed and pushed into the unconscious. The unacknowledged and undiscerned part of our self—our shadow, our debts—makes itself felt. After all, in the Christian tradition, sins (debts) include not only evil deeds, bad words, and perverse thinking but also the failure to do good, the burying of entrusted talents.

It is only when one has passed the tests of the noonday crisis—for example, when one is able to accept and integrate what one did not want to know about oneself and did not want to admit to oneself—that one is ready to embark on the journey of the afternoon of life. But one can squander this new stage of life by filling it with the mere continuation of morning activities, by continuing above all to forge one's career and achieve financial security, by dusting off and improving one's image in the eyes of others, by chasing honors and applause, by pinning more and more glittering orders on one's breast. One's persona can become so inflated that it eventually suffocates one's inner life. Even success has its pitfalls, and career and fortune can become a trap.

But the afternoon of life—mature age and old age—has a different and more important task than the morning of life—a spiritual journey, a descent into the depths. The afternoon of life is *kairos*, a time appropriate for the development of spiritual life, an opportunity to complete the lifelong process of maturing. This stage of life can bear valuable fruit: insight, wisdom, peace and tolerance, the ability to manage emotions and overcome self-centeredness. The latter is a major obstacle on the path from the ego, the center of our conscious life, to a deeper center, the inner self (*das Selbst*). By this shift from the "little self" to the most fundamental and essential self (we can call it God or "Christ in us"), the human being fulfills the meaning of life, attaining maturity and fullness. For Jung, completeness does not mean flawlessness but wholeness (in many languages the words "whole" and "holy" are related—whole and holy, or healthy and holy—*heil und heilig*).

By contrast, the failure to fulfill the task of this stage of life—"bad aging"—breeds rigidity, emotional upset, anxiety, suspicion, pettiness, self-pity, hypochondria, and terrorizing one's environment. Possibly all the psychological difficulties of people in the second half of life that Jung encountered in his extensive clinical practice were related, he said, to the absence of a spiritual and religious dimension to life—in the broadest sense of that word.

I believe that in one respect this inspiring metaphor of Jung's needs to be revised. Jung situates the noonday crisis and the shift to the afternoon of life around the age of thirty-five. But human life has lengthened in recent decades and is getting longer all the time; the cult of youth, brought about by the cultural revolution of the late 1960s, affects and absorbs middle age, virtually all productive life, slowing down and obscuring the aging process, which Jung believed should be the afternoon time of maturity. In contrast, the period of old age is getting longer and longer, which raises many problems and questions. Is old age to be an imitation of youth, or are the people of today and tomorrow being given the precious gift of the opportunity to develop a culture of spiritual life and spiritual maturing over a longer time and more profoundly?

As scripture says: "With the Lord one day is like a thousand years, and a thousand years are like one day."[3] For years now, I have been preoccupied with the question of whether and to what extent the metaphor of the day, which Jung used to explain the dynamics of individual life, can be creatively applied to the history of Christianity—and it has been a recurrent theme in my recent lectures, articles, and books. In order to understand the paradigm shifts in the history of Christianity—and especially the meaning and challenges of our time—I offer the following metaphor.

From its beginning until the threshold of modernity, the history of Christianity can be seen as a morning, a long time in which the Church built up its institutional and doctrinal structures. Then came the noonday crisis—with its epicenter in Central and Western Europe—that shook these very structures. It has lasted with varying degrees of intensity in a number of countries from the late Middle Ages through the modern period, from the Renaissance and the Reformation, the schism within Western Christianity and the ensuing wars that challenged the credibility of the various denominations, through the Enlightenment, the period of criticism of religion and the rise of atheism, to the period of atheism's slow development into the subsequent phase of apatheism—religious indifference.

I am convinced that today we stand on the threshold of the afternoon of Christianity; at the end of a long period of crisis, some features of a new, perhaps deeper and more mature form of Christianity are already shining through. But the afternoon form of Christianity—like all its earlier forms—will not be engendered and brought about by some impersonal and irreversible logic of historical development. It comes as a possibility, as *kairos*—an opportunity that will arrive and present itself at some point, but will only be fulfilled when people understand and freely accept it. Much depends on finding, at a particular moment in history, a sufficient number of those who, like the "wise virgins" of Jesus's parable, will be alert and ready for the *kairos*—the time when action is required.

Even in the history of Christianity, the possibility of "bad aging" looms. To miss the time for reform, or even to try to return to the time before the noonday crisis, could produce a sterile and repulsive form of Christianity. But equally dangerous are the attempts to solve the present crises in an indiscriminate way, by mere external reform of the Church's institutions, without deeper changes in theology and spirituality; these can only bring chaos and shallow results.

In this book I present a vision of the afternoon of Christianity, but at the same time I constantly stress that whether and to what extent this vision will be fulfilled is known only to the Lord of history, who is still creating history in dialogue with our deeds and our understanding. Seen through the lens of the theology of history, history is not merely the product of conscious and purposeful human activity, economic conditions, or social conflicts; it is not governed by blind fate or the laws of dialectics, nor is it guided by some celestial puppet master. It is a drama of salvation, of the mysterious interplay between God and human freedom. Insofar as people's free history-making acts are expressions of human self-transcendence (self-transcendence in love and creation), they open up space for what one rightly experiences as a gift that precedes, accompanies, and completes one's free action. In traditional theological terms, it is about the historical relationship between freedom and grace.

I use the metaphor of the noonday crisis to describe the long and internally fractured period of the gradual demise of *Christianitas*—a certain type of embodiment of the Christian faith in Western culture and civilization. Thousands of historical and sociological studies have been written about this period, and many different theories have attempted to explain it. There are different ways of dating, justifying, evaluating, and labeling this stage, such as the era of secularization, "disenchantment," desacralization, the era of "dechurching" or de-Christianization, the era of the " demythologization of Christianity," the end of the Constantinian era, or the era of the "death of God."

The classics of secularization theory have regarded secularization as the last stage of the history of Christianity or religion in general. Some heirs of the Enlightenment celebrated it as a victory of progress and the light of reason over the darkness and obscurity of religious superstition; some Christians, nostalgic for the past, lamented and demonized it. For a long time, the opinion that secularization could also mean a *kairos* moment for Christianity, a new challenge and new positive opportunities to renew and deepen faith, was quite rare.

In recent decades, however, the theory of secularization itself has been challenged. Some sociologists, philosophers, and cultural historians have described it as a scientific fallacy, an ideological myth, a product of "wishful thinking" by certain thinkers and sociopolitical circles.[4] It turns out that although they themselves mostly belonged to anticlerical circles (Émile Durkheim, for example) the classical theorists of secularization theory remained in many ways wedded to a narrow clerical conception of faith and religion; although they discussed various kinds of religion, they chiefly projected onto them the form of religion that they saw around them, and that was losing its vitality and appeal, especially the form of the Catholic Church at the turn of the twentieth century. They generalized the crisis of a certain form of faith and religion, declaring it to be a crisis of religion as such. For a long time, it escaped their attention that secularization did not bring about the extinction of religion but its *transformation*.

When, a long time ago—yes, it was in the last millennium—I celebrated my fortieth birthday, I responded to the toasts and congratulations with a very embarrassed, "Is there really anything to celebrate? Youth has departed!" One of my friends—it was the philosopher Zdeněk Neubauer—immediately retorted with vehemence: "Youth is not just one transient period of life, youth is a dimension of our personality!"

It all depends on what we do with our youth. We can betray and reject the young person we once were and repress it within ourselves; we can also foolishly try to hold onto our youth, frantically feigning it, and resisting adulthood and old age. But we can also integrate it, incorporating it organically into the ongoing story of our lives or returning to it, as a composer returns to a motif and lets it resonate creatively in new variations. In a sense, what we have been through continues to accompany us and remains within us—but it can operate in various ways. It depends on how we have fulfilled the task that a particular stage represents—not only in the life of individuals but also in the life of nations and cultures. The time in which our life story and history unfolds is not unidirectional, and our living space is multidimensional; even a past that is over, forgotten, and displaced can turn out to be only apparently dead and only temporarily closed. Psychoanalysis has taught us that what has been forcibly displaced has a tendency to recur in an altered form.

Almost the same applies to postmodernism and postsecularization. Cultural epochs are also dimensions of the life of a society rather than simply successive periods of time that come to a definite end at some point. The relationship between modernity and postmodernity, secular and postsecular, is more complicated than the alternation of times of day or seasons. Even the metaphor of the day (the morning, noon, and afternoon of history) must be treated with great care: when it is noon and spring here, elsewhere on the planet it is morning or evening and a dismal autumn. In our globally interconnected society, premodern, modern, hypermodern, and postmodern ways of life coexist and sometimes surprisingly collide.

In these cases, the prefix "post" does not imply a simple temporal succession or a qualitative leap. To advocate an evolutionary notion that postmodernity and postsecularization are automatically higher stages of development would reveal that we are still stuck in a culture of modernity, since the myth of evolution as constant unidirectional progress was one of the hallmarks of modern thought. Accepting evolution as the principle of all life does not mean uncritical acceptance of the ideology of progress. If we want to escape the bondage of modernity, we must discard the naive view of history as an unstoppable one-way movement toward a better tomorrow, governed by certain historical laws. In secular ideologies, the idea of progress, governed by external laws, concealed an unacknowledged theological, deistic model; for communist ideologues in particular, progress was a hidden god, manipulating history from outside—and they themselves were its prophets and instruments. One of Nietzsche's many insightful ideas was his observation that many modern ideals are merely the shadow of a dead god.[5]

The era of many "posts" raises a number of questions. What is the relationship of postmodernism to modernity? Will the postmodern age be truly transmodern, transcending and surpassing modernity, or is it rather supermodern (that is, just an intensified continuation of certain tendencies of the modern age in new conditions)? By analogy, aren't many of the persistent aftereffects of the communist era and many features of people's behavior under totalitarianism apparent in the postcommunist era, but simply in new clothing? As with postmodernism and postcommunism, so also in the case of postsecularity, the prefix "post" does not imply a total dissociation from the previous era. The contrary is more likely: the very fact that no new proper name for this new chapter of history has yet been adopted suggests that we are still, in a sense, living in the wake of our past. The Enlightenment thinkers were not long in finding a proud name for their culture. They then attached pejorative labels to the history of the past—they named the Gothic era after the barbaric Goths, the Middle Ages earned their name as being an uninteresting and somber interim period between noble Antiquity and their own enlightened epoch; according to Hegel, when we are interpreting centuries of medieval philosophy, we should don seven-league boots and run through this boring landscape as fast as possible. Maybe the fact that we are unable to find a completely new, proper name for our times suggests that it is only a time of transition, an in-between time. Only in that sense is our age a "new middle age."

When will the postsecular age finally manage to detach itself from the Secular Age? When will it find its own theme and give it a name? Perhaps the past era presented a challenge that we have not yet fully come to terms with. Have we provided adequate answers to the questions raised by the experience of secularization? Have we reflected thoroughly enough on this phenomenon of our cultural history? No religion has endured such a cleansing fire of criticism as Christianity. Have we extracted from this treasure everything needed to promote greater maturity and adulthood in the Christian faith? Have we allowed ourselves to be inspired by those texts in the Hebrew Bible—such as the account of Jacob's nocturnal wrestling match and the entire book of Job—that tell us that God loves those who wrestle with God?

The world of religion is a world of paradoxes. If we want to understand this world, we must discard dogmatic adherence to the principle that "a" cannot be "non-a" at the same time. We would do better to follow the rule *aut-aut*, not only, but also, which my teacher Josef Zvěřina maintained was the fundamental principle of Catholicism.

Are our times secular or postsecular, modern or postmodern? Is it a time of crisis of religion or revitalization of religion? Both are true. The one aspect should not cause us to overlook the other; giving a fair assessment of the one need not mean underestimating the importance of the other. Secularization and modernity have had a lasting impact on the history of faith and marked it in certain ways, but they were not what their radical proponents thought they were—that is, the culminating and final phase of historical development. Secularization was not the end of the history of religion; it was not, as the ideologues of secularism imagined, the victory of the light of reason over the darkness of religion. Rather, it was a transformation of religion and a step on the road to a more mature faith. One of the tasks of this book is to encourage us to take full advantage of this opportunity.

FIVE

Religious or Nonreligious Christianity?

The focus of this book is the transformation of the Christian faith, but it is also about the transformations of religion and the changing relationship between faith and religion. I distinguish three phases in the history of Christianity: first, the morning, premodern; second, the time of the noonday crisis, the time of secularization; third, the impending afternoon of Christianity—a new form that is already being heralded in this era of postmodern disintegration of the modern world.

However, over the course of history, religion also changes—both the meaning and use of the word and the sociocultural phenomena and roles that it can denote. I distinguish between two different concepts of religion in particular. The first is religion as *religio*—an integrating force in society and in the state, a common "language." The term *religio*, from which the term "religion" is derived in most Western languages, was first used in ancient Rome at the time of the Second Punic War. Religion as *religio* had a predominantly political meaning in the ancient Roman Empire, signifying a system of rituals and symbols expressing the identity of society; it was close to what sociology today calls civil religion. According to Cicero, *religio* was "the sound and sober reverence of those deities accepted by the state";[1] the opposite was *superstitio* (superstition)—the religion of others. As we will show, it was not until the fourth century after Christ that Christianity was cast into the role of *religio*.

Second, I speak of religion as it arose and is now generally understood since the Enlightenment: religion as one sector of society and culture among others, as a "worldview" concerned mainly with "the other world" and represented in the earthly realm by specialized religious institutions (churches).

But nor should we forget the archaic form of religion as a relationship to the sacred, experienced especially in nature. This "pagan" form of religiosity was first suppressed by the biblically defined belief in a God who transcends the world. Then it was largely integrated and "baptized" by popular Christianity, especially in the Middle Ages. Then the modernization and secularization of Western society attempted to eradicate it (along with popular Christian religiosity), but it was resuscitated by Romanticism. Today, the motif of the sacredness of nature is making a comeback in various transformations, from Heidegger's notion of the sacred to diverse ecologically oriented New Age spiritualities. Pope Francis's encyclical *Laudato si'* may be seen as an attempt to "baptize" this contemporary sensitivity vis-à-vis nature; its very title rightly invokes the tradition of Franciscan spirituality of creation.

I put forward the hypothesis that the Christian faith has outgrown previous forms of religion, and every attempt to squeeze it back into one of the earlier forms is counterproductive. Likewise, the dictum that "you cannot step into the same river twice" also applies to the living river of history and the flow of tradition (creative transmission).

Christianity as *religio*, embodied in the cultural and political form of *Christianitas* ("Christian civilization"), is definitely a thing of the past, and its nostalgic imitation results only in traditionalist caricatures. Secularization then created a second, modern type of religion: *Christianity as a worldview*, as a *denomination*—and over time Christianity became established in this form of religion as well. But the modern age (modernity) is over, and the type of Christianity that identified itself with religion in the modern sense of the word is also on its way out.

Atheist critics of religion—such as Nietzsche, Freud, and Marx—focused their criticism primarily on the type of religion from which faith needs to be liberated; therefore, critical (not dogmatic) atheism can be a facilitator of faith rather than its enemy. The harbingers of the transformation facing Christianity in our day have been prophetic figures in the ranks of Christians, such as Pascal with his critique of the "religion of the philosophers," Kierkegaard with his critique of bourgeois Christianity, and Teilhard de Chardin and Jung with their critique of a Christianity "that has lost its generative power." Neither the medieval nor the modern form of religion can be the permanent social and cultural home of the Christian faith.

Christianity in late modernity has found itself in a kind of cultural homelessness, which is one of the causes of its present crisis. In this time of changing civilizational paradigms, the Christian faith is only now finding a new shape, a new home, new means of expression, new social and cultural roles, and new allies. Will it become embodied in one of the existing or newly emerging forms of religion, or will it become, as some theologians have declared, a nonreligious faith? Perhaps the very dynamism and diversity of postmodernity that frightens many Christians is the incubation phase of the Christianity of the future.

If we are to reflect on possible future scenarios at the end of this book, let us now try briefly to recall the major stages in the historical development of Christianity in respect of the changing relationship between faith and religion.

At the beginning of its history, Christianity was not a religion in the sense of the ancient *religio*. It was rather a "path of following Christ," one of the Jewish sects of a messianic type. But it builds on the "universalist" ideas that the prophets in particular brought to Judaism. For them, the Lord was not just a "local" God of a single nation, a chosen people, but the Creator and Lord of heaven and earth and ruler of all nations. We can observe the development in Jesus's preaching: initially he considers himself sent primarily or exclusively "to the lost sheep of the house of Israel," but then he sends his apostles out into all the world to teach all nations; he declares, "all authority in heaven and on earth has been given to me."[2]

The apostle Paul represents the "first reformation": he takes young Christianity out of the confines of the Judaism of his day. He radicalizes Jesus's dispute with the rigid interpreters of the Mosaic Law. He frees the Gentile converts from the obligation to become Jews first (accepting circumcision and many other ritual regulations of the Mosaic Law) and gives center stage to faith, manifested in the practice of love of one's neighbor.[3] In so doing, he opens the way for "pious Gentiles" (Hellenistic sympathizers with Judaism, among them adherents of philosophical monotheism) to enter Christian communities, while at the same time allowing these communities, now freed from many of the demanding Jewish regulations, to enter more easily into the wider world of the culture of antiquity. As Paul conceived it, faith transcends all boundaries: all are now equal in Christ, they are a "new creation."[4]

By emancipating himself from the mission of Peter, James, and other early disciples of Jesus, by his emphasis on faith as a "new existence" and on Christian freedom, Paul preserved the emergent Christianity from assuming the form of a legal system. Religion as primarily a legal system played a major role in Judaism and later in Islam. But the temptation of legalism is also a constant thread running through the history of the Church; the great reforming figures—from Luther to Bonhoeffer—always invoke Pauline freedom from the law.

The pillars of the Jerusalem apostolic community—James, Peter, and John—were able to make concessions to the radical reformer Paul and thus avoid a schism by dividing their responsibilities and recognizing each other: the Jerusalem apostles would continue their apostolic work among Jews and Judeo-Christians, but they would confer on Paul the trust and freedom to conduct missions among the Gentiles at large.[5] We should bear in mind that what we now call

Christianity grew primarily out of Paul's courageous reform mission, while the various currents of Judeo-Christianity gradually petered out. We can only conjecture whether this was due to the external historical events or, instead, to the difference between the "conservatism" of the Jerusalem community and the intellectual dynamism of Paul's missionary vision.

Paul brings his version of Christianity and Christian universalism to a world shaped by Hellenistic philosophy and Roman politics at a time when Greek mythology and Roman political religion were in a crisis of credibility. However, the idea of a "new Israel" without borders eventually runs up against the limits of this culture of antiquity; instead of an Israel without borders, the Church became a "second Israel" and a third "religion" alongside Judaism and Hellenistic paganism. In addition, it also had to define itself vis-à-vis the Gnostic currents and the schools of wisdom and piety (*pietas*) of that time, as well as many religious cults. The representatives of the Roman state religion regarded the strange spread of Christianity as a politically dangerous phenomenon. They persecuted it and thus consolidated it as a counterculture, as religious-political dissent. In so doing, they transformed it into an alternative to the surrounding religious world.

Christians who refused to participate in Roman pagan rituals for religious reasons (considering them a form of idolatry) were persecuted as disloyal and therefore politically dangerous citizens, as "atheists" who were depriving the empire of the protection of the gods (*pax deorum*).

Nevertheless, the witness of the heroic sacrifices of Christian martyrs and the mutual solidarity in Christian communities, as well as the later efforts of early theologians to incorporate the faith into the intellectual concepts of Hellenistic philosophy, would eventually, as a result of the political calculations of the emperors, lead to a change in the status of Christianity in the empire—the conversion of Constantine. First tolerated and then privileged, Christianity assumed the political and cultural role of the *religio*. But it also transformed it; it transformed not only its "object" and ideological content but it also substantially enhanced its form. In its Christian form, the *religio* brought together a number of previously separate spheres—ritual, philosophical, spiritual, and political.

Pagan Rome was also familiar with what many people of our day associate with the term religion—namely, piety and a certain philosophy of life, a worldview—but it did not associate it with *religio*. Piety, spirituality—*pietas*—was more a question for the Mysteries; the "search for the meaning of life" and questions about the origin and nature of the world fell within the purview of philosophy, especially the philosophical interpretation of myths. These phenomena lived side by side separately; it was only in Christianity that religious belief, moral practice, spirituality, and philosophical reflection, as well as private and public rituals, were combined into a single entity, represented and administered by a single institution.

In the second century before Christ, the pagan philosopher Marcus Terentius Varro distinguished between three kinds of theology: *theologia naturalis* (philosophical theology), *theologia civilis* (the juridical and political aspect of worship), and *theologia mythica* (traditional religious symbols and narratives); at the turn of the third century after Christ, Tertullian, the Christian theologian and influential creator of Latin theological terminology, integrated all these aspects into the concept of *religio*.[6] In order to distinguish themselves from Roman pagan *religio* (and from Judaism, which long before Christianity had acquired the legal status of *religio* in the Roman Empire), Christian apologists now designated their faith as *religio vera*—the *true* religion.

With Constantine's legalization of Christianity and Justinian's proclamation of Christianity as the state religion, the path of following Christ became a religion in the sense of a Roman political *religio*, a "common language" and the central cultural pillar of a powerful civilization. Faith thus acquired the protective (but also limiting) shell of religion, reminiscent of the role of the *persona* in Jung's concept of the human personality: a mask that allows external communication while protecting the intimacy and integrity of the interior. But if this mask becomes hypertrophied and hardened, it suffocates life. This applies not only to individuals but also to spiritual and social systems.

As the Christian faith became increasingly embodied in philosophy (or, more precisely, as it allowed faith to be fertilized by philosophy, combining the Hebrew spirit with the spirit of Hellenistic thought), it acquired the form of metaphysical Christian theology with different emphases in its Roman and Greek versions. Faith was increasingly understood as a teaching, as a doctrine. Jesus's listeners reacted to his preaching with astonishment: "What is this? A new teaching full of authority."[7] The question arises whether the fusion of faith with political power and the incarnation of faith in the form of "doctrine" does not gradually bring about a weakening of that divine power that had so captivated the first disciples of Jesus. Already in antiquity Christianity also fulfilled the role of spirituality: the systematic cultivation of the deeper dimension of faith. This happened in particular thanks to the desert fathers, that radical alternative version of Christianity, initially dissenting from the mainstream "imperial Christianity," whose power and privilege quickly established itself. This movement of men and women who went to the deserts of Palestine, Syria, and Egypt and formed communities of "alternative Christianity" was later integrated into the "greater Church" and institutionalized in the form of monastic life and monastic communities. It acquired a legal form alongside other Church structures, but it is from the monastic milieu that the impulses for reforming the Church emerged over the centuries.

Christianity, as a combination of political *religio, fides* (based on philosophical thought), and schools of piety (*pietas*), bore enormous cultural fruit and achieved political success, building and consolidating over centuries one of the most powerful empires in the world. It succeeded in integrating many new stimuli from different cultures and philosophies; it survived the fall of Rome and later the great schism between Rome and Byzantium; it also resisted external invasions and expanded into parts of the world that were gradually being rediscovered. The Christian faith (especially in the form of doctrine and liturgy) became the common language of much of the world.[8]

Nevertheless, the romantic notion of the Middle Ages as a kind of golden age of faith must be taken with a pinch of salt. More detailed historical research shows that it was primarily specific layers of society that were affected by Christianization and evangelization. In particular, it affected those who (especially in the monasteries and later in the universities) actively shaped the culture by which we often form our image of that period. The spirituality and ethos of Christianity only slowly and gradually made inroads into the broad strata of the population, however, and for a long time they intermingled significantly with ancient pre-Christian religiosity. Paradoxically, the Christian faith had its greatest impact on the lower classes during the rise of modernity, when the Church lost its political power. At that time, bishops, who had previously been mainly feudal lords who were able to manage large estates, began to be chosen from the educated urban classes, who then became more concerned with the education of the priests and the people.[9]

Within *Christianitas*, however, a major divergence occurred after the dark tenth century (particularly after the great crisis of the papacy): the reform movement, emanating especially from the monastery of Cluny, provoked a clash between the monks and the secular clergy; the movement sought to reform, elevate, and discipline the clergy by assimilating them as monastics, emphasizing discipline, obedience, the order of prayer, celibacy, and education. The protagonists of the Cluniac reform rose to the top of the Church hierarchy and unleashed a "papal revolution" in the dispute over investiture (the right to appoint bishops). This would break the monopoly of imperial power and create a duality of authority: secular and ecclesiastical, imperial and pontifical, which would profoundly affect the political culture of the West. A by-product of this conflict was the emergence of a secular culture, the realm of "the profane," that gradually emancipated itself from the sphere of ecclesiastical power and control.

In the Renaissance, this new culture received a powerful impetus in the form of scholarly interest in the study of Greek, due in part to the influence of emigrants from Byzantium at the Florentine court of the Medici after the fall of Constantinople. On the one hand, this interest encouraged the study of the New Testament in the original, prompting translations of the scriptures from the originals into the vernacular languages, thereby strengthening the self-confidence of the nations and also paving the way for the reform of the Church. On the other hand, it revived the study and popularization of classical culture and thereby contributed to the emergence of Renaissance humanism. The shift from Latin to Greek and especially to national languages undermined the medieval cultural empire (preparing the ground for the emergence of nation-states), as well as the hegemony of scholastic theology in the intellectual sphere.

Medieval *Christianitas* would suffer a fatal blow in the form of the great schism in Western Christianity, especially when theological disputes spilled over from the intellectual to the political sphere and gave rise to the devastating wars of the seventeenth century. No less fateful, however, was another schism: the separation of traditional theology from the emancipating world of the natural sciences. The power and prestige of the Christian religion was diminished by the aforementioned double schism, caused by clinging to an ossified theological system incapable of interpreting and integrating both reformist theological impulses and new scientific findings in a creative yet critical manner.

Disgusted with both warring camps of the Church, critical Christian intellectuals—of which Erasmus of Rotterdam is the prototype—sought to create a "third way for Christianity." Rejected by both camps, they became increasingly alienated from the traditional Christianity of the Church. Eventually, that current would culminate in the Enlightenment, which assumed many different forms. Some Enlightenment thinkers sought to humanize religion, others confused the God of the Bible with the "god of the philosophers" and Christianity with deism, while others replaced religious faith with the cult of human reason.

The culmination of the third branch of Christianity in the form of the Enlightenment and modern secular culture would seem to fulfill a scenario rooted in the very nature of Christianity: according to Marcel Gauchet, Christianity is "a religion that emerges from a religion," moving from the political infrastructure of society to the superstructure—to culture.[10] After the Enlightenment, this process was consummated: culture was no longer part of religion, but religion was part of culture.

Bit by bit, the institutions of the Church were losing their political power; the strength and vitality of Christianity now lay mainly in the moral and intellectual influence of faith on the cultural mentality of society.

However, the cultural mentality of modern society was changing and Christianity, as represented by the churches (especially in the eighteenth and nineteenth centuries), was gradually losing its intellectual influence.

The process of modernization was a process of fragmentation, of emancipation of individual elements that were previously integrated into a single entity. *Christianitas*, "Christian civilization," was disintegrating and nation-states and national cultures were growing. Latin lost its privileged position; translations of the Bible into national languages, promoted especially by the reformers, helped the development of national languages. Self-confident young natural sciences rejected the dominance of theology. Systematic rational inquiry, to which medieval scholasticism had made a strong contribution, was now supplemented by experimental methods and turned against scholastic theology.

The age of secularization was dawning: the Christian religion ceased to play the role of *religio* in the modern period.[11]

Secularization does not mean the end of religion or the end of the Christian faith. It means the transformation of the relationship between faith and religion: it is the end of the long-standing "marriage" between Christian faith and religion in the sense of *religio*.

Religion in the sense of *religio*, the integrating force of society, is not disappearing, but this role is no longer played by the Christian faith. Other phenomena are becoming the "common language" of modern societies. However, after the break with religion in the sense of *religio*, the Christian faith did not become nonreligious but was gradually incorporated into another form of religion—one created by the secular culture of modern times.

The role of *religio*, religion as the "common language" and shared cultural basis of European civilization, began to be played by the natural sciences and secular culture, especially the arts (suffice it to recall the religious cult of artists and geniuses, from the Renaissance through the Romantics to the postmodern cult of pop-culture stars), as well as nationalism and later "political religions" such as Communism, Fascism, and Nazism.

Capitalist economics, the all-embracing global market, could be described as the *religio* of today. Numerous sociologists and philosophers of culture have addressed the pseudo-religious role of capitalism,[12] replacing monotheism with "money-theism," the capitalist cult of money.

Some "secular religions" have their own mystique, offering a certain "ecstatic" relationship with transcendence understood in a variety of ways. Observing the burgeoning market in chemical, psychological, and spiritual drugs—remedies for tranquilization as well as for excitement—we are tempted to stand Karl Marx's famous statement on its head: today opium is the religion of the people.

Although these phenomena have in many ways taken over certain psychological and social aspects of *religio*, they do not, however, perceive themselves as religions or label themselves as such. The term "religion," as it evolved and, in particular, became established during the process of secularization, now has a completely different meaning and content.

Since the Enlightenment, the word "religion" has referred to one sector of social life alongside others. Religion, as understood in modern times, is no longer an all-encompassing entity, a language that is understood by everyone and unites almost everyone; it is no longer a *religio*. In the modern understanding, religion has become just one of the language games, to borrow a term from Ludwig Wittgenstein. The community that this game unites and that accepts its rules is gradually shrinking.

Religion is now seen as a "worldview," just one alongside others. Apart from religion, there are now many other areas of society that want to follow their own rules. Religion has ceased to be ubiquitous and is therefore no longer "invisible" like the air that everyone breathes; it has stopped being something to be "taken for granted"; it is possible to maintain a critical distance from it; since the Enlightenment, religion has become a subject of study and criticism. Medieval theology was understood as the "science of God"; since the Enlightenment (witness Schleiermacher), theology has become a hermeneutic of faith, moving more toward a "science of religion."

On the threshold of the modern age, Christianity was enfeebled, among other things, by its disintegration into "denominations" or "confessions" held by different churches; then it was discredited by the destructive wars between those denominations. Since the Reformation, even within the West, Christianity has existed "in the plural": there are several "Christian religions." Gradually, the reformed streams of Christianity ceased to see themselves as innovations within one Church and began to dissociate themselves clearly from the "old" Church—mentally, theologically, and organizationally. Protestantism stood alongside Catholicism, and the Protestant camp itself became diverse. Unlike the *religio*, which bonded the whole, the *confessio* is the concern of *a part*; it is—though usually loath to admit it—just one language game among others.

Then came the next step: Christianity itself acquired the status of one religion alongside others. The explorers and colonizers of non-European continents began to perceive the rituals, customs, and narratives of these places in the light of their experience of contemporary Christianity as analogous to Christianity, as *religions*; for them they were "other religions." Also, Islam, which Christianity had to confront for centuries, only gradually ceased to be seen by Christians as a Christian heresy (a form of Christianity distorted by demons) and began to be seen as "another religion."

During the modern period, Christianity has fitted itself into what is meant by religion in the modern secular age: even for many Christians, it is seen as a worldview, concerned mainly with "the other world" and, in this world, concerned mainly with morality. As the sociologist Ulrich Beck has shown, after the initial disputes between natural scientific rationality and Christian religion, scientific rationality recognized that it could not master and fulfill all dimensions of individual and social life, and it permitted "religion" to become an expert on the "otherworldly" and "spiritual," to provide an aesthetic and rhetorical adornment to certain private, familial, and, exceptionally, social celebrations.[13]

This notion of Christianity persists to this day in the general consciousness not only of the secular public but also of many Christians: Christianity is understood as a religion (one of the religions), as "a system of beliefs and practices that unite all its adherents in a single moral community called a church."[14]

Christianity in the modern period is poorer, "leaner" than its medieval form. Many of the cultural and social roles that the premodern Christian religion filled and had a monopoly of have been assumed by secular institutions. While Christianity did become embedded in modern culture, the dominant element of that culture tended to be secular humanism, that "unwanted child" of a Christianity that was moving further and further away from ecclesiastical Christianity. While Christianity in its ecclesiastical (especially Catholic) form became a de facto part of the modern world, for a long time it could not come to terms with modernity (and its defining philosophy, Enlightenment humanism) and even waged many cultural wars with it that were lost in advance.

It was precisely because of the culture wars with the ideologies of late modernity that the modern form of Christianity was further deformed: the faith itself became highly ideologized. The form of the Catholic Church and theology of the "Pian era" (between the pontificates of Pius IX and Pius XII, mid-nineteenth to mid-twentieth century), a counterculture that stood in opposition to Protestantism, socialism, and liberalism, would become "Catholicism"—that is, to a large extent an "-ism" among other "isms." In other words, it became ideologized.

The Second Vatican Council in the second half of the twentieth century was not only an attempt at a "gentlemen's agreement" between the Catholic Church and modernity but also an effort to move from Catholicism to Catholicity and in the direction of an ecumenical Christianity—an attempt to de-ideologize the faith and de-clericalize the Church. The reform-minded council wanted to liberate the Church from nostalgia for premodern *Christianitas*, and it outlined a way to move the Church out of its narrow confessional form of modern times toward greater ecumenical openness.

But the effort to reconcile the Church with modernity came too late, and paradoxically it came at a moment when modernity was already on its way out. The Church's effort to achieve ecumenicity in a threefold sense—unity among Christians, dialogue with other religions, and rapprochement with secular humanism, with "nonbelievers"—never got more than halfway: continuing on this path remains a task for the afternoon of Christianity. We will return to all these ideas later in this book.

We have seen that the modern form of religion was not the first and will probably not be the last sociocultural incarnation of the Christian faith in history. This form of religion was created by the secular age early on, but its plausibility was eroded and collapsed at the very end of the modern secular age (which occurred at the turn of the 1970s).

It seems to me that this process is coming to a head in our time, with two phenomena that are, however, more its symptom than its cause or essence. One is the exposure of the pandemic of sexual, psychological, and spiritual abuse in the Church, and the other is the experience of churches being shut and services suspended during the coronavirus pandemic. The former points to a crisis of the status of the clergy, calls for an end to clericalism and a rethink of the role of priests and the relationship between priests and laity in the Church.

The second was a call for Christians not to rely solely on the service of the clergy but to seek new forms of experiencing and celebrating the mystery of faith beyond the traditional liturgy and sacral spaces.

We have said that the Christian faith already seems to be at odds with the second historical form of religion. Will it find or create another form of religion, or is the time coming for a nonreligious Christianity? Was the religious form of Christianity only one phase of its historical development?

The idea that the Christian faith can and should live apart from religion, that it is even "antireligious," was expressed most clearly in so-called dialectical theology in Germany. It opposed both liberal attempts to reconcile faith with the culture of bourgeois society and the flirtation and collaboration of the nationalist Deutsche Christen with Nazism. Karl Barth attempted to lead the Christian faith out of the shallows of nineteenth-century liberal theology with a pathos and radicalism similar to that with which Martin Luther once sought to free it from the web of medieval scholasticism, the accumulation of moral merit, and reliance on the intermediary activities of the hierarchical Church. For Barth, religion was a blasphemous attempt by humans to attain to God by their own efforts and manipulate God by using human devices such as theological speculation and moral endeavor, as well as any other means of anticipating and de facto supplanting the unmerited gift of divine grace. Karl Barth conceived faith as God, in complete freedom, bending down to humankind through the Word, through God's self-giving in the words of the Bible and especially in the incarnate Word, Jesus Christ crucified.

For Dietrich Bonhoeffer, religion was primarily associated with the idea of a strong, powerful God, an idea that, in his view, obscured and falsified the true face of the God to whom the Bible bears witness. That face was evident, on the contrary, in the "God of powerlessness"—in Jesus's self-surrender on the cross. The adult must dispense with God as a scientific hypothesis, with a God who scampers hither and thither in the light of rational knowledge before taking refuge in the holes of "mystery." The adult Christian must accept the world without religious, metaphysical, and quasi-scientific explanations and live in it "as if there were no God" (*etsi Deus non daretur*); he must discard "religious pre-understanding" just as St. Paul rejected circumcision as a prerequisite and condition of Christianity. Without the patriarchal notion of God, it is possible to live honestly, responsibly, and maturely before and with God.

Thus, in a sense, Bonhoeffer picks up the gauntlet thrown down to traditional Christianity by the critique of religion from the lips of Feuerbach, Marx, Nietzsche, and Freud. Bonhoeffer's theology of nonreligious Christianity was not born in a university study; its urgency is heightened by the fact that it was reflected upon and written down in letters in a Nazi prison before his execution.[15]

Bonhoeffer's critique of a bourgeois Christianity that had betrayed the radicality of the Gospel and conformed to the establishment is reminiscent of Kierkegaard. In his rejection of religious images of God, Bonhoeffer comes close to what the medieval mystic Meister Eckhart expressed in his prayer, "I beg God to deliver me from God."[16]

Nonetheless, Bonhoeffer's "nonreligious Christianity" also had strong social and political aspects. The only authentically Christian transcendence Bonhoeffer recognized was human self-transcendence in sacrificial love. He affirmed his understanding of faith through his political involvement and the sacrifice of his life. The Latin American liberation theologians may be considered heirs to this political aspect of Bonhoeffer's concept of Christianity.

The effort to liberate the Christian faith from "religion" in the form of metaphysical "ontotheology" and from the mentality of the Church, so entrenched in the bourgeois society of late modernity, was definitely a legitimate attempt to revive the radicality of the Gospel message from beneath all sorts of ideological and social overlays and accretions. It is important to remember, however, that the efforts of reformers to present "original Christianity" tend to be projections of their own ideals back onto history. It must be acknowledged that these are further historically conditioned interpretations of the Gospel, which can be very valuable, but should not be understood as reconstructions of some pure, "naked" Christianity.

This is also why I believe that a completely "nonreligious Christianity" is a mere abstraction. In historical reality, we always encounter faith within a culture, a cultural system. Early Christianity took its first steps within the context of a particular religion, within the framework of the ideas and concepts of rabbinical Judaism. Then it passed through various forms of religion, as well as through the process of secularization of modern society. Just as in personal life we cannot step out of a particular situation without stepping into another, so faith is always "situated" and sooner or later finds some cultural and social form, some form of "religion." But it may be religion in a different form and in a different sense than what the word "religion" designated in the past.

In today's postsecular era—as we shall see—two forms of religion in particular are offered as the fruit and consequence of the transformation of religion in the process of secularization: religion as a defense of group (for example, national or ethnic) identity, and religion as a spirituality separate from church and tradition. While the first of these forms is primarily intended to strengthen group cohesion and is close to political ideology, the second offers a certain integration of the personality and is closer to the role of psychotherapy. The Christian faith should maintain a critical distance from both, so that the Christianity of the future is not transformed either into an identitarian political ideology or into a vague spirituality dissipating into esotericism.

I am convinced that those Christians who lived very intensely through the collective dark nights of the twentieth century—Teilhard de Chardin at the front during the First World War, Bonhoeffer in a Nazi dungeon, and my teachers of faith, the Czech theologians in communist prisons[17]—have, in particular, bequeathed to our time visions and intuitions based on those experiences of faith that need further theological reflection in order to inspire the afternoon of Christian history.

Religion in its premodern political form of *religio*, or in its modern ideological form, can hardly be a living space for faith any longer;

those forms were too narrow, and it would be stifled. Faith must be brought into a new space, as when Paul brought Christianity out of the confines of the Judaism of his day.

The substantive *religio* is usually derived from the verb *religare*, to reunite. Religion in the sense of *religio* is an integrating force in society; that which integrates society is its religion (*religio*). However, the noun *religio* can also be derived from the verb *relegere*, meaning "to read again." This can lend the concept of religion a new meaning.

I believe that the Christianity of tomorrow will be above all a community of a new hermeneutic, a new reading, a new and deeper interpretation of the two sources of divine revelation, scripture and tradition, and especially of God's utterance in the signs of the times.

We will return to these ideas at the end of this book.

SIX

Darkness at Noon

In this chapter I talk about the noonday crisis in the history of Christianity. I have borrowed the title of Arthur Koestler's novel *Darkness at Noon*,[1] which was one of the first literary works to alert the world to the crimes of the Stalinist regime in Russia. The title was an obvious allusion to the Gospel narrative that at the crucifixion of Jesus there was darkness over the whole earth at noon. For me, the phrase "darkness at noon" associates and unites several important motifs: the cross of Jesus, dark nights on personal and historical journeys of faith, and the noonday crisis of Jung's comparison of human life to a day.

Before we try to understand the noonday crisis, it is necessary to ask whether it is appropriate to speak today of a crisis of faith, a crisis of the Church, a crisis of Christianity. The term "crisis" is one of the most frequently used words of our time; no wonder that many find it tiresome or offensive. Has there ever been a time without crises? Is there anything really special about the crises of our time? Isn't this sense of exclusivity an illusion that grips every generation? Is it not even a certain manifestation of narcissistic self-centeredness, that typical disease of our time, that if we cannot speak in superlatives about our achievements, then at least we refer to them as the "most" severe, serious, alarming, etc.? Do we not downplay and underestimate the crises of the past just because they do not directly affect us?

Let's face it, we can't answer these questions. They are questions for the Lord of History; we are not in a godlike position, we cannot step out of our time and judge it "objectively" from the outside. After all, the point is not to "objectively" compare the severity of the present crisis with those we have not experienced. According to the eschatological view of Christian theology, every moment is a "crisis" of sorts (a moment of decision and judgment), unlike the apocalyptic view, which always sees the ongoing crisis as the final one.

Statistics tell us that the number of Christians continues to grow, that never before have there been so many Christians on this planet as there are today, that Christians still represent the largest "opinion group" within humanity today. However, the number of Christians is growing primarily due to the high birth rate in non-Western countries. For these same reasons the number of Muslims is also growing, and at a much faster rate.

Let us now focus primarily on the largest of the Christian churches, the Catholic Church. When we study the history of the papacy, we encounter many appalling scandals there. Today it is different: during the last half-century at least, a succession of respectable personalities has occupied the See of Peter. Although the Church today faces many scandals, it can be said that the moral authority of the papacy has never been as high internationally as it is in our time. Nevertheless, it is one of the paradoxes of our time that Pope Francis—a compelling pastor, an undisputed global moral authority who is respected and loved far beyond the Church—is subjected to more attacks and open dissent within the Church than any pope in modern history. The very Catholics who have always pledged unconditional loyalty to papal authority are now taking an aggressive stand against a pope who does not conform to their taste and does not interpret their views.

The crisis of "organized religion" particularly affects the mainstream churches. In many Western countries, churches, monasteries, and seminaries are becoming depopulated, church buildings are being closed and sold, and the number of people formally leaving churches or giving up regular attendance at services is increasing. At the time of the empty and closed churches during the coronavirus epidemic in the spring of 2020, I wondered if this was a kind of prophetic warning of what these churches might look like in a few decades' time.[2]

The notion that the decline of the large churches is confined to part of Europe and that it is the result of the liberalization of Christian theology and the weakening of Church discipline, while the Church flourishes on other continents, is a delusion held by certain Church circles. The United States of America is no longer the Christian "city on a hill" that the alliance of conservative Catholics and evangelicals used to contrast with secularized Europe. Western conservative critics of secular culture used to hold up as a model for the West first the postcommunist countries (*ex Oriente lux, ex Occidente luxus*) and then, after the demise of that illusion, they pointed to the alleged flourishing of Christianity in the so-called developing countries. Some of them hope for a revival of traditional Christianity in the West from Christian immigrants, especially from Africa. Realistic African theologians, however, warn us against idealizing African Christianity and a fascination with the number of those baptized; they point out that the growth in the number of Catholics in Africa is due more to population growth than to the success of evangelization. African theologian Alain Clément Amiézi has written: "We are producing baptized people but not Christians."[3] He observes that African churches often maintain people in a state of infantile religiosity rather than offering a catechesis that offers depth, and they settle for a syncretism in which identification with African culture greatly overshadows Christian identity.

With the unstoppable process of globalization, it is to be expected that developments similar to those that accompanied the secularization of Europe will occur, after a certain delay, on other continents, including in many so-called developing countries. There, secularization has begun with their Western-educated elites and young people using the internet. The highly simplified image of Western living standards and lifestyles, disseminated by films and electronic media, is changing value orientations in poor countries and giving rise in their relationship with the West to a mixture of desire, envy, and imitation combined with rejection, fear, and resentment. Likewise, in some Muslim countries, I have encountered this ambivalent relationship with the West: the power of attraction of the forbidden and the desire to subdue this temptation through demonization and aggression. Religious fanatics want to destroy the aspects of a foreign culture that both attract and terrify them.

The Catholic Church has lost many members in countries in Europe and Latin America that were traditionally the most "Catholic." In my travels to Latin America, I repeatedly heard the view that as a result of the Church's reliance on the inertia of tradition and its neglect of the education of the faithful and solid spiritual formation, there has been a mass exodus of Catholics to Pentecostal sects and conversions to their simple fundamentalist theology and often very superficial emotional religiosity. The exposure of many cases of sexual abuse by the clergy and Church institutions has contributed to the secularization of Ireland. Meanwhile, in Poland, strong Catholicism is rapidly collapsing due to an unfortunate alliance between nationalist politicians and the conservative majority of the hierarchy—they have succeeded in causing far more damage to the Church in two years than the Communist government tried unsuccessfully for decades to cause, even when using all the means at its disposal.

Wherever the action of the Church is limited to the administration of the sacraments and religiosity is not transformed into personal faith, Christianity becomes a mere "cultural religion" that quickly fades and disappears with the change of the sociocultural paradigm.

Throughout Western civilization, there is a severe crisis of the clergy in the Catholic Church. The widely discussed sexual abuse scandals are only one aspect of this much broader and deeper crisis of the clergy as a body. What constitutes the identity of the priest and his role in the Church and in society? Previous answers to this question have been undermined by the changes in society and especially by the crisis mentioned above.

It is not only in the public opinion of secular society, which mostly considers priests to be a relic of the past, that we will have a hard time finding coherent and credible answers to the question of what the priest of the future should look like; the response of believers and even priests themselves is also often one of embarrassment. Pious platitudes often conceal insecurity. The traditional patriarchal role of the priest—the ideal image that the education in many seminaries is still focused on—clearly does not correspond to the reality and conditions of today.

The number of people interested in the priestly vocation is falling drastically, and the whole network of parish administration, as it was created several centuries ago, is being irreparably torn apart in many countries. The rescue attempts of the hierarchy—importing priests from Poland, Africa, and Asia, merging parishes, etc.—are not a realistic solution and will not stop or alleviate the deepening of this crisis; it is more like "shifting the berths on the Titanic." The satisfaction of seeing enthusiastic traditionalists applying to a number of seminaries and monasteries usually soon passes; traditionalism is either a temporary "infantile disorder" of immature converts or a cover for psychologically unbalanced people who will create serious problems for the Church structures. If decades of Church-wide prayer for new priestly vocations has gone unanswered, perhaps God is telling us that he expects us to look for other doors and other solutions instead of stubbornly pounding on the doors he himself has closed.

I believe that even the steps that will have to be taken sooner or later, steps that the Vatican is still hesitant to take and that therefore will probably come too late—namely, the ordination of married men and at least the ordination of women as deacons—will not solve this crisis sufficiently. The situation will not change unless the Church adopts a completely new model of pastoral ministry, different from that of territorial parishes, unless it offers a new understanding of the priest's mission in the Church and in society, unless it creates the conditions for a new style of training for the priesthood, and unless it creates even greater scope for the involvement of the laity, both men and women, in the life and activities of the Church.

Also, many suggestions from practice—such as the activities of the worker-priests or the experience of those of us who were priests of the underground Church in communist Czechoslovakia, whereby priestly ministry was combined with a civil vocation—deserve to be reevaluated. The model of synodality promoted by Pope Francis along with the decentralization of the Church can perhaps assist these changes because the specific solutions must always reflect the social and cultural conditions of each country.

Let us always bear in mind, however, that genuine renewal of the Church will not be generated at the desks of bishops, or in councils or conferences of experts; instead, it requires powerful spiritual impulses, thorough theological reflection, and the courage to experiment.

The most painful crises of recent years are the wounds inflicted by Church officials on defenseless people, especially children and adolescents; in doing so, they have also damaged the credibility of the Church in today's world, and these wounds will be slow and difficult to heal. The pandemic of sexual and psychological abuse, as well as the abuses of power and authority by members of the clergy, which have been gradually exposed after being covered up and downplayed for so long, were probably the last straws for tens of thousands of Catholics and led to their decisions to leave the Church.

Few topics have been discussed by the Church in recent centuries as frequently as sexuality. It is the area in which the Church threatened hellish punishments, imposed heavy burdens on people, and refused to listen with understanding and compassion to the problems that arose from trying to strictly observe all the Church's regulations concerning their sex life. This is probably why, after the hypocrisy of so many of the spokespersons of this kind of morality was exposed, the public, through the media, lashed out at the Church with far greater vehemence than at other institutions where abuses were also taking place. The Church has now paid the price for its tendency to treat the sixth commandment as the first and most important of all. After the embarrassing interrogation of the faithful in confessionals, confessors and judges are now having to confess before the judgment of the public and sometimes before civil courts.

The phenomenon of abuse is playing a similar role today to that of the sale of indulgences that precipitated the Reformation in the late Middle Ages. What at first seemed to be a marginal phenomenon, today—as then—clearly points to even deeper problems: the disorders of *the system*—namely, the relations between Church and power, and between clergy and laity, among many others.

In the case of sexual abuse, the Catholic Church's attitude to sexuality continues to be a major factor, especially for members of the clergy who are often unprepared to bear the psychological consequences of a commitment to permanent sexual abstinence and a life without a family environment. I believe that sooner or later the coupling of the priesthood with celibacy will return to where it originated: to monastic communities, which can compensate to some extent for the absence of family life with the environment of a "spiritual family" and perhaps also better sublimate spiritually the need for sexual intimacy than conventional seminary education is able to.

A striking phenomenon is the inability of many in religious authority to work with their own "shadow" (the unconscious component of their personality) and to cope with the pressure from superiors and the environment to maintain a rigid *persona*—a prescribed, enforced, and expected external role, lifestyle, and behavior. Sometimes, in order to preserve the desired image, those in positions of authority in the Church have distorted their humanity and banished their "weaknesses" to their subconscious. But the weaknesses do not cease to exist and exert their influence; on the contrary, they escape rational control. This has led not only to hypocrisy but also sometimes to a split personality—leading a "double life," the Jekyll and Hyde syndrome. Many of these phenomena are described in extensive psychoanalytic studies (for instance, Drewermann's once-provocative book *Kleriker*) or journalistic investigations (such as Martel's *In the Closet of the Vatican*).[4] It is worth remembering what Jesus said about the roots of this evil in his polemics with the Pharisees, whom he called "whited sepulchers," outwardly shining with purity but inwardly full of rottenness.[5] Pascal also pointed out that the desire to "be an angel" often leads to demonic results.

With regard to these phenomena, differences within the Church have become apparent: while Pope Emeritus Benedict blamed sexual abuse on the alleged laxity of clerical morality as a result of the sexual revolution of the 1960s, Pope Francis boldly diagnosed the profounder causes of these phenomena as being clericalism, triumphalism, and the way the Church deals with power and authority. Indeed, cases of abuse were widespread in the Church long before the 1960s. It would seem that some members of the clergy, especially after the Church was deprived of secular power, made up for this loss by exercising and abusing their own power and authority within the Church, particularly in relation to the defenseless, to children and to women, who did not enjoy their full rights within the Catholic Church, and still do not.

After this wave of scandals, the Church finds itself in a similar moral and psychological situation as the German nation after the revelation of the atrocities in the concentration camps. In saying this, I do not mean to equate the Holocaust with sexual abuse; I have something else in mind: just as the vast majority of Germans did not commit crimes in the concentration camps and did not know about them, so most Catholics, including most priests, did not abuse children and minors and did not know about these things—or at least the extent of them. Thinkers such as Karl Jaspers have asked how far the German nation as a whole bore responsibility for what some of its members did in its name, and they have distinguished between different degrees of complicity.[6] It is now legitimate to ask how the Church as such should be held accountable for the abuse of "sacred power" and authority by some of its representatives. Maybe the fact that it is in Germany that the local Church is asking these questions with such urgency—especially in the context of the so-called synodal path—is related to the moral sensitivity of German historical memory.

Sexual and psychological abuse in the Church is an abuse of power that evades scrutiny and criticism by referring to its unquestioned sacred origin. In marked contradiction with the spirit of the Gospel and its understanding of ministry, the romantic pseudo-mystique of the priesthood, by emphasizing the "sacred power of the priest," created a magical aura (*persona* in the sense of Jung's depth psychology) around the person of the priest, which often attracted candidates with psychological and moral problems.[7]

Jesus was not a priest but a member of the "laity." When there was tension between priestly, ritualistic religion and its prophetic critics, he sided with the prophets. His prophetic words about the destruction of the temple and the priestly temple religion cost him his life. Jesus did not make the circle of his twelve friends into priests in the sense of the temple religion of Israel. He wanted them to follow his example and strive to be "the least and servants of all." Jesus did not establish a "hierarchy"—a "holy government" in the sense of a ruling class in the midst of God's people. He empowered his disciples to be a provocative contrast to the world of power and to religious and political manipulation. When breaking bread on the eve of his death, he entrusted them with the task of imitating his *kenosis*—self-surrender, self-denial, self-giving.

The New Testament—in the letter to the Hebrews—calls Christ a high priest not in a sociological and historical sense but in a deeper, mystical, symbolic sense. The phrase *sacerdos alter Christus* (the priest is the second Christ) has been heard from the lips of several popes, it figures in many papal documents, and it is repeated in many first-mass sermons. It is, however, a dangerous phrase—it is fraught with the risk of great misunderstanding. There is no alternative, other Christ. There is one Christ and one only, one mediator between God and human beings. Christ is the only mediator, the representative of God to the people, and the representative of the people to God. Jesus is not a "second God" and the priest is not his substitute.[8] The priest is not a substitute Christ. Every Christian, through baptism, participates in the priestly role of Christ: to announce God's self-giving love to the world. The Catholic Church distinguishes between the *common priesthood* of all the baptized and the *ministerial priesthood* of the ordained ministers of the Church, but it nevertheless confesses that every Christian is called to make Christ present, to represent Christ in this world. The life of every Christian is in some sense eucharistic.

Christian existence is iconic: it is an art that makes the invisible visible through the witness of faith. However, a distinction must be made between the icon and the idol;[9] a priest must not be an idol. Wrestling with clericalism is a healthy kind of iconoclasm. Those whom the Church calls priests bear the indelible seal of the ministerial priesthood (the aforementioned common priesthood is based on the indelible seal of baptism) and are charged with fulfilling Jesus's command to be the last and the servant of all.[10] This is their way of following Christ. It is a significant aspect of "apostolic succession."

However, the most striking crisis phenomena—and the ones most discussed in the media—are not the really serious ones but rather their superficial aspects. The crisis of contemporary Christianity is not just about Church structures but about faith itself. I consider the claim that "faith is weakening" to be very premature. What is weakening, however, is not only the aforementioned power of the Church to control and discipline the life of faith but also, for example, the link between the language used in expressing the faith and the way it is lived. The crisis of the present form of the Church is not just the decline in the number of worshippers but the widening gulf between what the Church proclaims and how it proclaims it, on the one hand, and the ideas and opinions of the faithful, on the other. As Charles Taylor points out, Christians have been repeating many of the same words in the liturgy for millennia (such as when they recite the Creed), but they understand them differently[11] and some do not understand them at all.

Many of these wordings were created as part of a picture of the world that is very remote from our own. The Church and its theology have a hermeneutical mission: it is charged with the task of reinterpreting the message entrusted to it so that its meaning is not distorted by the changing cultural and social context. If preachers use biblical, dogmatic, and liturgical texts without making any effort to build a bridge between the world of these texts and the inner world of their hearers, if their knowledge of both worlds is only superficial, they reveal a lack of commitment, responsibility, and love for their mission; they are then like a "sounding brass."[12]

Whenever I read of cases in which the Congregation for the Doctrine of the Faith admonished or disciplined theologians when some subtle wording in their specialized books differed too much from the traditional language of Church documents, I would ask myself whether the relevant Vatican authorities were aware how dramatically the views and attitudes of a large proportion of even the "active faithful" differ nowadays from what they recite in the mass, what they learned in catechism classes, or what they heard in homilies.[13]

One of my great teachers of faith (but also of civic courage), the theologian Josef Zvěřina, who spent thirteen years in communist prisons and labor camps for his loyalty to Christ and the Church, summed up his relationship to the Church during the communist era with the words: "The Church—my love and my cross." At that time, as a young, enthusiastic convert, I did not understand how the Church—which I then perceived as a fighter for spiritual freedom against a totalitarian atheist regime—could be experienced as a cross, as a painful burden. Now I know.

During my recent illness with Covid-19, when, for a time, I was unable to work, read, or sleep at all, thoughts of the present state of the Church came painfully to me during those long sleepless nights. I kept coming back to the stories of the abused that I had heard in my conversations with victims, the feelings of disappointment with my bishop's attitudes, my disgust with Christians who support Donald Trump and other dangerous populists and nationalist demagogues who cloak themselves in Christian rhetoric ("defending Christian values"). I felt saddened by the hateful attacks on Pope Francis by such Catholics.

As I pondered on the Church, the words of the prophet Isaiah came back to me:

Why should you be beaten anymore?
Why do you persist in rebellion?
Your whole head is injured, your whole heart afflicted.
From the sole of your foot to the top of your head
there is no soundness—
only wounds and welts and open sores,
not cleansed or bandaged or soothed with olive oil.[14]

After evidence emerged that corruption and sexual abuses were committed by some members of the College of Cardinals and that the revered founder of a conservative religious order—a friend of the canonized Pope John Paul II—was an unscrupulous sexual predator, it was impossible not to think of Renaissance Rome, a visit to which once shook Martin Luther and confirmed him in his conviction that a radical break with this form of the Church was necessary. Is it possible to prevent a new reformation, which increasingly appears to be the necessary response to the present state of the Church, from happening without a schism?

During those sleepless nights, I tried to overcome the inner state of what St. Ignatius calls "the time of desolation" by constantly repeating a verse from the Apostles' Creed: *Credo in Spiritum Sanctum, sanctam ecclesiam catholicam, sanctorum communionem . . .* (I believe in the Holy Spirit, the holy catholic Church, the communion of saints . . .).

What does it mean that I believe in the Church? The very language of the Creed shows the difference between belief in God (*Credo in Deum, in Iesum Christum, in Spiritum Sanctum*) and the relationship to the Church (*credo . . . ecclesiam*): our faith does not relate to the Church in the same way as it does to God. Belief in the Church is not placed on the same plane as belief in God but neither is it something apart from our belief in God. Our relationship to the Church is part of our faith in the Holy Spirit, based on the trust that Jesus promised his disciples a Helper and Comforter, the Spirit of Truth, who would abide with them; the Church is the church of Christ insofar as the Spirit of Christ is at work in it. "Anyone who does not have the Spirit of Christ does not belong to him."[15] The statement of Jesus as rendered in Matthew's Gospel, whereby Jesus establishes his Church on the rock of Peter's confession—namely, the confession of Jesus's Messiahship—must be supplemented by the scene of the Pentecostal whirlwind of the Spirit, which is traditionally regarded as the "birthday of the Church." The Church is founded on a rock, but it must not become petrified. The Spirit, as the principle of its life, as the "circulation of the blood" that unites the various organs of its body, is the guarantor both of its unity and of its constant renewal.

As soon as I could do a bit of work again, I wrote in one of those sleepless nights a scathing text entitled "The Pseudo-religion of F."[16] I characterized a number of the phenomena that caused me pain—from religiously advocated hatred and violence to the advocates of a rigid legalistic religion, that "Catholicism without Christianity"—as a pseudo-religion that, despite all its differences, shares several common features. These are fundamentalism (the selective and purposeful use of sacred texts taken out of context), fanaticism (the inability and unwillingness to dialogue and to reflect critically on one's own opinions), and Pharisaism (the word is spelled with an "F" in Czech), clinging to the letter of the law, reminiscent of the attitudes of the Pharisees with whom Jesus waged a lifelong struggle. I was particularly concerned about the attempts of populist politicians in Poland, Hungary, Slovakia, Slovenia, and even in the Czech Republic to use religious rhetoric as a tool of populist, and often xenophobic and nationalist, far-right politics—and the collaboration of some Church leaders with such circles.

Isn't there something hiding behind the mask of religion that has nothing to do with faith as I understand it? Isn't this an instrumentalization and caricature of religion, a misuse of religious rhetoric to evoke strong emotions, to "unleash the genie" from the abyss of the unconscious? Where people experience something truly powerful, something that is *tremendum et fascinans*,[17] secular language is unable to express the power and intensity of that experience, and people (even "nonbelievers") spontaneously reach for religious terms and epithets. They can speak of divine beauty, but also of the demonic;

their enemies are no longer adversaries but "the Great Satan." Secular people, who as a rule underestimate the power of religion, do not realize what unconscious irrational forces these terms unleash; they cannot handle them, they cannot tame them. As Richard Kearney notes, the "Great Satan" can no longer be negotiated with: political conflicts are thus transformed into a scene of apocalyptic battles.

Where living faith is absent, there is scope both for cynical secular populists who exploit the "religious agenda" (such as a promise to criminalize abortion) to lure Christian voters and for fanatics who turn religious concepts into ammunition for culture wars. I can't help myself: it is impossible for me to walk under the same banners with those whose Christian rhetoric I perceive as "pseudo-religion F." When I observe that segment of Christians who have maybe never understood the Good News of Jesus and have turned Christianity into a militant religion, I begin to lose the hope that at some point in the historically foreseeable future it will be possible to unite all who claim the name of Jesus. I too have a sacred respect for the life of the unborn, but I cannot participate in the marches of those who have obsessively fixated on this one area and turned Christianity into a militant crusade to criminalize abortion and ban contraception. They have made this agenda the main and often the only criterion for judging the "Christianity" of politicians and how they vote in elections, thereby making themselves cheap prey for cunning demagogues. The gulf— not between churches but within them—is too deep at the present time. This division of Christians is one of the grievous features of the noonday crisis.

It is possible to view the noonday crisis in the history of faith as an epoch of atheism and "the death of God." The term "death of God" is most often associated with Nietzsche. But even before Nietzsche, Hegel had advanced a different version of the "death of God" in his *Phenomenology of Spirit*, a "biography of God" (*Lebenslauf Gottes*), inspired by Joachim of Fiore's three-age theory of history. For Hegel, the phrase "death of God" is a cipher for the historical moment between the "Age of the Son" and the "Age of the Spirit." Hegel ascribes a key meaning to this moment in the history of the Spirit: the experience of the radical eclipse of God's presence is a kind of updating of Christ's sacrifice on the cross (the "Good Friday of history"). In Jesus's voluntary sacrifice of love, death, which is essentially the negation of life and freedom, is negated by freedom and love, and thus this death becomes the negation of negation, the death of death. Atheism, which articulates the experience of that moment in the history of the Spirit, is thus for Hegel only a transitory historical phenomenon.

Atheism has been a concern of mine for years, and I will devote a separate chapter to it in this book. I have called existential atheism— the atheism of pain and protest against pain, evil, and suffering in the world—a mystical participation in the cross, in Jesus's cry of abandonment by God.[18] I am convinced that a mature faith must take seriously the experience of noonday darkness, which is part of both the Gospel story and the believer's spiritual journey, and be able to embrace and integrate it. The "atheism of protest" legitimately rejects the naive image of God as the guarantor of happiness and harmony in the world, as well as the convoluted theodicy that tries to trivialize the mystery of evil (*mysterium iniquitatis*)[19] with seemingly pious religious platitudes.

The noonday crisis in the history of faith has been explored theologically in remarkable ways by thinkers of "irreligious Christianity" (especially Dietrich Bonhoeffer), "the theology of the death of God" (especially Thomas Altizer), "Christian atheism" (such as Don Cupitt), and postmodern philosophers (such as Gianni Vattimo). They have all noted the inability of classical metaphysical theology to grasp the radical implications of historical and cultural transformations, and the need to take seriously the crisis of the existing perception of God, this noonday darkness and valley of the shadow of the death of the metaphysical God of the philosophers. They "grew ears" for the tidings of Nietzsche's Madman, who, with a lantern at noon, provoked the superficial atheists and the superficial Christians of his time.

Neither premodern theism nor modern atheism can adequately express the spiritual experience of our time nor provide an adequate response to its questions and challenges, which are giving rise to new impulses in postmodern philosophy and theology. New horizons and a new language are offered in particular by thinkers of continental and American phenomenological and hermeneutical philosophy of religion and philosophical theology, especially in connection with the so-called theological shift in French phenomenology.[20] Here I see a source of inspiration for that renewal of theology that I regard as a necessary part of the needed reform of Christianity.

Richard Kearney and his school of anatheism, which is very close to my heart, shows that thinking about faith in the wake of the break with traditional theism (the notion of God as the supreme being among other beings) can extract all that was valuable and valid in the modern critique of religion without accepting atheism as the only alternative. Anatheism means "to believe again"—in a new and deeper way, after faith has passed through the purifying fire of philosophical criticism. Anatheism is as far removed from traditional metaphysical theism as it is from atheism. God, according to Kearney, approaches us as a possibility,[21] as an offer; we are in a situation of free choice between belief and unbelief. This choice, however, is not merely a rational calculation, as in the case of Pascal's wager, but an existential choice. God often comes as a stranger and confronts us with the decision of whether to receive him with hospitality or with hostility.

It strikes me that the concept of anatheism provides a certain answer to the question of what sort of reflection on faith will carry us over the threshold of the afternoon of Christianity, once faith has weathered the noonday crisis, the dark night, and is looking for fresh expression. During the several decades of my pastoral practice, I have encountered a growing number of people who, in their mature age, are rediscovering the faith they once abandoned. They confess, "Today I believe again what I once believed, but I believe it differently." It is this "differently" that deserves our attention; it is this "differently" that provoked my reflections in this book.

I have said that the terms "noonday crisis" and "darkness at noon" remind me of the dark nights on personal and historical journeys of faith. We usually associate the term "dark night" with an eponymous poem and treatise by the Spanish Baroque mystic John of the Cross.[22] John writes first of the "dark night of the senses." At the beginning of the mystical journey, the soul is so captivated by the love of God that in the rush of passionate desire, like a lover's flight to her beloved on a summer night, everything "earthly" that might delay and distract love on this journey is plunged into darkness: the only light is desire itself. But God brings us out of these beginnings and leads us on. A soul accustomed to feelings of consolation, to knowledge and experience gained by contemplation, would be in danger of "spiritual gluttony." That is why God places it in a state of "contemplative aridity": it is incapable of reflective contemplation. The soul finds itself "in darkness," experiencing aridity, but at the same time an abiding desire to remain in solitude and *silence* with God.

But then comes the bitter and painful "night of the spirit," the night of faith, when, on the contrary, God is lost in the darkness of silence and the soul is afflicted by God's absence. Faith at this stage of the spiritual journey has no external support, and within the self there prevails the aridity and loneliness of the desert instead of the irrigating river of consolation in prayer. Even the most fundamental certainties of the spiritual pilgrim are shaken. Teresa of Avila lapsed into the conviction that her entire spiritual life had been and still was the work of the devil; John of the Cross felt eternally rejected by God; Thérèse of Lisieux felt that God did not exist and consciously stood in solidarity with the atheists of her time. But for John of the Cross, it is precisely this section of the journey that is the important transformation of the spiritual life into a form of "naked faith" in which its true core is laid bare and awakened.

Similarly, long before him, the medieval mystic Meister Eckhart had spoken of the faith of the "inner person" who, along with the outer (superficial) person, lays aside the "external god" and discovers "the God behind the god" with whom the soul, freed from "images" and fixation on external things, encounters "as the naked with the naked."

As I ponder on the thinking of these classics of Catholic mysticism, a question arises: Does such a maturing of faith not also take place in the "collective dark nights" of Church and social history? Certainly the dark nights of history include the tragic events of the twentieth century, especially the two world wars, the Holocaust and the Gulag, together with the terrible crimes of the Nazi and Communist dictatorships—and also the terrorism of our own time—what Pope Francis has called a "fragmented Third World War."

In the final essay of his last book, aptly entitled "The Wars of the Twentieth Century and the Twentieth Century as War."[23] Jan Patočka provided a very thought-provoking spiritual reflection on the experience of war, on the "leaning out of life into the night," the leaning out of the world of day, reason, and power into the night of nonbeing, chaos, and violence. Here Patočka also recalls the frontline experience of Teilhard de Chardin. I see this essay by Patočka—including the call for "solidarity of the shaken"—as an example of a kairological approach to history, an example of a spiritual reading of the meaning of historical events. The "dark nights of the spirit" and the "eclipse of God" in *late modernity* are evidenced in the works of many writers of existential literature, philosophy, and theology who have reflected on the loss of religious certitudes in secular society.

However, in considering the "collective dark nights" of history, we cannot confine ourselves solely to our own history, the history of Christianity. The unforgettable chapter of modern history is the Holocaust—the criminal attempt at total genocide of a people to whom belong the irrevocable promises and blessings of the God of our common faith. Some Christian theologians—J. B. Metz, to name just one—have rightly devoted themselves to a "post-Auschwitz theology" and have listened carefully to Jewish reflection on this attempted genocide of a chosen people.

The very decision of the Church to accept the Hebrew Bible, the Bible of Jesus, as the authoritative Word of God was a declaration that the memory of the people of Israel was part of its own historical memory. For that reason, Christianity cannot erase from its own memory even the tragic events of modern Jewish history. Many of the ways in which the Jewish faith continues to come to terms with the mystery of radical evil are also inspiring for Christianity, which in many places in today's world is exposed to cruel violence, and already the Christian victims of today outnumber the martyrs of the first centuries.

Some Jewish thinkers—one thinks of Hans Jonas, for example—have come to the conclusion that the experience of the Holocaust cannot leave our image of God and our language about God unchanged.[24] Isn't the idea of a powerful God just a projection of our power aspirations onto the heavens? Jonas returns to the kabbalistic idea of a Creator who voluntarily withdrew into himself to make room for creation and, consequently, also for human freedom and responsibility. Other theologians see the dark hour of Jewish history as *hester panim*, the veiling of (God's) face—an expression we encounter in the Psalms. Elie Wiesel sees faith after the Holocaust as an expression of loyalty to those who kept the faith even in the hell of Auschwitz.

For Christian thinkers, the crisis of the image of God as an impassive, omnipotent director of nature and history is an opportunity to rediscover the theology of the cross: to discover a God who shows his *pathetic* love (a passionate and suffering love) in Jesus who surrendered himself on the cross.

Here I anticipate one of the main ideas of this book: the Christian faith identifies itself by repeatedly entering into the Easter drama of death and Resurrection. Also, before entering a new, afternoon phase in the history of Christianity, the lengthy darkness of noon is a kind of *anamnesis*, a reminder of Easter. Each celebration of Easter is an opportunity to touch the very heart of Christianity afresh and to understand it more deeply. I am writing this text shortly after the second Easter that Christians in much of the world were unable to celebrate in the usual way due to the coronavirus pandemic. Perhaps this new experience was also an invitation from God to gain a fresh understanding of the mystery of Easter, which we commemorate each year.

SEVEN

Is God Coming Back?

Let us first return to reflection on secularization. We should differentiate between three phenomena: *secularization* as a certain sociocultural process, *secularism* as a one-sided ideological interpretation of secularization, and the *secular age* as a certain chapter of history in which the process of secularization took place in various ways in a number of European countries.

The *secular age* is my term for the stage of history that roughly coincides with the age of "modernity," the modern age. In this period, especially in central, western, and northern Europe, the form and role of the Christian religion in society and culture changed. However, the *process of secularization* has its roots in a much earlier period than the age of modernity and continues to operate beyond it. Since the end of the twentieth century, we can speak of a postsecular age.

The *process of secularization* has its roots in the biblical "disenchantment with the world": in the demythologization of nature in the creation narrative in Genesis and in the desacralization of political power encountered in the book of Exodus and in the prophetic critique of those in power.[1] The *age of secularization* encompasses the modern age—but it does not begin with the Enlightenment of the seventeenth and eighteenth centuries, or even with the Renaissance; it was already prepared by the division of the spheres of ecclesiastical and state power after the "papal revolution" in the dispute over investiture in the High Middle Ages. This was followed by centuries of coexistence, as well as mutual tension and open conflict between ecclesiastical and "lay" (secular) political power and spheres of influence. These clashes were particularly dramatic in France from the Revolution to the Dreyfus Affair at the turn of the twentieth century.

The beginning of the *postsecular age* was announced by Jürgen Habermas in his celebrated lecture at the Frankfurt Book Fair in the autumn of 2001, shortly after the terrorist attack on the Twin Towers in New York on September 11, 2001. He declared that the long-dominant ideology of secularism, which sees religion as a fading phenomenon receding into the past, was no longer sustainable: religions would be important actors to be reckoned with in the coming chapter of history.

Classical theories of secularization, predicting the weakening or early demise of religion in the course of modernization, were influenced by the ideology of secularism, and in the last quarter of the twentieth century they completely lost their persuasiveness. Books on secularization have been replaced on the shelves of bookstores by a rich literature on the new flowering of religion, on the "de-secularization" or deprivatization of religion; books with such titles as *The Return of Religion* or *God Is Back* have appeared.[2]

Is religion really making a comeback? I disagree with the proposition for at least two reasons. First, religion is not coming back because it never left. It didn't go away, it didn't disappear, it was still there; throughout its history it simply kept changing and transforming itself. It merely temporarily escaped the attention of academics, the media, and the public of the Western world due to the influence of the self-fulfilling prophecy of secularization theories. However, most of these theories, as already mentioned, focused solely on certain forms of religion and overlooked others.

The second reason is that in much of our world what now fills the spiritual space vacated by traditional religion, or after the era of harsh secularization in communist countries, is by no means the same as what was there in the past, in premodern times. Indeed, the alleged "return of religion"—in reality, the emergence of new, transformed forms of religion—has come as a great surprise both to the proponents of the theory of radical secularization, who no longer expected any future for religion, and to those representatives of traditional religious institutions who do not acknowledge the historical, changing nature of religion.

Both "traditionalism" and fundamentalism—which is also one of the forms of the contemporary religious scene—are not simply a continuation of the premodern religion they invoke; they are a modern phenomenon, and their attempt to imitate and preserve a certain form of the religion of the past is actually antitraditional: they deny the very essence of tradition, which is a creative process of recontextualizing religious content and adapting it to new contexts.

The premodern form of religion had—like all other forms of religion—its own sociocultural climate, and this is gradually disappearing even where it survived for a long time (such as now in Poland). The transition from a predominantly agrarian to an industrial and urban civilization, and from community (*Gemeinschaft*) to society (*Gesellschaft*)[3] coupled with the dominance of natural scientific and technical thinking in culture, has caused a shake-up of traditional religiosity. It has required a transformation of the Christian religion, particularly of its status in culture.

During the "Pian era" (from Pius IX to Pius XII, from the mid-nineteenth century to the mid-twentieth century), the Roman Church committed intellectual self-castration by silencing many creative thinkers within its own ranks during the unfortunate antimodernist struggle. Thus, when modernity was reaching its peak, the Church lost its ability to engage in honest dialogue with the philosophy of the day, or with the science that was then booming.

The trauma of the Jacobin phase of the French Revolution and of other subsequent revolutions (which sometimes involved the genocide of monasteries and mass murder of the clergy) drove the Roman Church into injudicious political alliances; fear paralyzed its capacity for critical discernment and it began to build defensive trenches and walls against the entire complex of modern culture. Pian Catholicism adopted a strategy of counterculture vis-à-vis the modern world, based on the principle "party against party, press against press, societies against societies." The "ideal Catholic" of the time was to spend his entire life—from the baptismal font in the Catholic church to the grave in the Catholic cemetery—in a clerical ghetto. The calls for greater lay activity—such as from the lips of Pius XI, the inspirer of "Catholic action"—did not deviate from the clerical model of the Church because they were always linked to the principle that all lay activity must be directed and controlled by the hierarchy.

Nineteenth-century retro-Catholicism was based on uncreative imitation of the past, such as neo-Gothic and neo-Romanesque styles in the visual arts and neo-scholasticism in theology and "Christian philosophy." The neo-Thomists lacked the courage of St. Thomas Aquinas, who radically innovated the theology of his time with the help of the ideas of the pagan philosopher Aristotle whose teachings were forbidden by the Church authorities at the time. In their efforts to construct a solid system of "scientific theology," the neo-Thomists were in effect aping the unfortunate mindset of their contemporary adversary: positivism. The neo-scholastics denied the historical dynamics of faith and hindered creative philosophical and theological reflection on it, much like the positivists and "scientific materialists" of the time who sought dogmatically to squeeze scientific knowledge into their sterile philosophical system. Both sides failed to realize that faith and science are both living streams and can only be understood in the context of their historical development, in which paradigm shifts and legitimate conflicts of interpretation can occur.

At that time, the teaching office of the Church (magisterium) hastily and unwisely condemned many valuable insights and prophetic suggestions, relying "presumptuously" on the mechanically conceived assistance of Providence—and then was obliged to revise its attitude clumsily and with difficulty so as to make up for lost time with a characteristic delay.[4] Many representatives of the Church's teaching ministry took their role as guardians of tradition and orthodoxy more seriously than the equally important task of maintaining scope for prophetic openness and sensitivity to the signs of the times. At times of social and cultural change, they repeatedly took an anxiously defensive stance, resisting those who attempted to creatively interpret new approaches to the world and integrate them into the spiritual world of Christianity.

The Church's efforts in the nineteenth and the first half of the twentieth century to create a parallel *polis* against Protestantism, liberalism, and socialism led to the ex-culturation of Catholicism and thus contributed significantly to the secularization of modern societies. However, that form of Catholicism must be credited with the fact that the Catholic Church opposed the totalitarian ideologies of Communism and Nazism in a timely and explicit manner, and that that opposition was sealed by the martyrdom of many Catholics on execution grounds and in Nazi concentration camps in Germany as well as in communist labor camps in many countries of Europe and Asia. Nevertheless, much of the Catholic hierarchy was not nearly so vigilant against the temptations of fascism in the Romance and Slavic countries (Spain, Italy, Portugal, Croatia, and Slovakia). Even today, many Catholics in postcommunist countries are attracted by an alliance with nationalism and right-wing extremism.

While acknowledging that this parallel world of "integral Catholicism" gave rise not only to the debilitating and doomed cultural wars against the modern world but also to the aforementioned heroic resistance to totalitarian ideologies and regimes, we cannot overlook the fact that in these struggles late modern Catholicism itself became to some extent a totalitarian (closed, intolerant) system of its own kind—and that this mentality still survives in some Catholics.

In the "Pian era" mentioned above, the Church failed to find a middle way of wise circumspection between two risks: uncritical fascination with new ideas or anxious, petty, a priori suspicion of everything new. Often it chose the latter path and paid the price with a sterile theology that reinforced the marginalization of the Church and its relegation from being the focal point for the creation of new forms of culture and society to becoming a sad vale of nostalgia for a vanished world. An exception to a certain extent was Catholicism in the United States, which was not paralyzed by the fear of modernity (the Enlightenment in the English-speaking world, unlike the French Enlightenment, did not have an antireligious tendency, and the revolutions there did not have a Jacobin phase) and found a modus vivendi in an environment of democracy, civil society, and religious pluralism; having been lambasted from Rome for the "heresy of Americanism," its experience greatly inspired the reforms of the Second Vatican Council.[5]

During the twentieth century, the voices of Christian thinkers gradually grew louder, recognizing that the culture of modernity that emerged from the Enlightenment carried many Christian genes, and that to recognize the "legitimacy of modernity"[6] need not mean the capitulation of Christianity or its loss of identity through absorption by modernity.

The Second Vatican Council (1963–1965) was a stellar moment for the efforts of the pioneers of renewal in the fields of theology, biblical and historical studies, liturgy, and pastoral practice. Theologians who had struggled to translate the content of Christianity into the language and thought of modern culture and who, until the Council, had encountered prejudice and suspicion, as well as frequent harassment and repression from Church authorities, were now accorded legitimacy and space.

The Council declared a position of receptive dialogue—not only with other Christian churches but also with other religions and with the secular humanism of global civil society. The Church remembered the once-rejected courage of Jesuit missionaries to inculturate the Christian faith, to incarnate it creatively in non-European cultures instead of merely mechanically exporting its European forms, thereby preparing the ground for a truly global, yet culturally pluralistic Christianity. This was also assisted by liturgical reforms, especially the introduction of national languages into the mass.

During the culture wars of the nineteenth century, the work of the Church in the West was gradually forced out of the public and into the private sphere. After Vatican II, ecumenical receptiveness and acceptance of the principle of religious freedom and tolerance seemed to open up the possibility for the Catholic Church to become an active co-creator of a pluralistic global civil society. Many Catholics saw the Council as a new springtime for the Church, a "new Pentecost."

However, the newly built churches, seminaries, and monasteries did not fill up; rather, there was a steady decline in applicants for the ministry. In the years following the Council, thousands of priests were so intoxicated by the spring winds of freedom that they abandoned their vocations, and sometimes even the Church, and this trend continues to this day. There is still debate about whether the crisis was due to the Council's reforms or to attempts to hinder them, whether the Church was too hasty or too slow and inconsistent in introducing the Council's reformist ideas into its pastoral practice.

However, even among the overwhelming majority of Catholics who accepted the conciliar reforms, two different tendencies gradually emerged. The American Jesuit theologian—and later Cardinal—Avery Dulles gave a name to both currents and their ways of interpreting the Council (and this position was later endorsed by Pope Benedict XVI in particular). He differentiated between a hermeneutic of continuity and a hermeneutic of discontinuity. The first current invoked the *letter* of the Council's documents and stressed that the Council had in no way deviated from the existing tradition; the second sought, in the *spirit* of the Council, to develop further the new approach that it represented in the history of the Church.

In the opening sentence of the constitution *Gaudium et Spes*, the Catholic Church promises solidarity with contemporary humanity in its joys and hopes, griefs and anxieties. The sentence sounds like a marriage vow of love, respect, and fidelity. However, "modern man" does not seem to have accepted this offer with much enthusiasm; perhaps he feels the bride now offering herself has aged somewhat and is not particularly attractive.

It was certainly praiseworthy that the Church stopped fearing and demonizing modernity. Nevertheless, one cannot avoid the critical issue of whether, paradoxically, the Church came to terms with modern culture at the very moment when modernity was coming to an end. Modernity, which had triumphed politically and culturally in Western civilization since the Enlightenment, was indeed at the zenith of its power in the 1960s, but the "end of modernity" was already looming. The Council had prepared the Church for dialogue with modernity, but had it sufficiently equipped her to meet and confront postmodernity, which was already on the doorstep?

The cultural revolution of 1968 was probably both the high point and the last word of the modern age. The global rebellion of the youth in European, American, and even Japanese universities against the paternal authority and disciplining "superego" of the prevailing social order was quelled politically, but it triumphed culturally. It injected into the prevailing mentality of Western society certain values that could be summarized by the slogans chiefly popularized by humanist psychology: namely, "self-fulfillment" and "self-actualization." However, since then modernity seems not to have come up with anything really new. Nineteen sixty-nine—the year that a man stepped onto the moon and the microprocessor was invented—can be described as the symbolic beginning of postmodernity, of the global "internet age."

In response to the cultural revolution of 1968, especially its sexual revolution component, efforts to impede reform in the Catholic Church intensified. Paul VI's encyclical *Humanae vitae* of the same year, which strictly rejected artificial contraceptive methods, was seen by many as the first signal of a "change of course." Efforts to implement it rigorously in pastoral practice contributed to the virtual demise of the sacrament of reconciliation in some countries: many Catholic laity felt too grown-up to submit the details of their married sex life to the scrutiny and strict judgment of celibate confessors. The gap between the teaching and preaching of the Church, on the one hand, and the thinking and lifestyle of a considerable number of Catholics, on the other hand, began to widen alarmingly.

In that same period, for a number of external and internal reasons, the image of Catholicism as a relatively unified cultural milieu[7] broke down in many Western European countries (for example, Germany). The process of the individualization of faith gained pace and intensity. The change in the value orientation of Western culture contributed to a split among Christians: a large part of them were strongly influenced by the mentality of the 1960s and loosened their ties to the Church and its doctrine and practice, while another part rejected this mentality and began to see the environment of the Church as a protective shelter from the influences of the outside world. These two currents in the Church were unable to dialogue with each other. In countries under communist rule, external pressure maintained a semblance of unity (apart from tensions between representatives of the Church who collaborated with the regime and Christians involved in political dissent), and the differences in religious mentality only became apparent after the collapse of the Soviet empire.

In an interview, Cardinal Ratzinger, the future Pope Benedict XVI, held the postconciliar developments in the Church partly responsible for the liberal cultural revolution of the late 1960s: the Church had ceased to play the role of a stable pillar of a solid social order.[8] But could and should it have played such a role? Did it still have the power and influence at that time to halt the ongoing civilizational trend? Would it have stopped it by insisting on unchanging principles, or would this have condemned it to the role of a marginal obscure sect on the fringes of society—as indeed had happened to the schismatic wing of the followers of the excommunicated Archbishop Lefebvre?

Although during the pontificates of Paul VI, John Paul II, and Benedict XVI a number of ideas from Vatican II were developed in papal documents (especially the social encyclicals), as well as in important initiatives in the field of ecumenical and interreligious dialogue, the necessary reform of the Church's structures did not take place. In addition, the Church's official moral teaching once again focused too much on certain issues of sexual ethics—in a manner that Pope Francis finally had the courage to describe aptly as "neurotic obsession." The perception of sexuality has changed in much of

Western society, and the Church's arguments, based on an ahistorical perception of unchanging human nature—ignoring, for example, the findings of medical science on homosexual orientation—have proved unconvincing.

But nowadays, the influence of the Church on the surrounding society depends entirely on the persuasiveness of its arguments; since the Enlightenment, the Church has had no other power to rely on. And yet, no common, mutually accepted philosophical basis has been found for a reasonable dialogue between theology and the secular liberal mentality (that is, that "third way" between outright rejection and uncritical acceptance). The secular public came to view the Church as an angry community, obsessively concerned with a few issues such as abortion, condoms, and same-sex unions, on which it repeated its *anathemas* in a manner that it was unable to comprehend; people knew what Catholics were *against*, but they ceased to understand what they were *for* or how they might benefit the contemporary world. The need to innovate theological anthropology is becoming increasingly apparent. For example, considering sexual ethics not on the basis of a static concept of "human nature" but on an ethics of interpersonal relationships perceived dynamically, and, in an age where sexuality is commercialized, encouraging an eroticism of tenderness and mutual respect.

The well-intentioned call for a "new evangelization" that was issued in the Catholic Church on the threshold of the new millennium did not meet with the expected response—probably because, among other reasons, it was not "new" and radical enough. The attempts of some "new movements" in the Church (*movimenti*) to focus on the emotional side of religion, to imitate the enthusiasm of evangelicals and the spirituality of pietistic groups, were clearly not the sort of thing to rouse weary Western Christianity from its midday slumber. Pope Francis returned to the reformist spirit of the Council after more than half a century. However, his attempts to reform structures and revive Church doctrine soon began to encounter resistance from the conservative wing, including parts of the Curia and the College of Cardinals. Pope Francis's call for a wise yet compassionate pastoral approach to people in "irregular situations," respectful of individual differences and fostering the responsibility of personal conscience, was met with the reluctance of much of the clergy to relinquish their role of judges, mechanically implementing the letter of canon law.

The Council's call to respond to the signs of the times by active participation in political life did not go unheeded. Catholics in many parts of the world, from Latin and Central America and some African countries to Europe, have been part of dissent against right-wing authoritarian regimes (such as in Spain and Portugal) and against communist dictatorships—and have been engaged in the struggle for human rights, social justice, democracy, and civil liberties, often contributing significantly to the nonviolent transition from authoritarian regimes to democracy. However, some Catholics have since been unpleasantly surprised, disappointed, and sometimes even suffered culture shock when, after the fall of dictatorships and the triumph of democracy in a new or renewed pluralistic environment, the churches gradually lost ground and increasingly encountered distrust and rejection on the part of secular liberalism. Their expectation that Christianity would fill the gap left after the fall of communism (as it did to some extent in Germany after the fall of Nazism, for example) has not been fulfilled. Pope John Paul II is said to have experienced the greatest disappointment when he discovered that, after the fall of the atheist regime, many Poles headed for supermarkets instead of churches.

It would appear that the Church, which on the whole had survived *hard secularization* under atheist regimes, was taken by surprise to a much greater degree by the subsequent *soft secularization* under renewed democracy. Some of them seem to have been unable to live without an enemy: after the fall of communism, they assigned the role to the "corrupt West." Jeremiads lamenting the "tsunami of secularism, liberalism, and consumerism" have proliferated in numerous sermons in postcommunist countries, aping without acknowledgment the anti-Western rhetoric of communist ideologues. These ecclesiastical circles were seized with vertigo and fear of freedom: agoraphobia—fear of open space, literally, fear of the marketplace.

During the half century after the Council there were unending disputes in the Catholic Church between conservatives and progressives. These debilitating conflicts have also brought the Catholic Church today to the brink of schism. For a long time now, I have had the overwhelming feeling that both sides of these conflicts, especially the radicals among them, lack a prophetic understanding of the signs of the times. The traditionalists' attempts to reject the Council's necessary reformist steps and return to the premodern world have done much damage to the Church and are ending, in the words of a classic, in farce rather than tragedy. But the many attempts of the progressives have also confirmed the validity of the adage that if you marry the spirit of the age, you soon become a widower.

Those who understood the *aggiornamento* demanded by the Council—the necessary revision of the serviceability of what the Church holds as her entrusted treasure—to be mere conformity to secular society and an ill-considered sellout of tradition, remained mentally trapped within the too-narrow confines of modernity. For this reason, some of the criticism by educated conservative Christians of superficial progressivism in the Church and theology provides useful feedback and is worth listening to carefully. But the fatal deficit of conservatives is that they are unable to offer a viable alternative.

The difference between proponents of a hermeneutics of continuity and a hermeneutics of discontinuity in interpreting the Council's message mirrors the more general differences between stabilizers and reformers in the history of the Church. The Church needs both types, in some situations more of one, and in others more of the other. Perhaps it was natural in the turbulent years after the Council that those who wanted to moderate the radicality of change once more became more vocal. Nonetheless, I am convinced that this is a *kairos* moment for fundamental reform and that it really is no coincidence that someone who represents the dynamics of the Latin American continent has been called to the See of Rome. I consider it an urgent task of the magisterium of theologians to carefully elaborate his reformist impulses.

Pope Francis sees a certain solution in reduced centralism in the Church and strengthening of the synodal principle, as well as in the greater autonomy and responsibility of local churches. However, the tensions within local churches present another problem. Are the superiors, especially the bishops, ready to give up the monarchical conception of their role and become mediators of dialogue within the Church? Are they sufficiently prepared to create and defend scope for the exercise of the charisms of individual believers, men and women? Are they ready to recognize the capacity of women to bear equal co-responsibility for communities of believers?

I continue to stress that the reform of the Church must go deeper than changes in institutional structures, that it must come from deeper sources of theological and spiritual renewal.

The afternoon of Christianity, the way out of the prolonged noonday crisis, will probably not be accompanied by the solemn trumpeting of the angels of the Apocalypse but rather will come "like a thief in the night."[9] Many have long been triumphantly crying "God is back"—but Jesus's warning applies here too: don't trust them, don't follow them![10] The afternoon of Christianity will probably arrive in the way that Jesus came after the Passover morning: we will recognize it by the wounds in its hands, side, and feet. But they will be transformed wounds.

EIGHT

The Heirs of Modern Religion

Secularization did not eliminate religion but transformed it. Religion has turned out to be a much more dynamic, vibrant, powerful, and, above all, much broader, more complex, and more multifaceted phenomenon than it seemed to be in the past two centuries. Religion has not died but is spilling over into new dimensions—now not only in the private sphere but once more into public space. Faith has left the old institutional shores behind. The churches have lost their monopoly on religion. During the Enlightenment they lost control of the secular sphere, now they have lost control of religious life. The greatest competitor to the churches today is not secular humanism and atheism but a religiosity that is beyond the control of the Church.

The secular culture of the modern age gave birth to religion as a worldview, and this form is now mired in postmodern radical pluralism. The crisis of traditional religious institutions continues, but the old dogmatic atheism is also on the wane. Three striking phenomena are worth noting in today's world: first, the transformation of religion into a political identitarian ideology; second, the transformation of religion into spirituality; third, the growing number of those who subscribe to neither "organized religion" nor atheism.

As a result of secularization, many of the phenomena that held the traditional form of religion together—doctrine, morality, ritual, personal piety, and so on—are now distinct and have taken on a life of their own.[1] In a pluralist postmodern society, these emancipated components of religion have become a publicly available resource from which individuals and human groups freely select and assemble their own collages.

Religious symbols, taken out of their original context, appear in contemporary art, including pop culture[2] and fashion accessories. Sometimes the original context of these symbols is forgotten and ignored, while at other times the deliberately provocative tension with the original context increases their poignancy and appeal. The authors of such works often count in advance on the fact that the religious authorities, who see the unconventional and provocative use of religious symbols as mere blasphemy, will publicly protest against them, thereby granting them free publicity and ensuring their commercial success. Sometimes, however, the unconventional, provocative, and seemingly blasphemous use of religious motifs has a paradoxical effect: it provokes reflection, research, and rediscovery of the original context.[3]

Both the political-ideological and the "purely spiritual" form of religiosity can be considered heirs to the two extreme poles of the earlier type of religion: namely, the public and the private. In the age of modernity, as the Christian religion became confessionalized, it lost its influence on modern society as a whole, moving from the public sphere into ever narrower spheres—the sphere of the church, the family, and then personal, private beliefs, thus becoming "privatized." Even Catholicism, as a counterculture against Protestantism, liberalism, socialism, and ultimately against the entire modern world, as I have discussed in previous chapters, was defensive rather than offensive.

During the last quarter or so of the twentieth century, however, the situation changed: religions went on the offensive in an effort to take advantage of the crises and weaknesses of liberal society and become major political players. Religions thus once more aspired to the role of *religio*, an integrating force, wanting to integrate a particular group (such as a specific ethnic group) and be the defender of its identity—but it was now defense by means of attack. These forms of religion have become intolerant and militant. In some places they stick to militant rhetoric (as is usually the case with Christian fundamentalism today), while in others—as in the case of radical political Islamism—they do not hesitate to incite and justify physical violence, wars, and terrorist attacks.

One of the first authors to draw attention to this global trend was the French sociologist Gilles Kepel with his book *The Revenge of God*.[4] Kepel showed that the radical Islamism that has come to the world's attention since Khomeini's revolution in Iran has parallels in the politicization of other monotheistic religions. Kepel's book quickly became a bestseller and has been followed by countless studies on the global repoliticization of religion, especially since the 2001 terrorist attack on New York.

An example of the political use and abuse of the symbols and rhetoric of Christianity is the American religious right, which helped put the amoral populist Donald Trump at the helm of the United States. In Europe, it is mainly so-called defenders of Western Christian values among the far-right political demagogues and nationalist populists in France and Italy, as well as in Hungary, Poland, Slovakia, Slovenia, and the Czech Republic. Their favorite target is the European Union and migrants from Islamic countries. These nationalist trends are being systematically fueled via fake news and social networks of disinformation by the current large-scale Russian propaganda industry. In the Putin regime's hybrid war against the West, Christian conservatives are specifically targeted; there is an endeavor to portray President Putin as the "new Saint Constantine" who will lead the Christian world in a crusade against the corrupt West. It exploits the fact that conservative Christianity's DNA harbors a dangerous liking for authoritarian regimes.

I am convinced that liberal democracy remains an unsurpassed form of political culture and that it offers a much more favorable environment for Christians than any "Catholic state." However, I also recognize the weaknesses of contemporary liberalism and believe that Christian social teaching, especially in the form of Pope Francis's social encyclicals, can inspire future political culture and act as a counterweight to one-sided neoliberalism.

Today's populism, especially in postcommunist countries, pits the ideal of illiberal (or managed) democracy—a code name for the authoritarian state—against liberal democracy. Wherever these populist forces come to power, they begin to destroy Western-style liberal democracy—attacking the freedom of the media, the universities, NGOs, and the courts, especially the constitutional court.

It is significant that the most vocal promoters of the "return of Christian Europe" often include people whose entire mentality and lifestyle are far removed from the Gospel and whose "Christianity" consists solely of their hostility toward migrants, Muslims, and sexual minorities. Even the leaders of the churches sometimes collaborate with populists and nationalists; they try to drown out, silence, and discredit the cautionary prophetic voice of Pope Francis. The question is whether these cases are about the politicization of religion or the sacralization of politics—the creation of a false aura around the deeply unholy and impious power interests of certain groups. The reason I return to the subject of politics and religion is because I consider this combination of the two to be an extremely dangerous phenomenon. As a result of the ideology of secularism, the world public has long underestimated the power of religion and failed to acknowledge and understand it. Religion is a force that can be used both therapeutically and destructively: in certain circumstances it can turn international political conflicts into a destructive clash of civilizations. That is why we need to look for ways to engage the moral influence of religion in the process of *tikkun olam*—"repairing the world." Can the other heir of modern religion—spirituality—contribute to this? If the world's religions develop their spiritual dimension, this can make a significant contribution to interreligious dialogue, which is one of the most urgent tasks of our time. It is in this area that the major religions are probably closest to each other.

The current attempts to bring religion back into public and especially political life are a reaction to the modern trend of privatization and individualization of faith; the postmodern shift toward spirituality is rather a manifestation and fruit of this trend of the personalization of religion. I am devoting a separate chapter to the perspectives and pitfalls of spirituality in our time.

The work of Harvard psychologist Gordon Allport offers an important key to understanding the great differences in the religious arena. In the mid-twentieth century, extensive empirical research was conducted in the United States to test the hypothesis that religious people have a tendency toward authoritarianism and a rigid understanding of the world, similar to the followers of the totalitarian ideologies of Fascism and Communism. The result was far from conclusive: it was true of some religious people, while others were found to have a strong propensity for altruism, tolerance, and creativity. Based on these findings, Gordon Allport distinguished between two types of religiosity: *extrinsic* and *intrinsic*.[5]

People with *extrinsic* piety, for whom religion is a tool to achieve some other goal (such as social approval or affirmation of group identity or group membership) tend to be really rigid and authoritarian. People of intrinsic religiosity, for whom faith is meaningful in itself, tend to be open, tolerant, flexible, socially sensitive, sacrificial, and have a sense of solidarity. Extrinsic religiosity was characterized by Allport as immature. He named a number of indicators of the maturity of intrinsic faith: its internal richness and articulation, its dynamism, its ability to form a complex philosophy of life, to bear doubt, to cope with evil and contemporary cultural and scientific knowledge, and to be a source of practical action. While extrinsic piety values the Church mainly for its sociocultural function and participates in its life only marginally, such as on major holidays, people of intrinsic piety regard the Church as primarily a community in whose life they are actively involved and whose worship they regularly attend.

The American psychologist Daniel Batson subsequently added another kind of religion to this typology—faith as a quest, as an adventurous journey, as a constant search, a journey into the depths.[6]

What is there to say about these theories in the light of our present experience? We encounter extrinsic religion at every turn. This includes the political instrumentalization of religious language and symbols (from Islamist radicals to right-wing "defenders of Christian values"), as well as commercialized spirituality—the mixture of religion and psychotherapy in spiritual wellness centers.

Allport identified a mature *intrinsic* religiosity mainly among faithful active members of religious communities, parishes, and congregations. However, this institutional form of Christianity, as we show in many places in this book, is today undergoing upheavals and crises that are unlikely to abate even with the end of Christianity's noonday crisis. Of course the parishes, congregations, and various institutions that have emerged throughout history will not disappear, but their position in society has already changed and will continue to change. Christianity is looking for a new home and new forms of expression in a pluralistic postmodern and postsecular society.

The vitality of the churches—and the vitality of *intrinsic* religiosity—would seem to depend on the extent to which they can communicate with that third form of religiosity, the faith described by Batson as a way that itself has no fixed institutional form. In addition to the dialogue between the Church and the secular world called for by the Second Vatican Council, there is a need for dialogue between the different psychological types of faith within Christianity: between faith as a way and faith as a certainty, between the Church as a community of pilgrims and the Church as a home, between the Church as a community of memory and narrative and the Church as a field hospital. Will the Church of the future be able to be a common home for these different aspects and forms of religiosity?

Many institutional forms of Christianity are in crisis, and faith is therefore looking for new forms. This is not to say that any institutional form of faith can be considered merely a relic of the past. The underestimation of the importance of institutions is a typical weakness of liberal theology and has certainly contributed to the fact that today's religious institutions have been largely taken over by Christian conservatives and traditionalists.[7]

Let us now turn to a third remarkable phenomenon on the postsecular scene: the ever-increasing number of people who, when asked what religion they subscribe to, answer that they subscribe to none. Sociologists have given this growing set of people the collective label of *Nones*.

Nones are the third-largest group on the planet today, after Christians and Muslims. They represent an extraordinarily diverse range of opinions and existential orientations (of *belief* and *faith*).

A notable example is the Czech Republic, which is often mistakenly considered one of the most atheistic, if not *the* most atheistic country in Europe, and perhaps on the planet. In fact, it is the country with probably the largest proportion of Nones; the Nones here strongly outnumber the people who subscribe to various churches and particular religions. The Czech lands have undergone a very complex religious development. Once a religious hotbed of the reform movements preceding the German Reformation, it seemed for a time, after the revolutionary upheavals of the Hussites and the Five Crusades, to be an oasis of religious tolerance thanks to a reconciliation of sorts between Catholics and Utraquists (at the Council of Basel and especially at the time of the Letter of Majesty of Emperor Rudolf). Soon after, however, the Czech lands became the setting for the devastating Thirty Years' War, and then underwent the Baroque Recatholization, followed by the Enlightenment reforms of Joseph II. This was followed by three different waves of secularization. At the turn of the twentieth century, a *soft secularization* first took place, mainly due to the cultural consequences of the Industrial Revolution. Then came *hard secularization* in the form of the persecution of religion under communist rule; this was very brutal in the 1950s and then more bureaucratic but more sophisticated in the 1970s and 1980s. After a brief hint of religious revitalization in the early 1990s, another wave of *soft secularization* followed, as a result of which Czech society outwardly resembles the postmodern cultural mentality of some heavily secularized Western and Nordic European countries.

But not even in the Czech Republic has this development resulted in a purely atheistic society, but rather in one that is strongly dechurched. Within it, apatheism (indifference toward religion), agnosticism, religious illiteracy (absence of even elementary religious knowledge), anticlericalism (allergy to many manifestations of the Church), and various kinds of alternative spiritualities and spiritual seeking are intermingled.

Sometimes what is too hastily described as the atheization of society actually means that people's spiritual life has evolved away from the forms offered by the churches; the demand for a more mature and specialized form of spiritual life outstrips what the churches have to offer, which is too narrow and stereotypical. Unlike in neighboring countries—Germany and Austria and, in recent years, Poland—the Czech Republic has not seen an increase in formal departures from the Church; the baptized, who are less and less willing to attend services or even to formally acknowledge their Church membership in the census, do not even bother asking to be deregistered from the Church.[8] There is a slight increase in the number of adults seeking baptism; however, it is far from certain that these believers, who have generally found their faith through reading, media programs, or the witness of friends or the minority of active parishes, especially student pastoral centers, will find a permanent spiritual home in traditional parish structures.

A certain number of Nones are people who have left the churches—and especially the Catholic Church. As we have already mentioned several times, it is especially the wave of gradual revelations of serious cases of sexual and psychological abuse in the churches that has caused many believers in recent years to decide to formally leave the Church. For many of them, this was probably just the last straw or the rationalization of a move that culminated in their disillusionment with the Church, which they no longer saw as a support for their lives, as—in the words of Pope Francis—"mother and shepherdess."

However, after breaking with the Church, people do not, as a rule, become atheists. It is especially those who were already atheists and whose relationship with the Church fell into the category of *belonging without believing*[9] who declare themselves atheists after leaving the Church. However, some of those who take faith and the Gospel very seriously are now also parting ways with the Church, and the motive for their separation is the conviction that the Church has become alienated from its mission.

In the past, those Christians who broke with the Catholic Church usually joined another church; today they tend to remain believers without a church affiliation. Even in the Czech Republic, a significant percentage of citizens who do not subscribe to churches nevertheless cite Christianity as their religion in censuses and surveys of religiosity.

In many countries in recent decades, the churches—and especially the Catholic Church, for well-known reasons—have increasingly lost credibility: they are regarded as incapable of giving competent, convincing, and comprehensible answers to essential questions, not only from nonbelievers but also from a significant number of their members. When I hear certain sermons, and read certain pastoral epistles and certain types of devotional publications, it strikes me that we should not only investigate why people leave but also where the ones who remain get their strength and patience from.

I consider the most interesting part of the Nones to be the spiritual *seekers*. Sociologists distinguish between *dwellers* and *seekers*. It would be wrong to divide people into believers and seekers, because dwellers and seekers are found both among believers and atheists.

I am convinced that the future of Christianity will depend primarily on the extent to which Christians relate to the spiritual seekers among the Nones.

What should that relationship consist in? I would strongly caution against *proselytism*, against a simple apologetic and missionary approach—against trying to squeeze these people into the existing institutional and mental boundaries of the Church. Rather, these boundaries need to be crossed and opened up.

Benedict XVI made a definite step toward spiritual seekers beyond the visible boundaries of the Church with his call—fittingly phrased for the first time on a plane en route to the Czech Republic—for the Church to create within its structures something akin to the "Courtyard of the Gentiles" in the Temple of Jerusalem, intended for "pious pagans." It was certainly a well-intentioned initiative and it is still a subject of debate in various parts of the world. However, the spiritual face of our world is changing rapidly, and this step falls far short of what is needed today. The "temple form" of the Church is definitely a thing of the past.

The closure of churches during the coronavirus pandemic that began in 2020 has contributed in some way to this. While a section of the faithful—especially where vibrant parishes had become a natural part of civil society and had developed all kinds of assistance during the pandemic—were eagerly awaiting the resumption of public worship, another section, for whom Sunday church attendance was more a matter of habit than of intrinsic need, fairly soon found other ways of spending their Sundays and did not return to the churches. Others became too accustomed to the convenience of watching services on television or on the internet. It remains to be seen whether people who were not churchgoers but whose confrontation with suffering, death, and human vulnerability during the pandemic evoked metaphysical, existential, and spiritual questions will head to churches and whether they will find answers, or at least understanding, there.

The Church today is no longer a temple that can afford to invite seekers into its anterooms. On the eve of his election as pope, Cardinal Bergoglio quoted Jesus's words "I stand at the door and knock,"[10] but he added that today Jesus knocks from within the Church and wants to go out, especially to all the poor, marginalized, and wounded in our world, and we must follow him.

One more form of faith in our world needs to be mentioned. Robert Traer, a disciple of Wilfred C. Smith, speaks of "secular faith." He cites many quotes from UN officials, and from key UN and international human rights documents, which speak explicitly of faith—

in particular, faith in the dignity of the human person and in its inalienable fundamental rights.[11]

Clearly it is not a "religious faith" in this case, but we could make many arguments for it being a *Christian* faith, even though it does not explicitly claim to be Christian.

The German constitutional lawyer Ernst-Wolfgang Böckenförde is often quoted as saying that democracy is based on value assumptions that have not been democratically voted on. It is based on a *belief* in certain values, on a belief that did not "drop straight out of the sky"; it is not the fruit of some ahistorical universal and all-encompassing human nature or an offshoot of "natural reason" but the fruit of one particular culture, Judeo-Christian culture, drawing on the Bible, Hellenistic philosophy, and Roman law.

It is still a stream of faith, running through history, onto which Christianity has imprinted many of its essential features. If one derives faith in the dignity of the human person and the legitimacy of human rights from the Enlightenment alone, one is mistaken; one should go deeper and ask where the Enlightenment drew these ideas from. Often these are Gospel ideas that have not been sufficiently developed in the theology of churches in the past, nor, in particular, in their practice, and sometimes they have been asserted in opposition to the political stance of church institutions.

In a number of his books, Charles Taylor has shown that many of the ideas of the Gospel became an integral part of European political culture only when the Church lost political power.[12] Similarly, Hans Küng points to the Gospel origin and Christian legitimacy of the rallying cry of the French Revolution: liberty, equality, and fraternity.[13] If today's Catholic Church wants to strengthen its catholicity—its universality—by way of a "third ecumenism"[14]—by way of an accommodating dialogue with the secular humanism that grew out of the Enlightenment—it can rediscover in this dialogue much of the heritage that it has often failed to make use of, or even misappropriated, in the course of history.

NINE

From Global Village to *Civitas Oecumenica*

The process of globalization is undoubtedly the most important social process to have determined the economic, political, cultural, and moral development of our world over several centuries. I belong to a generation that has witnessed both the peak of this process and its major crisis.

Reflections on the roots of globalization are beyond the scope of this book. Let us content ourselves with the hypothesis that they lie in European Christianity and its missionary expansion. The centuries-long effort to fulfill Jesus's call to "go into all the world" has made the Church a global player and contributed significantly to the process by which the scattered civilizations on this planet have become one "whole world"; tribes and nations have become "humanity."

However, the evangelization of "new worlds" (non-European cultures) often went hand in hand with their colonization by European explorers and conquerors. The zeal and dedication of missionaries, committed to the point of martyrdom, was not the only face of

European expansion. Its dark side was the plundering greed and violence of the conquerors—their power and commercial interests. The preaching of the Christian faith was often accompanied (and increasingly overshadowed) by the export of European material goods, science, technology, and political ideals. In the nineteenth century, both the preaching of the Gospel and many elements of Western civilization spread to virtually every corner of the globe, turning more and more of the planet into a likeness of itself. "Europe's suicide" in the two wars of the twentieth century that emanated from that continent meant that the helm of the globalization process was passed into the hands of the "heirs of Europe," in particular the United States of America.[1] The dynamics of globalization have been accelerated and intensified by technological development, particularly the development of means of communication. The process of globalization arguably entered its culminating phase with the end of the Cold War, the end of the bipolar world in which the two superpowers had divided up their spheres of influence.

The rapid and seemingly easy collapse of communism, which was the result of many circumstances but mainly the result of the inability of the "real socialist" regimes to compete in the global free market of goods and ideas, was not in itself as significant a cultural transformation as it first appeared. Timothy Garton Ash has called the political changes of the autumn of 1989—that *annus mirabilis*—"a revolution without ideas."

Ideologically, the revolt against communism was primarily inspired by the philosophy of human rights: that is, the heritage of Christianity and secular Enlightenment humanism. It espoused the Western intellectual heritage and brought to the fore a few inspiring personalities, such as Václav Havel, but it did not bring any new visions, no truly new political philosophy. In spiritual terms, it was nowhere near as influential as the French Revolution two hundred years earlier.

Due to the influence of John Paul II and Joseph Tischner, the Polish workers' uprising that gave birth to the Solidarity movement—

probably the only "proletarian revolution" that paradoxically removed a Marxist regime—espoused the ideas of Catholic social teaching. At that time, it succeeded in bringing together nonconformist intellectuals (who had been the main actors in earlier protests, such as the Czechoslovak Charter 77 movement) with the social demands of the workers. It was only the desire of the broad mass of the people to attain the material standards of neighboring Western societies—combined with an opportune international constellation, the influence of several prominent Western statesmen, and the moral authority of the pope from Poland—that bolstered the demands for spiritual freedom articulated by a limited circle of dissidents among the intellectuals.

However, the lack of new ideas mentioned above probably contributed to the fact that the ideological and political landscape of the postcommunist countries was soon dominated by the ideologues of market fundamentalism and the pioneers of unbridled capitalism, and subsequently by populists and nationalists. In the postcommunist countries of the 1990s, the opportunities of the global market that suddenly opened up propelled those who were prepared for competition—often members of the former communist elite, who were the only ones with the capital of money, contacts, and information—to power and prosperity. But it swept to the brink of poverty and insignificance those who were caught off guard by the changes in political, economic, and social conditions. Reliance on the invisible hand of the market has proved a dangerously naive illusion. The European Union has provided generous support to the new member states, but due to the lack of a legal culture in the postcommunist countries, much of this capital has been hijacked by corruption.

It was certainly a good thing that the revolutions in most of the countries of Central Eastern Europe—unlike in Romania and the countries of the former Yugoslavia—took place without violence, but they paid for the incredible ease of the transition from police-state regimes to free societies by neglecting the important political, psychological, and moral task of coming to terms with the past. It is certainly a good thing that the threshold of the new era was not sullied by violence and the spirit of revenge. However, the unwillingness to deal with the past was not due to the virtue of mercy and forgiveness but rather to the sin of omission, a sin against truth and justice.

Without sufficient reflection on, or even truthful naming of the evil to which society was exposed, and which caused its moral disintegration, it was impossible to overcome it. It is a pity that Karl Jaspers's previously mentioned book *The Question of German Guilt* or the experience of South Africa after the abolition of apartheid did not serve as guides for this section of the road to freedom. In the matter of coming to terms with the past in the postcommunist societies, even the churches—which are supposed to be "experts on forgiveness" and show that forgiveness and reconciliation is a difficult process that cannot be circumvented by merely banishing guilt into the darkness of oblivion and ignorance—have failed. Churches that did not find the courage to first deal with collaboration within their own ranks, to "remove the beam in their own eye," began to lose credibility and the moral right to engage in healing the unhealed scars of society.

The gift of freedom soon proved to be a challenging and difficult task for much of postcommunist society—including the churches in these countries. Today's electoral successes of populists in postcommunist countries (especially among the elderly with limited education) are largely the result of nostalgia for the "fleshpots of Egypt," for the security of authoritarian and totalitarian regimes that did not expose their citizens to the necessity of free choice and responsibility.

After the fall of communism, Francis Fukuyama announced, in the spirit of Hegel, the "end of history"—the planetary victory of capitalism and Western-style democracy. The world awoke from this illusion in the face of a series of disturbing phenomena over the next three decades: the terrorist attack of September 11, 2001, the rise of Islamic fundamentalism and of extremism of right and left, the collapse of the Arab Spring, the crises of postcommunist democracies, the global rise of populist politicians (including in the US and the UK), Brexit, financial crises, migratory waves, the arrogance of the undemocratic hegemons of China and Russia, the Russian invasion of Crimea, the Putin regime's hybrid disinformation war against the West, and the hot war in parts of Ukraine.

The process of globalization has begun to reveal its drawbacks, including the numerous problems that the existing economic and political system of global capitalism, which requires unlimited growth of production and consumption, is unable to solve. Climate change, environmental destruction, pandemics of infectious diseases, and rising youth unemployment pose serious threats, causing anxiety about the future; today's *risk society* is a postoptimistic society.[2]

An important tool of globalization has been the mass media, which handles the most precious commodity of our time: information. Particularly at the time when television was the dominant medium with one or only a few channels, it took over many of the important social roles of religion: interpreting the world, being the arbiter of truth and relevance, offering shared narratives and symbols, and influencing the lifestyles and thinking of much of society. What one saw on the television news "with one's own eyes" (but in reality through the perspective of the camera and the director) was true, and if it was given priority in the news (again, by editorial choice), it was universally considered important.

Electronic media still supply "bread and circuses": the required dose of information needed for survival and the entertainment industry. They also offer virtual participation in the sacred games of our time: sports matches, pop music concerts, and politicians' election contests.

In the 1960s, media theorist Marshall McLuhan predicted that electronic media would greatly enhance cohesion in society, gradually turning the entire world into one "global village."[3] This has only happened to a certain extent—people in different parts of the world watch the same (mainly entertainment) programs. However, the continued development of social networks is creating a plurality of media that reflects and deepens the fragmentation of the world rather than fostering a culture of communication and reciprocity. It tends to breed "bubbles"—many separate worlds colliding with one another.

The media has not created a "global village," as it has not offered what makes a village a village—a village square, a space of neighborly reciprocity, or even a communal church. Instead, it has demonstrated the truth of Martin Heidegger's idea that technology has overcome distances, but it has not created closeness.[4] It has created a kind of false closeness—people compete in how many so-called friends they have on Facebook. But how many of these "friends" would be a support in difficult life situations? Technical pseudo-proximity tends instead to obscure and exacerbate what existentialism highlighted during modernity—growing alienation, loneliness, disorientation, and anxiety.

Some authors—including Teilhard de Chardin—hoped that technology would allow people who were physically remote to see, perceive, and sympathize with each other more. Certain shared images changed the world. For example, the photograph of a weeping naked Vietnamese girl fleeing a napalmed village contributed more to the defeat of the Americans in the Vietnam War than the weapons of the communist guerrillas.

However, the overabundance of images of violence on television news does not arouse the conscience but instead numbs it; we all seem to have a limited capacity for perception and compassion.

Listening to the morning news each day at the beginning of the coronavirus pandemic, many of us felt that perhaps we were still dreaming some horrible dream, or that we were waking up to some media horror show, such as Orson Welles's famously evocative radio play about a Martian invasion (based on H. G. Wells's book *War of the Worlds*) that caused panic throughout the United States in October 1938. After more than a year, however, many viewers and listeners were jadedly skipping over the daily statistics about the number of dead and infected in the world.

Nevertheless, during the coronavirus pandemic when, in the space of a few weeks, virtually the entire world experienced a dramatic existential threat to life and health and socioeconomic security, something happened to our world: a deepening sense of loss of security and fear of global threat. In our time, the long-standing shake-up of traditional religious certainties has been joined by a shake-up of the certainties of secular humanism and confidence in the omnipotence of scientific and technological control and domination of the world. Mental stress and fear of the future have paved the way for racial and social unrest, and for the further growth of the ideological influence of populists and extremists on the political left and right, along with fake news and conspiracy theories and the search for culprits (scapegoats), as well as xenophobia and the demonization of everything foreign and unfamiliar.

The globalization process arguably peaked on the threshold of the new millennium. Our entire world is interconnected in many ways, but it is not unified. This interconnectedness reveals even more clearly the enormous social and cultural disparities and deepens them.

We are witnessing many antiglobalization protests and a counterculture against efforts to connect our planet even more intensively. In the non-Western world, the process of creating a global civilization is seen by many as more of a threat, a manifestation of the hegemonic aspirations of Western society and its elites. They do not see Western society as ideal or universal. In his well-known book, Samuel Huntington expressed this feeling when he wrote: "What is universalism to the West is imperialism for the rest."[5]

However, even in the West (and especially in the postcommunist world, which has politically become part of the West), fear of globalization has spawned conspiracy theories. Many people are unable to accept the fact that it is not a process controlled from a single center and is therefore rationally difficult to understand and manage; instead, they prefer to invent mysterious hidden centers of power and cast various groups and personalities in this role.[6]

Is there anything in our globally connected world that could create a culture of closeness and safe reciprocity? Is there anything that can bring our world even remotely close to Jesus's vision of the

Father's house in which "there are many mansions"? The integrating role—the role of *religio*—can no longer be played by religions in their traditional form, nor can it be fulfilled by any of the secular ideologies.

If Christianity wants to help foster a global society, then it will have to be a "kenotic" Christianity, free of any claims to power, and free of clerical narrow-mindedness. This world has no need of a "Christian empire " or a Christian ideology; it will be benefited only by a Christianity that is ecumenically open and ready to serve all those in need.

Teilhard de Chardin's argument that planetary civilization, the culminating stage of evolution, requires the energy of love sounds idealistic to the skeptics of our time, but it reminds us of something of enormous significance. Spirituality, as we shall show, is the name for spiritual passion—and there are tasks that cannot be accomplished without passion. "Love alone," wrote Teilhard de Chardin, "is capable of uniting living beings in such a way as to complete and fulfill them, for it alone takes them and joins them by what is deepest in themselves."[7] Love is a passionate desire for union.

Teilhard de Chardin saw the attempts of totalitarian regimes to achieve unity as a dangerous caricature of the true unity that only a free decision can bring about—and the ultimate expression of this freedom is love—freedom from selfishness. That is why he saw in this phase of evolution a special task for Christians, for the Christian concept of love.

I am convinced that spreading Jesus's concept of love is a task not only for individual Christians but also for Christian communities and churches, which are enmeshed in the great organism of humanity and have a shared responsibility for this entity.

A compelling form of Christian love, especially for these times, is *ecumenism*—the effort to turn the world into an *oikumene*, a habitable space, a home. By ecumenism, most people imagine efforts to bring Christian churches together. The Second Vatican Council encouraged a second ecumenism, interreligious dialogue, and even a third ecumenism, building mutuality between believers and people who do not share a religious faith.

Out of all the Church documents in Christian history, the most urgent call for ecumenical openness was made by Pope Francis in the encyclical *Fratelli tutti* on October 4, 2020.

I am convinced that, just as the democratization of the Church in the Reformation contributed to the democratization of European society as a whole, ecumenical efforts can outgrow the environment of the churches and contribute to what Pope Francis calls human fraternity, to the greatest task of our time: to transform the process of globalization into a process of cultural communication and sharing, of true closeness.

The fact that people all over the world use the same products and technical inventions, watch the same films and computer games, and perhaps pay with the same currency, does not make humanity one family. The process of uniting humanity or of uniting Christians is aimed not at unification or standardization but rather at mutual recognition and complementarity, at broadening perspectives and overcoming one-sidedness.

We must be wary of the ideological promises of "heaven on earth" made by totalitarian political projects; Christianity teaches us "eschatological patience" (and thus political realism): the complete unification of humanity will not happen during history but only at its culmination in the embrace of God. Only then will everything be subjected to Christ, Christ will be subjected to God the Father, and God may be "all in all."[8]

But the task of today and tomorrow—for the afternoon of Christianity—is to take certain steps along this path. I am convinced that a faith that steps out of its premodern "religious" and modern "worldview" roles can be the leaven of a *new ecumene*. The fact that, especially in our time, we perceive an inner dialectic of faith and critical thinking, of proto-faith and constant seeking, encompassing even doubt, creates scope for more humble self-reflection and thus a deeper reciprocity between cultures and religions. One of the main messages of this book is that the time has come for a deeper *ecumene*—for the self-transcendence of Christianity.

The current crisis of globalization presents the world with a choice between two alternatives, at the crossroads between the threat of a "clash of civilizations" and the hope of a *civitas oecumenica*.

At the time of the fall of Rome and the great Migration Period— in a historical situation somewhat similar to our own times after the collapse of the bipolar world, a period of migratory crisis and fear of tensions within a fatefully interconnected world—St. Augustine was confronted by a number of theological and political questions. Whom was God seeking to punish with these phenomena and for what? Augustine rejected those speculations and created his original theology of history on the threshold of a new epoch. He did not speak of a clash of civilizations but of a contest between two loves pervading the world and the Church—love of self to the point of rejecting God and love of God to the point of transcending self. These are the basis of the two communities: *civitas Dei* and *civitas terrena*.

Our age also needs a new theology of history, a new vision. If nations, cultures, and religions, in a world in which they can no longer isolate themselves from one another, cultivate "love of self" without respect for others and their interests and needs, they will create the *civitas terrena* of which St. Augustine wrote. States whose politics are dominated by reckless national egoism (in the spirit of Trump's "America First" slogan), and who surround themselves with walls of indifference to others and abdicate their shared responsibility for justice in the world, will become—to quote Augustine again—"great robber bands."[9]

Where is the opposite of today's *civitas terrena*, where is the path to *civitas Dei* leading us now? In church documents of the last decades we read many calls for a "civilization of love" and a "new political culture." The task of the afternoon of Christianity is to translate these words into deeds, into practical examples.

TEN

A Third Enlightenment

Pope Francis has described our era not only as an epoch of change but as a time of epochal change.[1] By "epoch" here he seems to mean a chapter of history marked by a certain set of external conditions of life, as well as the ways we understand them and respond to their changes. I regard epochal changes, including the present one, as *kairos*, a challenge and an opportunity—an opportunity to transform the way we think and act, to cross another threshold on the path of that transformation (*metanoia*) that Jesus called for in his first sermons. One of the reasons for the existence of the Church is to be constantly reminded of this call to transformation: "Do not be conformed to this world, but be transformed by the renewing of your minds, so that you may discern what is the will of God—what is good and acceptable and perfect."[2] *Metanoia* is inner renewal, not conformity to the external environment and its mentality. It presupposes the art of spiritual discernment.

It is necessary to ask again and again "what the Spirit says to the churches"[3] and to try to understand the signs of the times.

I wonder whether the last quarter of a century has not been the beginning of a cultural epoch that might be termed the "Third Enlightenment"—and how this epoch will affect our civilization, including religious life.

In the same way that reformations and renaissances of varying significance have recurred throughout history, so too there have been different periods and forms of enlightenment.[4] Enlightenment is what I call a certain type of cultural revolution or change of cultural paradigm, characterized by a revolt against existing authorities and traditions and a desire for freedom and emancipation—that is, always some form of *liberalism*. By this I mean transformations that are more radical than the changes in cultural mentalities that usually occur with the succession of generations. Even when the political forms of these revolutions are defeated, their cultural impulses are permanently inscribed in the life of society.

Periods of enlightenment have a dual aspect. We often associate the Enlightenment with the cult of reason. However, even that glorious Enlightenment of the seventeenth and especially the eighteenth century—let us call it the first Enlightenment—which invoked reason as the new messianic deity, displayed a certain dialectic of light and darkness, reason and madness. The Enlightenment of that era set the stage for the French Revolution, the radical phase of which was the period of Jacobin terror. The complementary shadow of the cult of rationality was the unleashing of the "demons" of revolutionary violence, those specters brilliantly portrayed in the drawings of Francisco Goya or Fyodor M. Dostoyevsky's *Demons*. Philosophers of culture such as Theodor Adorno, Max Horkheimer, Michel Foucault, Hannah Arendt, or Zygmunt Bauman, who cannot be suspected of conservative nostalgia for premodernity, have demonstrated very cogently the reverse side of the Enlightenment, which gave rise to the perverted rationality of totalitarian regimes.[5]

I use the term "Second Enlightenment" to refer to the revolt against authority in the late 1960s, which fostered a number of important emancipatory movements. The demand for authenticity and self-realization became an expression of the desire for freedom. This Second Enlightenment culminated in the cultural revolution of 1968, the radical phase of which saw student riots in France, Germany, the United States, and other countries.

A variant of the anti-authoritarian revolt of that time was the Prague Spring of 1968. When this attempt by reformist Marxists to transform the Czechoslovak communist regime into a more democratic "socialism with a human face" slipped out of the Communist Party's control and awakened the eager yearning of the mass of the population for real democracy, it was crushed by the tanks of the Soviet neo-Stalinists.

In the West, the revolt of the students and leftist intellectuals suffered political defeat, but it achieved a cultural victory that permanently marked the moral climate. Apart from an intensification of individualism, it is typified by the cult of youth. Whereas youth was traditionally considered simply a preparatory phase of life, it now became an attribute of ideal humanity. If Goethe's Faust can be considered the archetype of the first Enlightenment's ideal of knowledge as power, then Oscar Wilde's novel *The Picture of Dorian Gray* is a prophetic depiction of the great myth of the Second Enlightenment, the cult of eternal youth.

While the eighteenth-century Enlightenment sought to liberate reason from the domination of tradition and ecclesiastical authority, the Second Enlightenment sought to liberate what the rule of reason had undervalued—emotionality, libido, sexuality. In opposition to the Apollonian cult of reason, the Second Enlightenment held up the Dionysian culture—emphasized by Nietzsche—of night, chthonicity,[6] chaos, altered states of consciousness (also under the influence of psychedelic substances); it countered the censorship of the paternal and social "superego" with the power of libido discovered by Freud; the sexual revolution was part of the revolt against social conventions.

However, the revolutionary energy of the 1960s revolt was not quelled by the police crackdown on demonstrations but by the victory of the consumer mentality. It is an example of historical irony that many of the attributes of nonconformism and protest against consumer society at the time (such as clothing and hair fashions, music and provocative artistic expressions) soon became standard attire and the consumer goods of the mass entertainment industry. The sexual revolution, which was soon commandeered by the pornography industry, tended to trivialize and commercialize sex rather than humanize this important dimension of human life. In response to the desire to transcend the everyday, to escape boredom and to experience ecstatic states of consciousness, the market mechanism offered a broad range of drugs of every kind.

However, the moral and psychological climate of the Second Enlightenment—the questioning and shaking of traditions and authorities—also affected the religious scene of the 1960s. The atmosphere of general easing (including the easing of the Cold War) influenced the cultural context of the reformist Second Vatican Council and fostered a liberal trend in Catholic thought. At that council, the Church was able to integrate—especially into its social teaching—many of the previously demonized values of secular humanism associated with the first Enlightenment, including freedom of conscience and religion.

The other spiritual aspect of the 1960s was the boom in nontraditional spirituality in the form of new religious movements, ranging from the charismatic streams in Christianity such as the Jesus People, which first proliferated in American universities at the time, to the mixture of various elements of Eastern spirituality and humanistic, depth, and transpersonal psychology and psychotherapy, usually known as New Age. In contrast to dry, moralizing religion, these spiritual currents offered ecstatic emotional experiences, "intoxication with the Holy Spirit," as well as various meditation techniques and the use of psychotropic substances. Thus, the Second Enlightenment also assumed both a political and a spiritual form.

Is what we are now witnessing a manifestation of a Third Enlightenment? There are multiple aspects to what we are now experiencing. It is possible that the emotional, irrational, chthonic side of our time of change is being heralded by the antiglobalization protests, as well as by the current wave of violence and unrest, from the "tearing down of monuments" (symbols of the colonial past), which began in 2020 (a typically Enlightenment rebellion against the authorities of the past), and even the fascist attack on the Capitol, the symbol of American democracy, instigated in January 2021 by populist President Trump.

While the Second Enlightenment of the late 1960s rebelled primarily against the generation that immediately preceded it, who had lived through World War II and the beginning of the Cold War in the 1950s, the Third Enlightenment, such as with the aforementioned "tearing down of monuments," goes much further in its rejection of the past: it opposes the centuries-old legacy of Western civilization, which it accuses of racism, colonialism, machismo, and cultural chauvinism.

Distrust of the current economic and political world order fuels political extremism, populism, and fanaticism. As with the economic crisis of the 1930s, both the left and the right are becoming radicalized. In some postcommunist countries, as already mentioned, the nationalist right is coming to power, while, particularly on the campuses of some American and Western European universities, the proponents of the radical left-wing ideology of multiculturalism and political correctness (which was originally intended to defend pluralism and tolerance) treat their ideological opponents with a degree of intolerance, arrogance, and bigotry that is almost reminiscent of the ideological purges of the communist era. Compared to the 1960s, the process of globalization has radically accelerated in the current internet era; however, the interconnectedness of the world also increases the risks we face today—many hazards, from economic and financial crises to infectious diseases, spread like an avalanche across borders at lightning speed. Incendiary slogans, ideas, and social sentiments are also spreading at a similar rate.

To a large extent, the new cultural and political visions of the Third Enlightenment are still being shaped. But the values and slogans that appeal to the youngest generation tell us something about these ideas. If the first Enlightenment was an effort to *emancipate reason* from the domination of tradition and authority, and the Second Enlightenment the *emancipation of emotionality* (and also related sexuality) from the domination of social conventions, then the slogan of the Third Enlightenment is primarily the *liberation of nature* from the domination of human technological and economic manipulation, and *respect for minorities* (including sexual minorities) and for all those under threat (including animals). It is clear that today's young people, demonstrating against the destruction of nature and the extermination of animals, often project a sense of their own vulnerability onto a world that has no voice.

The first Enlightenment ushered in the era of modernity and the second was probably its last word. The current Third Enlightenment seeks light, freedom, and meaning in a confusing global postmodern world in which the fruits of the scientific and technological power of human rationality, especially the manipulation and devastation of nature, lead to feelings of human powerlessness in the face of the world's irrationality.

The first Enlightenment called for freedom and equality, as well as the sovereignty of the people and nation; it abolished the aristocratic and hierarchical states of the realm and paved the way for civil society. The Second Enlightenment, inspired in the West by a quirky interpretation of Marxism and Maoism, called for the abolition of "bourgeois democracy" and, influenced in particular by humanistic psychology, inscribed on its banner "It is forbidden to forbid"—the slogan of personal self-realization against all censorship and restriction. (The protest against censorship and state control—in this case by the much more rigid and repressive communist regime—played a significant role in the events of the Prague Spring.) The anarchist fervor of the Western student revolts came to an end. The ideal of individual self-realization and a hedonistic lifestyle without any restraints was seized upon by the unfettered market of global capitalism. But this economic system has brought humanity to the brink of ecological disaster.

That is why the Third Enlightenment places so much emphasis on environmental responsibility, especially in a period of undeniable climate change, and it vehemently rejects neoliberal capitalism and its ideology of unlimited growth. The movements associated with the proliferation of alternative lifestyles call for frugality, even a certain asceticism of eating and dressing. And they sometimes assume a pseudo-religious aspect. The emergence of the child prophet of this movement, Greta Thunberg, has received global media attention.

A large part of today's young generation is cosmopolitan; it accepts and welcomes cultural pluralism. As mentioned, it respects the rights of minorities, including sexual minorities,[7] and rejects racism, nationalism, and cultural chauvinism. Individualism and disdain for traditional institutions, including political parties and churches, have intensified. At the same time, however, there is a growing willingness among a significant proportion of the younger generation to engage in various civic initiatives and movements. At the time of the influx of migrants to Europe, as well as at the time of the coronavirus pandemic, many young people showed solidarity toward people in need and participated selflessly as volunteers.

When representatives of today's social (as well as ecclesiastical) establishment label youth movements simply as "neo-Marxist," they reveal their inability to fully grasp what is new in these movements. They often overlook the fact that these movements have a strong ethical thrust—but their emphasis is on different moral values than those of previous generations.

The present younger generation feels at home in a digital, postindustrial and postmaterialist society, attracted more by constant change and rich experiences than by high earnings and careers. Their main living space is the virtual world of internet networks. But there also lurks the danger of this civilization: the shallowness and superficiality resulting from an overload of information that cannot be sufficiently processed intellectually and emotionally, and the virtual pseudo-closeness of social networks.[8]

While the first and second Enlightenments were accompanied by eager anticipation of the revolutionary arrival of a better future, the present generation does not associate anger at the current state of society and its culprits with any hopeful inner-worldly eschatology: today's young people mostly view their future and the future of the world in very dark hues. There are some glimmers of hope in the aforementioned attempts at alternative, noncommercial lifestyles. Some of the radical manifestations of the current younger generation have led those who remember 1968 to believe that what we are seeing today is more like a relapse into the left-wing rebellion of those days. However, it is likely that today's moral unrest will gain an ideological and political face of its own in the coming years as it confronts social, political, and spiritual changes.

ELEVEN

The Identity of Christianity

Running through the reflections in this book is the conviction that a distinctive feature of postconciliar Christianity will be an increasing ecumenical openness. Bold steps toward crossing existing mental and institutional boundaries will always encounter concern among us Christians that we might be betraying Christianity. Are we not obscuring the identity of our faith in this way? This doubt—like most doubts that lead us to critical self-reflection—is healthy and helpful. It leads us to a question that must be asked again and again—and especially in situations of cultural paradigm shifts: what constitutes the Christianness of our faith; what constitutes the identity of Christianity?

The simple answer that the Christianness of Christianity resides in faith in Jesus Christ is certainly correct. However, its correctness must withstand confrontation with a number of other questions. What do we believe in, what faith do we profess, when we claim to believe in Christ? Do we believe in Christ's divinity and in his Resurrection, these stumbling blocks even for those "unbelievers" who share with us an admiration and love for Christ's humanity and humaneness, but who part company with us there? Or do we believe the faith of Jesus, what Jesus believed (*fides qua*) and in what Jesus believed in (*fides quae*)? Is our faith primarily trust in the truth of Jesus's witness to the one Jesus called his Father?

For centuries, the preparation of candidates for the priesthood in Catholic theological faculties consisted of studying philosophy and "natural theology" before studying theology as such. This structure of study, however, led them to have a ready-made answer when asked whom Jesus meant when he spoke of his Father in heaven: the God whose nature and attributes they had learned a great deal about in their metaphysics courses. I fear that this initial understanding has led to a fatal misapprehension, and indeed a distorted understanding, of the very heart of the Gospel.

Jesus did not believe in the God of the philosophers but in the God of Abraham, Isaac, and Jacob, the God who spoke to Moses in the burning bush. Pascal glimpsed this difference in his "night of fire." The premise of Christian theology, on the contrary, must be the courage to radically "forget," or to "bracket," all our human ideas about God, from metaphysical constructions to our personal fantasies, and with the humble acknowledgment (or wise recognition) that we don't know who God is, we don't know what people (including ourselves) meant and mean by the word—we must *seek* to know whom Jesus meant when he spoke of the Father. We long to enter into Jesus's relationship with the Father—that is, to attempt what is impossible unless Jesus himself sends us an Advocate and Helper.

In order to counter biblical fundamentalism, on the one hand, and vague emotional fideism, on the other hand, the First Vatican Council taught that it is within the capacity of human reason, by reflection on creation, to arrive at a firm conviction about the existence of a Creator. However, this conviction should in no way be confused with faith—a virtue in which the divine gift of grace and the human freedom to receive it are intrinsically intertwined; a faith in which divine openness (Revelation) encounters human openness, the capacity to listen to God and obey God (*potentia oboedientialis*). Our faith is not based on the metaphysicians' views of God. At the heart of

Christianity is Jesus's relationship with the Father. The Gospels present this to us by preserving Jesus's words and telling his story, which testifies to this relationship.

Jesus says to his disciples, "Have the faith of God!"[1] Cautious translations have weakened and distorted this phrase: Have faith in God! But Jesus is saying something more: God is not the "object" but the "subject" of faith. The classic school textbooks of theology say that Jesus did not have the virtue of faith, he did not need it, since he was God. But Jesus was "the pioneer and perfecter of faith," scripture maintains.[2] In his faith is the faith of God himself, his risk-taking trust in us. God awakens our faith and accompanies it with trust in our freedom, trusting that we will respond to his gift with faith and faithfulness. God is faithful because he cannot deny himself.[3] God is faithful even when we are unfaithful. God believes in us even when we do not believe in God. God is bigger than our hearts—than the human heart, in which faith and unbelief, faithfulness and unfaithfulness, are always wrestling.

In Jesus's story, God's faith, trust, and love for us humans is crucified, killed, and buried by us humans. But it does not remain lying in the grave. The Czech poet Jan Zahradníček, who like few others experienced the darkness of Gethsemane, wrote that the earthly powers are still desperately trying "to keep history from moving beyond the morning of Good Friday."[4] But the Easter story does not allow hell and death to have the final word. It ends with the message that love is stronger than death.

In the Gospels we read how slowly and with difficulty the light of the Easter morning penetrated the darkness of the apostles' sorrow and doubts. Jesus comes to them changed beyond recognition by the experience of death. Sometimes it seems to me that even we have not yet "grown ears" for this message. Whereas the message of Nietzsche's Madman about the death of God has already taken root among us, the message of the Resurrection is not yet fully understood and accepted. It often comes in a banal form (either as a report of the mere reanimation of a corpse, or as a mere symbolic statement that "the cause of Jesus marches on") that is easy to dismiss.

This message becomes credible by the witness of Christians' lives to the fact that Christ lives in them, in their faith, in their hope, and above all in the strength and authenticity of their solidarity of love. "To have faith in their Redeemer . . . his disciples would have to look more redeemed!," Nietzsche tells us Christians.[5] Our freedom—our redemption from slavery of all kinds—is the most compelling testimony to the resurrection of Christ, to this cornerstone of our faith.

The statement "Jesus is God" is ambiguous, and some interpretations of it have given rise to many misunderstandings and heresies, especially the heresies of monophysitism and docetism, the denial of the true humanity of Jesus. The idea that Jesus is God *alongside* God has led to conflict with Jews and Muslims who suspect Christianity of betraying monotheism, the belief that there is only one God. These heresies have damaged not only Christian thought and theology but also Christian spirituality and social practice. Christian humanism, the humanity of Christians, found it hard to breathe in the shadow of such an emphasis on the divinity of Jesus that obscured or questioned his true humanity. The orthodox belief in Jesus's true, radical humanity can best be confessed by Christians through orthopraxy, a radically enacted humanity and co-humanity. Here rests one of the pillars of Christian identity.

And what are we to make of the confession of Jesus's divinity? In the Gospels we encounter it explicitly in just one place, when the doubting apostle Thomas, on touching Jesus's wounds, exclaims: "My Lord and my God."[6] I think we should relegate belief in the divinity of Jesus from many theological interpretations and dogmatic definitions to this scene where it has its "Sitz im Leben." We should test the authenticity of all statements that have often departed from this foundation in the flame of Thomas's resurrected faith.

I often recall the moment of my "awakening" when I personally gained a new understanding of this phrase—and also of my faith in Christ, in his Resurrection and in his unity with God the Father. It was during a trip to Madras, India, where I visited a Catholic orphanage full of hungry and sick abandoned children near the place where legend has it that the apostle Thomas was martyred.[7] There it came home to me: These are the wounds of Christ! Whoever in our world ignores the wounds of misery, suffering, and pain of all kinds, whoever closes their eyes to them and refuses to touch them, has no right to cry out: "My Lord and my God." Let us reclaim our faith in the divinity of Jesus back from dogmatic definitions, whose language is incomprehensible to many of our contemporaries, back to the orthopraxy of our openness—in solidarity—to the theophany (the revelation of God) in the suffering of people in the world. Here, in the wounds of our world, we can authentically see the invisible God in a Christian way and touch an otherwise barely touchable mystery.

If we are looking for Christianity's contribution to the history of faith, we cannot ignore the teachings of Jesus—and especially his emphasis on the union of love for God and love for man. Many New Testament texts reiterate that those who claim to love God (whom they have not seen) and do not love their brother are hypocrites and liars.[8] Conversely, supportive love of one's neighbor implies faith in God. In Jesus's account of the Last Judgment, we read that it was those who showed effective love for the needy without an explicitly "Christian" motivation who demonstrated the authenticity of their faith and attachment to Christ. They were unaware that they were serving Christ himself in doing so.[9] Jesus claimed that it is not the one who invokes his name and calls him "Lord, Lord," who is his true disciple but the one who does the will of God.[10]

This is an important corrective to the common understanding of Jesus's words that he is the only door giving access to God the Father[11] in an "exclusive" (exclusionary) way. A strictly exclusive understanding of these words is to deny non-Christians the possibility of salvation. But the account of the Last Judgment in Matthew's Gospel shows that Jesus's "I" is broader: it includes all the "least" with whom he identifies. This means that all those who render them a service of solidarity and love thereby go to God *through* Christ, even if they do not name or recognize him. Christ is hidden within them.

As Paul teaches in Philippians, Christ "emptied himself."[12] He is the door—an open door is an *empty space*—and therefore can be a passageway, allowing access.[13] It is *kenosis* (self-giving, self-obliteration) that causes the Father to "exalt" Jesus and to give him a mighty name: to make him the "universal Christ," the almighty and omnipresent Lord.

Let us return to the theme of implicit faith in the Epistle of James: Those who talk ceaselessly about faith, but whose faith is not supported by any acts of love, are hypocrites, they have a dead faith, while others can exhibit a faith that is implicitly, anonymously, and un-spokenly present in their way of life.[14] So if we are to seek the Christian faith as depicted in the New Testament, there is no need to look for it only where it is associated with an explicit commitment to Jesus, nor exclusively within the confines of the Church as traditionally understood. There are also "disciples who don't walk with us," "anonymous Christians," the "invisible church."[15] Jesus told his overzealous and overly narrow-minded disciples not to forbid those "who do not walk with us" from freely witnessing to him in their own way.

The human story of Jesus is framed in the New Testament narratives by the theology of the Pauline and Johannine writings, in which the man Jesus is first and foremost the Christ. In both Paul and John, this means much more than being the Jewish Messiah promised by the prophets. Jesus's earthly humanity, the Church teaches, is a proto-sacrament, that is, a symbol, a potent sign, which points to something beyond and above itself, and at the same time is a self-expression of God himself. For John's Gospel, Jesus Christ is the Word who is intrinsically united with God himself; through him and with him and in him God is the creative principle of all things, "the world was made through him."[16] Therefore, in this Gospel, the Self of God shines through in Jesus's statements about himself, which are prefaced by the words "I am" (*ego eimi*): "I and the Father are one."[17] Jesus Christ, according to John's Revelation, is the alpha and omega, the beginning and the end of the history of all things; he is their first and last purpose.

For Paul, Jesus crucified, resurrected, and received into the Father's glory is the cosmic, universal Christ, Lord and Judge of heaven and earth. The universality of Paul's Christianity is based on the universality of Christ, not just the person, stories, and teachings of the man Jesus of Nazareth. What fascinates Paul far more than the historical Jesus ("according to the flesh") is the Christ "according to the Spirit" who breaks down all boundaries and even overcomes and supplants the apostle's own ego, for "I no longer live, but Christ lives in me."[18]

If Christianity is to be a universal proposition again in the context of today's global society, its Christology must, as in Paul, the Greek Church Fathers, the mystics, Franciscan spirituality, the spiritual theology of the Christian East, and the mystical cosmology of Teilhard de Chardin, present a disproportionately "greater Christ" than that portrayed in much of the sentimentally moralizing or scholastically dry preaching of recent centuries. One of the bold and inspiring attempts at a Christology drawing especially on Franciscan theology and mysticism is the concept of the "universal Christ" in Richard Rohr's book of the same name.

In my opinion, this vision of an omnipresent and almighty Christ, in whom the unity of the divine and the human is achieved and the consummation of the Incarnation through the Christification of matter, harmonizes not only with Teilhard's teaching of Christ as the Omega Point of cosmic development but also with Karl Rahner's well-known theory of "anonymous Christians": we encounter Christ in all people, baptized and unbaptized, believers and unbelievers. According to Rahner, all people are already connected by their humanity to the one in whom God has accomplished the deification of humanity as such.

The deification of humanity through Christ is a characteristic feature of the theology and spirituality of the Christian East in particular. Moreover, this "Christmas mystery" is also pronounced by the priest at every mass in the Western Catholic liturgy: as water is united with wine, may our humanity be united with the divinity of the One who took on our humanity. Richard Rohr says: "Christ in everything and everyone else."[19]

The idea of Christ as the mysterious eschatological destination of history and of every human life opens up new possibilities for a second and third ecumenism: it makes it possible to come closer to other religions and to "nonreligious but spiritual people." In a dialogue with Judaism and Islam, we can show that our faith is not a pagan cult of the man Jesus, whom we are attempting to pass off as a "second god" and thus threaten the purity of faith in the one God. In dialogue with secular humanism, we can again show the mystical depth of our reverence for humanity. Our relationship with nonreligious humanism must not remain a superficial alliance of convenience; it must be theologically and philosophically reflected upon and matured in common meditation. Only then can it be a mature contribution to the common search for an answer to the challenging age-old question "what is man."

But let us go further and deeper. The Church and its faith is Christian insofar as it is an Easter faith: it dies and rises again. There are many forms of faith, both on a personal level (our childhood faith, faith as a mere "inheritance," but also the initial enthusiasm of converts) and in the Church's journey through history, and these must all die at some point. When their habitual form of faith is dying, believers sometimes experience a Good Friday darkness, a sense that God has abandoned them. But those who persevere through these dark nights (the trials of personal faith, but also the collective nights of faith in history) may sooner or later experience the light of Easter morning and the transformation of their faith.

For the Easter drama includes a mystery, expressed in an important line in the Apostles' Creed: "He descended into hell." In the Passion story, Jesus descends first into the hell of human cruelty and violence and then into an even deeper hell, a hell of the deepest abandonment, abandonment by God himself. Reverence for the wounds of Jesus is part of Good Friday folk piety and especially of Franciscan spirituality, but we must not forget the deepest wound, the wound in the heart, articulated in the poignant question: "My God, why have you forsaken me?"

If in the pain and misery of people we touch the wounds of Jesus, then in the darkness of the pierced, crucified, and dying faith of many people we touch this wound without which the Easter story would not be complete. Only two of the evangelists have the courage to quote this statement. In John, he is suffused with light—his understanding of the Passion already links the cross with the Easter victory: "Into your hands I commend my spirit," "it is finished." But in many people's lives this wound remains open and unhealed—the question of the meaning of suffering remains unanswered.

Nor, I fear, is our faith complete and fully Christian unless it dares to enter into this darkness of the cross and the silence of Easter Saturday. Jesus's death on the cross as the "death of God" is the subject of many sophisticated theological and philosophical treatises and mystical poetry. The thought occurs to me: When folk piety contemplates God's tomb on Easter Saturday, is it possible that it also knows in some way about the "death of God"?

In Byzantine icons, we see depicted the meaning of Jesus's descent into hell: Jesus leads the procession of the dead out of hell with a dancing step. In front of this icon I always think that the risen Christ is leading out into the light of salvation even those whom our too-narrow faith has sent to hell for centuries: all that humanity that "believes differently." Indeed, no dogma forbids us to hope that after Jesus's passage through hell, hell remains empty.

I cowardly deleted the original title of this chapter: Jesus in Hell. Nevertheless, I believe that the phrase "descended into hell" is an important part of our faith, and that the passage to the afternoon of Christianity is through the darkness of noon, which includes the experience of abandonment that Jesus shouted into the noonday darkness of Golgotha and which he shares with many spiritually anguished people in our world.

Living Christianity is in movement, it is happening, it is becoming, it is still unfinished, it is only on the way to its eschatological consummation. Christianity truly is about being "born again,"[20] about transformation (*metanoia*). I understand this transformation somewhat differently from many Pentecostal "born again" Christians or from those who understand conversion merely as a change of mind or "moral improvement"; all these are, at most, only partial aspects of the path to "becoming a Christian." Rather, they are something that naturally accompanies conversion; they are a consequence of it, but conversion itself cannot be reduced to them. The life of faith is not reducible to belief, nor to morality, nor to the emotional experience of the "second birth"; *metanoia* is the total existential transformation of the human being.

Christ came not to offer a "doctrine" but a journey on which we continually learn to transform our humanity, our way of being human, including all our relationships—to ourselves and to others, to society, to nature, and to God. This is his "teaching"—not a doctrine, or theory, or teaching "about" something, but a process of learning, of learning "something." This is Jesus's educational and therapeutic practice. His "new teaching" is "teaching with authority,"[21] and this authority lies in the ability to transform a person, to change his motives and goals, his fundamental orientation in life. Jesus is a teacher of life (a *"Lebensmeister,"* to borrow Meister Eckhart's term), rather than a rabbi or a philosopher or simply a "moral teacher." The faith he teaches, this existential response to the call to conversion, is participation in the ever-ongoing event of the Resurrection.

The Resurrection of Jesus cannot be reduced to the "resuscitation of a corpse" and the resurrection of believers simply to a postmortem event. Paul speaks of the resurrection of believers as their radically new life in the here and now.[22] Resurrection—the Resurrection of Jesus, the resurrection of believers (conversion), and the resurrection of the church (reform and renewal movements)—are not a return to the past, a repetition of what has passed away. Resurrection is always a radical transformation.

The depiction of the Last Judgment in Matthew's Gospel tells us that Christ passes through history and our lives anonymously, and only on the threshold of the eschatological future does he shed his many disguises: yes, the poor, naked, sick, and persecuted people—they were me! Already, on our journey, the *parousia*, his Second Coming—and at the same time his judgment on us—is occurring in those in need. The last crisis, the Last Judgment, will only be the consummation of this hidden process. Our life and the history of the Church is an adventure of searching for the hidden Christ. Let us not close our ears to the cries of the suffering, the exploited, and the persecuted, let us not close our eyes to the wounds and pains of our world, let us not close our hearts to the poor and the marginalized—we might miss the voice of Jesus in them. We might miss Jesus in them.

The Resurrection does not end on the morning after Easter. Like the ongoing creation (*creatio continua*), we can also speak of *resurrectio continua*, the ongoing Resurrection. Jesus's victory over death, guilt, and fear continues in history, in the faith of the Church, and in the stories of individual people. The hidden life of the Risen One (Jesus did not appear to "all the people")[23] is like an underground river that bubbles to the surface in the events of individual conversions and the reforms of the Church.

St. Augustine maintained that to pray is to close one's eyes and realize that God is now creating the world. I add: to believe, to become a Christian, is to open one's heart and realize that Jesus is now rising from the dead.

TWELVE

God Near and Far

The history of faith, of which the Christian faith is an important part, can be imagined as a river flowing through the landscapes of different cultures. Faith can also be likened to a collective memory in which the experiences of believers and communities of believers are inscribed.[1]

How does this river flow into individual lives? How do individual people become believers? Who participates in the life of faith and how? And how do they become Christians?

The answer of canon law is simple: one becomes a Christian by baptism. Except in exceptional cases, an adult can be baptized only after proper catechetical preparation and after having made a profession of faith. Young children can only be baptized if the Church—represented at the ceremony by parents and godparents, and preferably by the entire gathered parish community—vouches for them with its faith. Children are baptized "into the faith of the Church," which they are then to acquire through education; in the Catholic Church the sacrament of confirmation, preferably administered on the threshold of adulthood, is a kind of seal of baptism—an occasion when a person, baptized as an infant, consciously subscribes to the faith of the Church by his or her personal faith.

A significant step in the process of ecumenical efforts was the decision of a number of Christian churches to mutually recognize the validity of baptism. American theologian David M. Knight recently raised the quite logical question of why, then—if it recognizes that by valid baptism non-Catholic Christians live, like Catholics, "in sanctifying grace"—the Catholic Church does not admit them to the other sacraments on the same terms as its own members.[2] Are not these sacraments themselves of greater value than their theological interpretations? Might they not unite us even before we clarify those interpretations and old disputes that divide us—although to most Christians they no longer have any meaning?

Another aspect of the theological debate about the sacrament of baptism—baptism as a condition of salvation—emerged early in the history of the Church. Can catechumens be saved who have believed in Christ but have not received baptism because they died during the catechumenate—and especially those who died a martyr's death? Though unbaptized, they gave the greatest conceivable witness to their faith, the sacrifice of their lives! The Church of that time—from the lips of St. Cyprian, for example—answered these questions by teaching "baptism of blood" and later also "baptism of desire"; it saw them as validly, though extraordinarily, baptized.

The idea of baptism by desire, which Thomas Aquinas wrote about, for example, was developed in the twentieth century by the Czech theologian Vladimír Boublík, in exile in Rome, with his theory of "anonymous catechumens."[3] He presented it as an alternative to Rahner's well-known doctrine of "anonymous Christians." Like Rahner, he argued that there was a hope of salvation for those who, for various (at least subjectively legitimate) reasons, had not received baptism and had not formally been admitted into membership of the Church, but whose conscience led them to seek truth, goodness, and beauty in the course of their lives. The doctrine of the possibility of salvation for the unbaptized and those without explicit faith in Christ became a firm part of Catholic dogma through the documents of the Second Vatican Council.[4]

Thus, the absence of explicit belief need not be understood as a rejection of it. Even a verbal rejection of Christ and the Church in some cases can be (and often is) merely a rejection of the false ideas that the person has come to hold (such as by generalizing their own personal negative experiences with the milieu of believers). On the other hand, the American Jesuit Leonard Feeney was excommunicated from the Catholic Church for his insistence that non-Catholics could not be saved—in other words, for radically and explicitly invoking the phrase *extra Ecclesiam nulla salus* (outside the Church there is no salvation)—long before the last council in fact.[5] Questions about the boundaries of the Church and the relationship between the visible and invisible Church have been the subject of theological debates for centuries, and these cannot simply be concluded by a single dogmatic definition; the Spirit of God guides the Church through history, transforming it, bringing it unceasingly into the fullness of truth, and inspiring its theological self-reflection, including theological reflections on its historical transformations. This action of the Spirit in the Church will only come to an end with the consummation of its history in the embrace of God; to deny it and not listen to it would probably risk blaspheming against the Holy Spirit, against which Jesus so emphatically warned.[6] Not only in the teachings of the Second Vatican Council, but also in the writings of eminent Orthodox theologians, one can encounter the statement "we know where the Church is, but we cannot be sure where it is not."[7]

Let us add one more thought to our reflections on baptism. Insofar as we are advancing a process theology of faith in this book, let us also adopt a process approach to the sacraments, especially the sacrament of baptism. By no means is the mystery of baptism, the event of "immersion in Christ," exhausted or brought to an end at the moment of the conferral of the sacrament. The life of God ("grace") is infused by baptism into the whole existence and personality of the baptized; it is meant to permanently irrigate all that is "formless and desolate" in them and to erode the boulders of sin and unbelief throughout their lives; it is meant to penetrate into ever deeper layers of their consciousness and unconsciousness, into their thinking, feeling, acting, and into the sanctuary of their conscience. Baptismal grace is the life of God in the person, the energy of the promised Spirit of the Creator (*Creator Spiritus*) and Advocate (*Paraclete*), and effects a lifelong movement of *metanoia*—transformation. Baptism is an irrevocable sign (*signum indelibilis*); in other words, it lasts even where the baptized are themselves unaware of it and do not actively cooperate with this grace; it does not cease to be a gift even when the recipient does not value it.

Nowadays, theologians are returning to a broader concept of sacraments and sacramentality predating the medieval definition of the seven sacraments at the Council of Lyons in 1274. Also, the Second Vatican Council expanded and deepened the doctrine of the sacraments by viewing Christ and the Church as a *proto-sacrament*—here, too, a "visible sign of invisible grace." At the same time, however, the Catholic Church teaches that the action of the Spirit in human beings is not bound to the sacraments alone (*Deus non tenetur sacramentis suis*), nor confined to the boundaries of the "visible Church." If the Church replaces a narrowly juridical understanding of itself with wonder at the generosity of God's freedom and all-pervading love, it may provide impetus for the development of ecumenism in all three of its dimensions, as we have already mentioned.

The question of how the river of faith flows into the lives of individual people, how people become believers and how they become Christians, cannot be adequately answered in canon law alone. We have mentioned that baptism presupposes a confession of faith (at least by proxy in the case of children), and the Church requires that this confession not be a formal "confession with the mouth" but be backed by a conscious, free, and informed act of faith, a conviction of faith (belief), and a determination to put this conviction into practice in one's life.

The personal faith of particular individuals is, of course, a mystery beyond "ecclesiastical control"—the baptizer can never be fully certain that the faith of applicants for baptism is authentic, and neither can the witnesses, who are asked to declare at the time of admission to the catechumenate that the applicant comes with good intentions, nor can the believers themselves. The faith of the individual person, as one of the liturgical prayers states, is known and can only be fully judged by God alone. When we talk about the faith of specific people, but also when we think about our own faith, we sometimes have to resort to words of hope: I believe that they (or I) have faith.

Faith is a journey, so I can say that I am on a journey of faith, even though I am troubled by a sense of its weakness and insufficiency; my very desire to believe and "to believe truly" is an important step on this journey. Faith is a journey toward certainty, but perfect certainty, the fullness of faith, comes only in the embrace of God beyond the horizon of this life and world, in the beatific vision (*visio beatifica*) in which faith and hope are both consummated and brought to completion: they are engulfed by a love that does not cease even then.[8]

If my faith relates to God, it relates to one whom I cannot possess or even fully comprehend: *si comprehendis, non est Deus*—you can be sure that if you think you've understood it, it isn't God—St. Augustine taught.[9] And if we consider Augustine's definition of love as desire—*amo: volo ut sis* (I love; that is, "I want you to be")—then we can say that at the heart of the Christian faith in God is the desire for love.

"I want" in this case is not an imperious command of the human will but a humble confession of desire that enters with hope even into the terrain of uncertainty, into the cloud of mystery.[10] Desire, as John of the Cross taught, is an inner light even in the night of faith. Desire, passion, yearning for fulfillment constitutes that mysterious sap of faith that we can call spirituality, the spiritual life.

Who, then, is an "authentic believer"? One who loves. And since God, who is not an "object" (and therefore cannot be an "object of love"), is present in everything and at the same time transcends everything, love for God includes everything; it is a boundless love. Human love of God is not some kind of exclusive relationship with a "supernatural being" beyond the horizon of the world but is to resemble in its boundlessness and unconditionality the love of God, who embraces and sustains everything in existence through love; it should resemble God, who is present in everything with love and as love.

This commandment of love (inseparable love for God and one's neighbor) is a task that can never be finished in this world and in this life; like faith, it has the character of an invitation to a path that is always open. The Christian is called to be like God, from whose love no one is excluded.[11]

So the grace of faith is poured into the life of a particular person not primarily at the moment when that person gives rational assent to the articles of faith, "when he or she begins to think there is a God" (as many people imagine conversion), but rather when there is transcendence (self-transcendence, transcending selfishness and self-absorption) in his or her life—that is, what Christianity means by the word "love." Convictions of faith (beliefs), opinions about God, are part of the act of faith only to the extent that their context is the practice of love. Outside that context they are cold "dead faith."[12]

Without faith, coupled with love, even the reception of grace (that is, the life of God) in the sacraments would be an empty ritual akin to magic.[13]

The Church has long defined faith as an act of human will, brought about by God's grace, which causes reason to assent to the articles of faith presented by the Church. Faith is thus an "infused virtue" in which the gift of God meets the freedom of man; God's initiative is primary in this, but human freedom is also indispensable. However cumbersome this description of faith may be, it nevertheless preserves the experience that faith is dialogical, that it is a meeting of the divine and the human.

Psychology offers an answer to the question of whether and to what extent this theoretical model corresponds to the actual experience of human stories. The psychology of religion has often focused primarily on the period of adolescence, during which people's outlook on the world is usually shaped. Adolescents may consciously *assent* to the faith in which they have been raised, or they may *reject* or deviate from it; alternatively, they may better understand and accept it in a new, more mature way than the way it was presented to them in childhood. The transition to adulthood is when conversions most often occur: a believer may change one religion for another, or abandon a religious life; or, conversely, a person who has not yet believed may embrace a faith. In our civilization, however, even traditional believers often undergo a "conversion" of this kind when they realize that their religion is not universally accepted as something normal and, in spite of that, they freely choose to remain in the tradition they received. The British sociologist Grace Davie argues that while in the past many believers saw their attendance at church services as an unquestioned obligation imposed by tradition, today church attendance is primarily by those who want to be there by their own free choice.[14]

The absence of social pressure to "go to church" and to declare one's faith has deterred a certain number of "cultural Christians"[15] from participating in the life of the church (except perhaps for infrequent attendance at church services on major holidays or family events). However, this "bloodletting" has instead tended to reinvigorate the churches and their faith. If religiosity is not just a habit, if believers think about faith and make it their personal faith, then they usually reinterpret its content to some extent, recontextualizing it in light of their expanding education and personal maturation. A received faith, unless it is *internalized*, unless it has taken root in the inner emotional and intellectual world of the person, is unlikely to withstand the crises that it will probably encounter in a secularized world.

However, depth psychology and psychoanalysis-influenced developmental psychology have challenged the notion that adolescence is the key period for religious life. Erik Erikson coined the term "basic trust" (*Ur-vertrauen*) to refer to the underlying attitude toward life that is formed in the earliest stages of life when a newborn child first comes into contact with its mother or significant others. Ana-María Rizzuto, a Harvard psychologist of Argentinean origin, produced a very inspiring developmental psychology of religion.[16] Children's religious ideas are formed spontaneously at the earliest age on the basis of early experiences; they reflect basic trust or basic disbelief. Subsequent religious ideas may build on that basic trust or may correct the basic distrust. A pathological image of an evil god may develop from basic distrust, and this may cause mental and spiritual disorders. The psychological reaction to this image can be atheism; as a rule, it is first a protest against a certain type of religion before developing into an aversion to religion as such.

Children's spontaneous, personal, emotional, poorly differentiated, and mostly unconscious image of God sooner or later encounters the cultural concept of God, which is mediated to them through the religious life of a given society, especially through religious education in the family or at school. In the process, their spontaneous childhood image of God may be complemented harmoniously by this cultural image (which promises a more robust religiosity in later life) or they may not accept it and retain their own image of God. In other cases, by contrast, children can reject their spontaneous image or leave it in their unconscious, accepting instead the concept offered by culture.

I think this theory can also shed some light on the religious situation in countries like the Czech Republic, where most children have not been exposed to any type of religious education for generations (and often still have not). Hence people either have "their own god" or they became atheists when they grew out of their spontaneous infantile religiosity and did not encounter any other form of religion afterward. The absence of a credible religious upbringing—especially the failure to interact with the specific mythopoetic religious life of the child—contributes to the proliferation of the Nones discussed in one of the chapters of this book.

Faith is gradually incorporated into individual life stories. It is a life-long dynamic process: for a person who undergoes conversion from unbelief to belief in adulthood, the earlier period of unbelief is part of the story of faith. Theologically speaking, everybody has a God story, believer and nonbeliever alike, and God is present in their belief and in their unbelief: "Am I a God only when I am near at hand, but not when I am far away?"[17]

What the Epistle to the Hebrews describes as happening in the history of salvation—"in the past God spoke to our ancestors through the prophets at many times and in various ways, but in these last days he has spoken to us by his Son"[18]—also happens on a personal level in the stories of converts: God has already spoken to each person many times and in many ways before that person gives the Gospel message the "yes and amen" of their personal, conscious faith.

This is why prayer is important for faith—which is a constant search for God—not as a means of influencing God to do one's will but as a means of creating an inner silence in which one tries to be aware of the presence of the hidden God and to discern God's will. Unlike the "blessed belonging" (*visio beatifica*) of the saints in heaven, faith does not possess the evidence, or the certainty of complete and explicit knowledge. If it is humanly authentic, faith will retain legitimate scope for critical questions that help it to grow and cooperate more fully with its divine aspect (faith as a gift of God's grace). The doubt that is a healthy corollary to faith and makes it humble is not doubt about God, or doubt about whether God exists, but doubt about myself, about the extent to which as a believer I have properly understood what God is saying to me.

The profoundest mystery of faith is not related to the existence of God. Strictly speaking, the Christian does not believe in a God who might not exist. Only contingent (accidental) existences, "objects," are able not to exist. A God who might not be, God as an existence among existences, truly does not exist—such a God as object would be an idol, not God. The God we believe in as Christians both contains everything and *transcends* everything.[19] There is no sense in asking whether the whole of everything exists, but it is natural to ask what the character of this whole is, and whether it is possible to communicate with it in any way, if it is infinitely greater than all our statements and ideas about it.

Faith does not become Christian by believing that God exists; we have become Christian believers not by believing in God's existence but, as scripture says, by the fact that "we have known and believe the love that God has for us."[20] The objection that we must first believe in God's existence before we can believe in God's love contradicts the logic of the Gospel: *only those who love can understand what is meant by the word God.*[21]

Love is not one of God's attributes but God's essence, God's very name. Maybe one of the reasons why it was forbidden to speak the name of God was that love cannot be encapsulated in words. Love can only be expressed through one's own life. Words of love, not validated by one's own life, amount to taking God's name in vain— sinfully.

I have already mentioned Jesus's challenge: Have the faith of God![22] Have the faith that God has! God loves us and trusts us, so we can participate in this faith by trusting in it. The content of our faith is not opinions about God's existence but the response of our trust to God's trust, the response of our love to God's love. Faith is therefore inseparable from love, and we have both faith and love only in the form of hope and desire, not that of possession.

I believe in order to understand (*credo ut intelligam*)—but at the same time I need a certain kind of understanding to provide a space in which faith can live (*intelligo ut credam*).[23] But faith itself, as a specific existential experience, is a kind of understanding, an interpretation of the world and of life. Between faith and understanding, as between faith and love, there is a hermeneutical circle: they interpret each other and cannot be separated.

Jesus promised his apostles that if they had faith like a grain of mustard seed, that faith would accomplish unimaginably great things.[24] This phrase is usually understood as a rebuke to the apostles for not having enough faith. In one of my books, I offered a provocatively different interpretation: our faith may be incapable of doing great things because it is not small enough.[25] Lots of incidental things—our ideas and desires—have been heaped upon it. Only naked faith, free of all ballast, is "the faith of God." For we know from St. Paul that what is great in human eyes is insignificant in the eyes of God, and vice versa.[26]

In John's Gospel, Jesus says that the grain of wheat must first die before it can produce any fruit; if it does not die, it remains in itself and perishes without fruit.[27] Isn't that also true of our faith? Does not our faith have to imitate the *kenosis* of Jesus, to die to its previous condition and become empty, so that it can be filled with the fullness of God?

Just as we celebrate Easter repeatedly throughout our lives and throughout our history to understand its meaning more deeply year after year, so our faith must also revisit the Easter mystery of death and resurrection. The dark nights of faith, as the mystics well knew, are the schools of its maturation. This is obviously true both in our stories of faith and in its history. Let us not be afraid of the moments when our faith is nailed to the cross of doubt, when it descends into the hells of pain and abandonment and some of its forms wither and are laid in the grave. Sometimes God speaks in a Pentecostal storm, sometimes in a quiet, barely audible breeze, such as to Elijah on Mt. Horeb.[28]

Sometimes our personal crises of faith coincide with those of history, since our life stories are woven into the stream of history. Our personal faith participates not only in the light and joys of the faith of the Church but also in its dark hours. Carl Gustav Jung confessed that during one of his deepest depressions and personal crises, he was helped by the realization that his crisis in some way anticipated the crisis of our civilization, the world war.[29] Perhaps we too can be helped by the knowledge that the pains of our faith are a mysterious participation in the pains of the Church and thus in the ongoing mystery of the cross of Jesus. St. Paul wrote that our sorrows are what remains to be completed in history from the sufferings of Christ;[30] thus, in addition to *creatio continua* and *resurrectio continua*, the first and greatest of Christian theologians presents the doctrine of *passio continua*.

The call to *sentire cum ecclesia* (to think and feel with the Church) is usually presented as a call to obedience to the Church's authority, but I also understand it as a call to put my questions, pains, and doubts, my nights of faith, in a wider context, in the faith of the whole Church. The Church, as a community of faith, is also a community of shared experience of the journey through the dark valley of the shadows. Not only our personal stories of faith but the history of the Church has its springs and its long, cold winters.

In what way does the Church participate in the fullness of God's truth, this certainty of all certainties? How and to what extent does it pour this water of life into the hearts and minds of individual believers? I think here we can use the verb *subsistit* (abides, dwells, is contained). This word lent an important ecumenical dimension to the doctrine of the Church in the documents of the last council. During the heated debate of the council, in the sentence that states that the Catholic Church is the Church of Christ, the verb *est* (is, is equal to) was replaced by the verb *subsistit*. In the empirical Catholic Church that exists here and now, there is present (*subsistit*) the Church of Christ, that mysterious bride of Christ whose full glory and beauty will be revealed only in the eschatological horizon of eternity.

This also implies that this specific Roman Catholic Church does not "fill the whole space" of the Church of Christ, that there remains a legitimate place for other Christian churches. This important theological foundation of Christian ecumenism was finally accepted once and for all at the council, though later statements of the magisterium cautiously tempered this generosity with the addendum that in those other churches the Church of Christ *subsists* in a somewhat different, more modest way, than in the Roman Catholic Church.[31]

By analogy, we might possibly say that the Truth, which is God himself, *subsists* in the doctrine of the magisterium without, however, fully exhausting the fullness of the mystery of God at any moment in history. The assertion that the official teaching of the Church presents the revelation of God authentically and to a degree sufficient for salvation, and that no further revelation is to be expected, certainly does not mean that the Church wishes to prohibit the Holy Spirit from further influence. There is always room for the free flowing of the Spirit, which, until the end of history, is gradually bringing the disciples of Christ into the fullness of truth. The point is, however, that openness to new gifts of the Spirit does not mean an ungrateful and foolhardy loss of respect for the importance and binding nature of the treasure of the earlier gifts of the same Spirit; Jesus praised the wisdom of teachers who select both new and old things from this treasure.[32]

Likewise, in the faith of an individual Christian or a particular Christian group (for example, a theological school), the faith of the whole Church, the fullness of Christian doctrine, *subsists*, but the faith and knowledge of an individual Christian or a particular Christian group always has its human (historical, cultural, linguistic, and psychological) limits, so that it is unable to absorb the whole faith of the Church in its fullness. This is why, moreover, individual believers and particular schools of faith and spirituality also need the whole of the Church and its teaching ministry to complete and possibly correct them. Individual believers participate in the faith of the Church insofar as their personal limited capacity to embody the treasure of faith in their understanding, thought, and action allows. St. Thomas Aquinas already taught about implicit faith: no one believer can encompass everything the Church believes; he or she can understand and accept only part of it explicitly. Believers implicitly participate in that which is beyond their understanding and knowledge through the act of trust in God and God's revelation and in the Church which presents that revelation. This awareness should lead to humility and to the recognition of the need for communication and dialogue in the Church.

Moreover, the Christian faith never (even with the saints and mystics) completely fills the whole space of the human soul—the conscious and unconscious part of the psyche. It is in this sense that I construe Cardinal Danielou's statement that "a Christian is always a partially baptized pagan." Baptism has the nature of an indelible sign (*signum indelibilis*) and of a real participation in the mystical body of Christ, but the grace of baptism works dynamically in people, making them grow and mature in faith, insofar as they open the space of their freedom to it at all levels of their existence. If the faith of the Church does indeed *subsist* in the spiritual life of believers, but the religious knowledge they have received does not fill the whole space of their spiritual life, then there remains legitimate room in their minds and hearts for searching, critical questioning, and honest doubt. It is healthy for them to humbly question whether their faith journey is authentic, faithful to tradition, but also faithful to how God guides them in their conscience. Therefore, the final addressee of their questions cannot be the ecclesiastical authority alone, but God, present in the sanctuary of their conscience, God who speaks to them not only in the teachings of the Church but also in the signs of the times and in the events of their own lives.

The gift of faith, whether mediated by upbringing, by the influence of environment, or received as the fruit of a personal search, is an immensely precious gift of God's grace, but equally precious is that "restlessness of the human heart" of which St. Augustine speaks. This restlessness does not allow one to rest in any particular received or attained form of faith, as one is always seeking and longing to go further. Even critical questions, doubts, and crises of faith can be a valuable stimulus on this journey. They, too, can be seen as a gift from God, a "helping grace." The Spirit of God does not only illuminate people's reason but also acts as "intuition" in the depths of their unconscious—this knowledge is valuable for reflection on the "faith of unbelievers"; even people who have not had access to the proclamation of the Church, or who have not received it in a form they can honestly accept, may have a certain "intuition of faith," and the dialogue of the faith of the Church with this "intuitive faith" of people distant from the Church can be mutually helpful.

"God is greater than our hearts," we read in St. John's epistle.[33] But "our heart" is greater than what our reason, our religious beliefs, or our conscious and reflective act of faith, and our profession of faith, know about God. But let us beware of narrowing the concept of the heart we find in the Bible, in Augustine, and in Pascal to mere emotionality.[34]

Jung argued that the conscious and rational component of our psyche is like a tiny part of an iceberg jutting out of the sea; the much more powerful and important part lies in the unconscious, not only the personal, but also the collective: it is there that ideas, inspirations, and ulterior motives for our actions are born. Perhaps depth psychology may be said to be describing the experience of the mystics that "there is no bottom to the soul," only in different words or from a different perspective: the depth of the human being is penetrated by the depth of reality itself, which we call God; in the words of the Psalm, "deep calls to deep."

The psychology of religion, based on depth psychology, argues that faith—as an existential *trust* in that depth of reality that is completely beyond our control—permeates the totality of human existence and is rooted psychologically deep within the unconscious. Spiritual theology, reflecting on mystical experience, complements this view from the other side, as it were: God addresses the entire person, but what depth psychology calls the unconscious, and what the Bible and mystics from Augustine to Pascal and the spiritual writers of our time most often describe using the metaphor of the heart, is more capable of understanding God than our *mere* rationality. The role of reason in the life of faith is neither to be underestimated nor overestimated.

The "grace of faith" is obviously a greater and more dynamic gift than how we usually understand "faith." Faith reaches into the deepest layers of our being and goes far beyond what we "think" or how we "exercise" our faith in ordinary religious practice by going to church and keeping the commandments. Especially in times of upheaval (for example, when it is impossible to attend church during infectious disease pandemics, or when people find themselves in extraordinary life situations in which the usual moral textbooks and stereotypical pulpit lectures are of little help), this is not enough. To do God's will faithfully, especially in borderline situations, requires something more—the constant cultivation of one's own conscience, creativity, courage, and personal responsibility. And isn't the overall situation of humanity today borderline?

If God, who "is greater than our hearts," enters into our lives, he infinitely expands the depth and openness of our being, which we describe by the metaphor of the heart. Something more significant and greater is happening within us than we can comprehend and than we can "grasp" and "exhaust" with our regular religious practice. Therefore, it is important not to be stuck within its framework, not to be satisfied with the habitual form, but to keep searching, even if this search is accompanied by crises and difficult questions arise that go beyond the set of catechism answers offered by tradition.

The young man who had kept all the commandments from his youth was looked upon with love by Jesus—but probably also with sorrow, for the young man was too rich. Perhaps he was not only rich in material goods but also in piety and righteousness in the sense of the Mosaic Law. He was not inwardly free enough to leave all this wealth behind, to set forth and follow him.[35] Our piety and virtues, especially if we are duly proud of them, can also become a trap and a shell—that heavy armor of Saul that the young David had to remove in order to face Goliath. This is true threefold of the shiny and heavy shell of theology, which is supposed to protect us from all the questions it cannot answer. Let us remember again Meister Eckhart: we must meet God "as the naked meet the naked."

In the rite of admission to the catechumenate, we bless the ears, eyes, mouths, hearts, shoulders of those who have believed and are embarking on the journey to the baptismal font; we bless their outer and inner senses, their bodies and souls; we pray that they will be open and attentive to God's action, to the variety of inconspicuous charisms that God has prepared for them and often concealed in the astounding little things, in the ordinary events of everyday life. They will find them more easily and use them more abundantly if they seek and receive them, knowing that these different aspects of the gift of faith are given to them in order to serve others, to be either the eyes or the ears, the mouth or the heart of the community of believers.

THIRTEEN

Spirituality as the Passion of Faith

In many churches, one can still hear lamentation, panic, and alarm about the danger of a "tsunami of secularism and liberalism." But atheistic secular humanism has long since ceased to be a major competitor to traditional ecclesial Christianity; today it is equally aging, enfeebled, and short of breath. In both cases, it is most readily discernible in their language: the loss of spiritual vitality is always first betrayed by a jaded use of language, speech cluttered with a plethora of clichés and platitudes.

The main challenge for ecclesial Christianity today is how to turn from religion to spirituality. While the traditional institutional forms of religion often resemble drying riverbeds, interest in spirituality of all kinds is a surging current that is eroding old banks and carving out new channels. Even the Second Vatican Council would seem to have been more about preparing the Church to align itself with secular humanism and atheism, and it seems not to have envisaged a great expansion of interest in spirituality. The mainstream churches were not prepared for the hunger for spirituality and are often still unable to respond adequately to it.

Let us spell out one of the main arguments of this book: the future of the churches depends largely on whether, when, and to what extent they understand the importance of this shift and how they can respond to this sign of the times. Evangelization—the central task of the Church—will never be sufficiently "new" and effective unless it penetrates the deep dimension of human life and human culture, which is the habitat of spirituality. If evangelization consists in sowing the seed of the Gospel message in good soil, then this soil must be something deeper than the rational and emotional component of the human personality. It has to be that innermost region that Augustine called *memoria*, Pascal called the heart, and Jung called *das Selbst*; it is the womb from which people must—in the spirit of Jesus's words to Nicodemus—"be born again."[1]

The task awaiting Christianity in the afternoon phase of its history consists largely in the development of spirituality—and a newly conceived Christian spirituality can make a significant contribution to the spiritual culture of humanity today, even far outside the bounds of the churches.

This begs a whole set of questions. What is the cause of the current interest in spirituality? What challenge does this phenomenon pose to Christianity and the Church? What are the risks and pitfalls of this trend? Is the interest in spirituality evidence of a revitalization of religion, or is it, on the contrary, a substitute for a declining religion? What is the relationship of spirituality to faith and religion?

Such questions are difficult to answer because they depend on different definitions and conceptions of religion, faith, and spirituality; it is clearly unrealistic to expect universally acceptable definitions in this area. On the matter of whether spirituality belongs to the sphere of religion, whether it is a dimension of religion, or whether it is part of the secular sphere and more of a "substitute for religion," I would refer to a recent inspiring lecture. According to Israeli researcher Boaz

Huss, spirituality is a separate phenomenon that belongs neither to the realm of religion nor to the secular world.[2] Based on his study of spirituality, Boaz Huss questions the relevance of the concepts of religion and secularity: he argues that both the concept of religion and the concept of secularity (and thus the theory of the relationship between the religious and secular spheres) emerged exclusively in the European Christian context, at the threshold of modernity, at the time of the Reformation, colonization, the emergence of nation-states and capitalist society. These concepts and theories were later adopted to describe the situation in the non-European world for which, however, this division is completely alien and whose languages lack an adequate equivalent of either the concept of religion or the concept of secularity. Huss argues that the relevance of these categories is limited not only locally (geopolitically) but also temporally. They denote phenomena belonging to an era that has already passed, even in the West, and are therefore no longer suitable for describing the contemporary Western situation. However, in this author's opinion, the term "spirituality," even though it is also a product of modern Western culture and even postdates the terms religion and secularity, is suitable for describing today's spiritual situation.

This theory is also borne out by numerous studies of Nones, including the international research project Faith and Beliefs of "Nonbelievers," which I have been working on with colleagues from the Czech Republic and abroad.[3] As I mentioned earlier, not only the concepts of religious and secular, but also the analogous categories of believers and "nonbelievers," theists and atheists, are proving inadequate to describe today's spiritual situation. The transformation of religion in the age of globalization has relativized even these boundaries; contemporary society is not divided along these lines. People today, at least in Western civilization, are rarely entirely clear-cut in their views. Not only beyond the bounds of the churches but also among their members, there is a growing number of those who could be called *simul fidelis et infidelis*—in their inner world there is an intermingling of faith and skepticism, of basic trust and doubt, of critical questions and uncertainties.

Thus, the inner world of a large number of our contemporaries both reflects and co-creates the prevailing mentality of society and the "outer" cultural landscape. Postmodern culture has in its genes both Christianity and the modernity and secularity that grew out of Christianity, and this heritage is extremely intermingled. The vast majority of practicing Christians in the West are deeply influenced culturally by modern secular society. However, most atheists could also be described as (culturally) "Christian atheists" because they carry with them much more of the heritage of Christian culture than they usually care to admit.[4]

For centuries, ecclesiastical authorities have sought to control the spontaneity and vitality of spiritual life, to guard the orthodoxy of the creeds, to control the formal expressions of belief, and to discipline the morals of the faithful. Spirituality, as a dynamic inner dimension and form of faith, more easily evaded that control. This is also why, throughout history, the ecclesiastical authorities have often treated this form of faith with caution and suspicion, wanting to restrict it to a limited space (especially behind the walls of monasteries) and designated time (for example, prescribed times of contemplation in the lifestyle of the clergy). The ecclesiastical authorities tried to discipline and institutionalize nonconformist spiritual movements—such as that of Francis of Assisi and his followers—as much as possible. However, monastic spirituality often radiated out from the monasteries to the laity, and this radiation took the institutionalized form of brotherhoods and "third orders."

Many of the pioneers of the new spiritual currents, who were later declared saints by the Church, such as Teresa of Avila, John of the Cross, and (initially) Ignatius of Loyola, also confronted mistrust, harassment, and suppression in the Church. But, as psychoanalysis teaches us and as many examples from history have demonstrated, everything that is suppressed and displaced always returns in some altered form.

Often, in times of crisis in institutional religion, there has been a great revival of spirituality in lay Christian circles. For example, when the form of the Church was in deep crisis in the High Middle Ages, and various tensions were growing within the Church, as well as conflicts between the Church and the secular authorities, the hierarchy made excessive use of the interdict, a kind of general strike of the Church apparatus, as a punishment. When the operation of the Church, including the celebration of the sacraments, came to a halt, lay Christians were forced to look for alternative paths—and one form was the revival of personal spirituality. This contributed, among other things, to the individualization of faith that then developed into the Protestant Reformation and secular spirituality. In times of crisis in the strictly hierarchical medieval Church, lay brotherhoods grew and they disseminated a quiet pietistic piety as well as, at other times, a revolutionary-chiliastic spirituality of passionate anticlerical resistance.[5]

The revival of interest in spirituality at the end of the second millennium of Christianity may also be related to some extent to the culminating crisis of power, authority, and influence of traditional religious institutions and their credibility. Precisely because spirituality—out of the entire broad spectrum of religious phenomena—is the least controllable by ecclesiastical authority, it is the area that is most easily emancipated from the ecclesial form of religion. Today the relationship of spirituality to religion is the subject of much debate.

If art and many other cultural phenomena have gradually freed themselves from the embrace of religion, why shouldn't spirituality follow suit and establish itself as a separate domain governed by its own rules? If the Church, in the documents of the Second Vatican Council, recognized the legitimate autonomy of science, art, economics, and politics, and renounced its aspirations to dominate these sectors of life, should it not similarly recognize the emancipation of spirituality from religion in its ecclesiastical form? But what would remain of the Church and of religious life without spirituality? "Faith without works is dead," says the apostle.[6] But faith without spirituality is also dead.

Spirituality, a living faith, precedes intellectual reflection (the doctrinal aspect) and institutional expressions of faith; it transcends them and sometimes revives and transforms them in moments of crisis. The impulses that animated theological thought and led to Church reforms most often emanated from centers of spirituality. Tragic upheavals in the Church occurred especially when the ecclesiastical authorities were unable and unwilling to listen to the impulses of these centers,[7] viewing them a priori with the distrust and sometimes arrogance of those who possess the truth and wield power.

At the turn of the third millennium (in the epoch sometimes referred to as the new Axial Age), various circumstances contributed to the vitality and attractiveness of spirituality not only in lay Christian circles but also beyond the confines of the churches. One reason was certainly the need to compensate for the noise, stress, and superficiality of an overtechnologized lifestyle by delving into silence, inwardness, and depth. A number of contemplative monasteries began to open their doors for time-limited silent retreats with the possibility of spiritual accompaniment for seekers. Trying out monastic life for a time is now one of the most popular offerings of the Church in heavily secularized countries. Many monastic communities are aging and dying out, but the exception tends to be the most rigorous, purely contemplative ones—those that offer something that "the world" cannot give. And these monasteries, monasticism, and hermitage are not losing their appeal to the people in the world (and not only to romantic souls).

New religious movements and communities have found a home in some of the abandoned historic monastery buildings; in some places, lay people and priests, men and women, families, and temporarily or permanently celibate people live together. In a number of instances, the silence of hermitages has inspired the spirituality of people who live amid the din of cities but experience them as spiritual deserts, places of desolation within the crowd.[8] One of the first Catholic religious to reach a wide twentieth-century audience with his books from his hermitage near a contemplative monastery in Kentucky was the American Trappist Thomas Merton.[9] From the 1960s to the present day, more and more authors of books on contemplation have emerged; they often attract the interest of readers who might be described as seekers rather than religious believers and churchgoers.

The 1960s were a stellar moment in the emergence of many new religious and spiritual movements. As already mentioned, a very dynamic charismatic movement emerged in evangelical groups on American campuses in the late 1960s, and after a while, there emerged its counterpart in a Catholic context, the charismatic renewal movement. Later, especially in Latin America, Pentecostal churches began to attract members of the traditionally strong Catholic Church on a large scale. Where the life of traditional parishes was in the doldrums, Pentecostal groups impressed with their vitality and emotionality. Where the Catholic Church had neglected the education of the faithful and the catechesis of adults, the simple fundamentalist theology of the evangelicals was rapidly reaping success.

The process of globalization, the interpenetration of worlds, has also contributed to the revival and enrichment of spirituality in the West. The postmodern turn to spirituality has drawn much inspiration from Oriental spirituality. This trend was also viewed, and in many places still is viewed, with great suspicion by many church authorities and conservative Christians, and sometimes they even demonize it. Since the 1960s, interest in spirituality—especially Far Eastern spirituality such as yoga, Zen, and other schools of meditation—has found fertile soil in circles of humanistic and transpersonal psychology and psychotherapy, as well as in personal development courses and in nonconformist culture (for example, the beatnik movement). The colorful wave of this subculture, whose promised land was mainly California, was subsequently termed the New Age movement. It was certainly understandable and legitimate for Church authorities to take a critical stance toward the syncretism of this movement; to their detriment, however, they failed to ask what needs and signs of the times these movements were responding to and whether the Church was capable of responding more competently.

In the Christian milieu, only since the first wave of "Christian Yoga" and "Christian Zen" has there been a renewed interest in the study of the classics of Christian mysticism, and many centers are springing up and putting Christian meditation into practice. Some centers of Christian spirituality are ecumenical in character and renounce any proselytism—the ecumenical Taizé community, for example, has inspired a worldwide Christian youth movement that reaches out to many "seekers."

As we shall demonstrate later, at a time when in many countries' churches are emptying out, the numbers of priests are dwindling, the parish network is becoming increasingly fractured, and there is no sign that this trend will not continue, the spiritual accompaniment of seekers is clearly a form of ministry that the Church can offer not only to its faithful but also to the growing world of Nones. Let me preface this by saying that this is not a classical mission of recruiting new Church members. It is not very realistic to expect most Nones to find a permanent home within the current (mental and institutional) borders of the Church. However, centers of open Christianity, especially those devoted to courses in meditation, can expand these borders.

The most valuable service to the credibility and vitality of the faith will probably be rendered by those Christians who have the courage to go beyond the present mental and institutional boundaries of the traditional churches and, following the example of St. Paul, succeed in being all things to all people and venture out as seekers with seekers onto new paths.

When we are speaking about the growing interest in spirituality, it is also necessary to mention its downsides. The negative aspect of the popularity of these paths is the tendency to commercialize and trivialize them. One manifestation of the economization of life in contemporary civilization is the fact that the global marketplace of goods and ideas has quickly responded to the demand for "spirituality" with a flood of cheap goods: kitsch imitations of Oriental spiritualities, cheapjack esotericism, occultism, and magic, and charlatans with recipes promising instant enlightenment, healing, ecstatic experiences of happiness, or magical powers. Pseudo-mysticism has become part of the market for drugs of all kinds (chemical and psychological) and also of the entertainment industry. Self-proclaimed "spiritual teachers," magicians, and gurus have often committed spiritual manipulation, psychological abuse, and the fleecing of gullible people in their "ashrams." Sexual abuse has also thrived here.

In spiritual wellness centers, "meditation" is practiced as a noncommittal leisure activity or a dilettante substitute for both pastoral care and psychotherapy. This is the best outlet for spiritual goods with fake exotic "made in the Orient" labels. After visiting an amusement park of Western pseudo-Buddhism, my Japanese Buddhist monk friends told me with sad irony, "What these people mistakenly pass off as Buddhism is just mutilated Christianity—a cheap Christianity, devoid of what they dislike about Christianity because it requires something of them; it is a comfortable Christianity without church, without dogma, and without Christian morality. But they have no idea that Buddhism is also a demanding path."

Smart entrepreneurs of spirituality offer a quick way to get "spiritual experiences" or the acquisition of extraordinary abilities. By contrast, in monasteries where honest spiritual practice is cultivated, they welcome those interested in spiritual practice with the words: "Remember that you have come here not to gain anything but to put many things aside."

When I spent some time dealing with the freak show of religious populism, I had to ask myself to what extent the Christian churches, which, over a long period of time, presented Christianity as a religion of precepts and prohibitions, were also responsible for this situation. They failed to respond in time to the sincere desire for spirituality and give access to the treasures of Christian mysticism, kept hidden in a locked vault to which they themselves have often lost the keys. And in so doing they allowed the opposite of faith—superstition and idolatry—to flood this space. Interest in spirituality—this great sign of hope for a positive transformation of our world—may be a missed opportunity and may soon fade away again if the culture of the spiritual life is replaced by esotericism, which is a debased form of gnosis that amounts to a banalization and trivialization of spirituality.[10]

Not only in Christianity but certainly also in the traditions of many other religions, as well as in secular culture, there are often forgotten, extremely valuable sources of spirituality that can add depth, sparkle, and therapeutic power to contemporary civilization. If this potential is developed within different religions, it can open up a space for sharing and mutual enrichment. I observe with great interest the coming together of people across religions who are responsibly engaged in serious spiritual practice and who draw on the treasures of mysticism. The cultivation of their own spiritual facets could be the way by which these traditions can become a positive alternative to fundamentalism and to the trivialization and commercialization of religion, as well as to the ideological and political abuse of "religious energy" to foment nationalism, prejudice, hatred, and violence.

Spirituality—more than academic theology, liturgy, and moral precepts—is the source of religion's long-underestimated power. But let us not separate it from the other dimensions of faith. If the awakened power of spirituality is to lead to peace and wisdom, it must not be divorced from rationality, nor for that matter from moral responsibility or the sacred order that the liturgy brings to life.

We talked about the relationship of spirituality to religion and the Church. Let us return to the question of what is the relationship between faith and spirituality. As an indirect answer, I will quote Augustine's commentary on the Gospel of St. John: "I say it is not enough to be drawn by the will (*voluntas*); you are drawn even by delight (*voluptas*)." Here Augustine surprisingly chose a word that could be translated as libido (pleasure, passion, ardor, lust, desire)— and certainly not only because of the pun on *voluntas/voluptas*. He adds: "Or is it the case that, while the senses of the body have their pleasures, the mind is left without pleasures of its own? . . . Give me a man that loves, and he feels what I say. Give me one that longs, one that hungers, one that is travelling in this wilderness, and thirsting and panting after the fountain of his eternal home; give such, and he knows what I say. But if I speak to the cold and indifferent, he knows not what I say."[11]

Doesn't St. Augustine mean by this passion of faith precisely what we today call spirituality? Don't we find in these sentences an answer to the question about the relationship of faith to spirituality? Spirituality gives passion, vitality, attraction, and ardor to faith; therefore, in transmitting faith, the flame of spirituality must not be forgotten; it must not be extinguished but tended if faith is not to become a rigid and cold religion. We must not forget that fire is also dangerous—just like life itself.

FOURTEEN

The Faith of Nonbelievers
and a Window of Hope

I approach the writing of this chapter with great misgivings. In the
next few pages my interpretation of belief and nonbelief will be
(even) more personal and subjective than in the rest of this book. But
haven't theologians from Augustine to Gerhard Ebeling, or religious
philosophers like Martin Buber, taught us that the authentic language
of faith is necessarily personal? Augustine demonstrated the hermeneutical circle between self-knowledge and knowledge of God, and
he wrote his most influential theological book—one of the most
influential religious books ever—in the form of an autobiography.
Ebeling warned against a "naturalistic," objectivist, object-oriented
language about God; he argued that the language of Christian theology must come from one's own conscience as it listens to God—
that it must involve personal commitment.[1] Reading the books of
Martin Buber, I came to understand that if God is not a personal
Thou for us, but only a "he" or an "it" (an object about which we can

speak impersonally, with detachment, without personal involvement, "objectively"), then we are not talking about God but about an idol.

I make no secret of my closeness to existentialist philosophy and theology or my disdain for neo-scholasticism. I have carefully investigated where my allergy to "metaphysical realism" stems from. Did my personal traumatic experiences with some of the neo-scholasticists and the neo-scholastically molded theological faculty in Prague in the early 1990s have something to do with it? It was then that this attempt at "scientific, objective" theology began to remind me of both the "scientific atheism" of Marxism and scientistic positivism's arrogant yet naive claim to "objective knowledge of reality." Theology, groomed into the form of an incoherent, closed system of syllogisms, in which there is no trace of the drama of the personal search for God or the struggle between faith and doubt, has always seemed to me as cold and inert as a dead body without a soul.

The claim to know and present the "objective truth" is something I have always suspected of pride and narrow-mindedness, of a naive and also insolent claim to assume the "position of God," of an inability to humbly acknowledge the limits of one's own limited perspective. I have always feared the "possessors of truth" who leave no further room for doubt, critical questioning, or further searching. One of the things that makes me respect Nietzsche—and why I do not fear the supposed "relativism" of postmodernism—is his realization that all of our seeing is itself already an interpretation. I was first reconciled to some extent with the notion of objectivity in the philosophy of science by my friend, the philosopher and natural scientist Zdeněk Neubauer, with his sentence: "objectivity is the virtue of subjectivity," that it is the virtue of impartiality and justice.[2] In the realm of theology, I understand this virtue to be *kenosis*, the "bracketing" and relativizing of one's own experience and perspective, because this "self-denial" helps us to listen better to the experience of others and to seek a platform of mutual understanding. Relativism also must not be absolutized.

I would guess another reason for my extreme reticence and suspicion of "positivism in theology" and its claims to objectivity as "impersonal truth" is that art was the key to my understanding of the world—and the world of faith. Indeed, literature in particular offers the possibility of participating in the experience of others. Art, more than science, led me onto the path of never-ending search for truth. In the history of philosophy, I was closest to those thinkers who were also great writers: the existentialists and their two great predecessors, Nietzsche and Kierkegaard. I grew up in the family of a literary historian, and one of the reasons I intuitively chose to study sociology and psychology is probably that the best writers in both fields operate at the intersection of science and literature.

It was its aesthetic aspect that first attracted me to the world of religion; for me, the first door to the world of faith was art: the architecture of the old churches of Prague, those treasure troves of works of art, and sacred music—those indelible traces of the sacred amid the uniform grey of state-imposed primitive materialist ideology. My intellectual initiation into Christianity, which happened only after that emotional enchantment, was not offered by theological books or catechisms but by literature: the essays of G. K. Chesterton and the novels of Fyodor M. Dostoyevsky, Graham Greene, Heinrich Böll, George Bernanos, François Mauriac, Leon Bloy, and many others, as well as the poems of Czech Catholic poets, especially Jan Zahradníček and Jakub Deml. From the very first years of my missionary zeal as a convert I introduced many of my friends and colleagues to the then forbidden world of Catholicism particularly through the dissemination of this type of literature, as well as through meditations on works of art with religious themes in galleries, or by listening together to music ranging from Gregorian chant, Johann Sebastian Bach, and George Frideric Handel to Igor Stravinsky and Olivier Messiaen. It was much later, through the cracks in the iron curtain of communist censorship, that I gained access to contemporary theological and philosophical literature, which is now my main reading matter and my spiritual world.

In later years I would also put catechisms into the hands of potential converts, but always with the cautionary proviso that neither perfect acquaintance with the articles of faith, nor even intellectual assent to them—that we hold them to be true—can be considered faith, but at most an antechamber to faith. I then went on to study dogmatics, the architecture of the cathedral of Catholic culture, with great intellectual pleasure, but with the benefit of the history of dogma, which makes it possible to know the historical context and the struggles out of which the articles of faith were born. But if the study of dogmatics is not accompanied by the cultivation of a strong and healthy spirituality, if the work of the intellect is not accompanied by the "intellect of the heart," then this cathedral is for us only a museum, not a living house of God. Some of the theology students and aspirants to the priesthood whom I met seemed to me like people who sit for days over the scores of operas but have never heard music and have never been to a theatre.

In some postcommunist countries that underwent both hard secularization under the communist regime and soft cultural secularization before and after it—especially in the Czech Republic and East Germany—it is still very easy for people to identify themselves as atheists. Their atheism tends to be more a manifestation of conformity to the majority mentality than an expression of a clearly defined opinion and a carefully considered position. The phrase "I am an atheist" most often means: I am *normal*, I am not a member of any obscure society; I am like almost everyone else around me; I have nothing against religion, but I consider it to be something that has long since been a "done deal" and passé, something that does not concern me personally in any way.

After a futile effort to find interesting atheists to debate with, it seemed to me that I might have to find the atheist in myself and resort to talking to myself. It was then that it finally dawned on me that the prerequisite for a fruitful dialogue with atheism is to first discover the atheist, doubter, or nonconformist within oneself and to engage in an honest conversation with that person. Nietzsche claimed to have "two opinions about everything." I grew accustomed to an internal dialogue between different perspectives on faith. Faith—like the Church, the Bible, and the sacraments—is a meeting of the divine and the human, it has both aspects. As a sociologist and psychologist, I was more interested in the human side of faith; as a theologian, in the divine side: faith as a gift, as grace, as the life of God in man. I have always found the inner dialogue between the two perspectives interesting and useful.

J. B. Lotz's book *An Atheist Lurks in Every Person*[3] strengthened me in my search for whether an atheist also lurked in me. Although I did not find an atheist in myself, several traumatic experiences with the Church brought about not only a crisis in my relationship with the Church but also a certain crisis of faith, accompanied by many critical questions and doubts. Solidarity with the persecuted Church was one of the godmothers of my conversion; in other words, my love for the faith was deeply connected with my love for the Church. If one of these loves was wounded, the other would also be hurt and suffer pain. But that crisis brought my faith to a deeper level; it brought it to a greater maturity and to a more adult relationship with "Mother Church."

Gradually, I learned to perceive faith and doubt as two sisters who need each other, who must support each other so that they do not fall off the narrow bridge into the abyss of fundamentalism and bigotry—in which doubt helps faith—or into the abyss of bitter skepticism, cynicism, or despair—in which case faith as a kind of basic trust helps us. I say that I found my way to faith through doubt; if we are consistent on the path of doubt, then that path will teach us to doubt our doubts too.

When the flood of literature on religion, spirituality, and esotericism on the shelves of bookstores (especially in English-speaking countries) began to be matched by books by the "new atheists," especially the Oxford popularizer of science Richard Dawkins, I looked forward to an opportunity for interesting dialogue at long last. I was disappointed, however. It seems to me that the militant atheism of a few vocal apostles of neo-Darwinism represents a naive atheism similar to the vulgar scientific atheism of the Marxist-Leninists. It is based primarily on a misunderstanding, on a mistaken target: these atheist militants confuse religion with fundamentalism, and belief in a Creator God with the primitive natural-science hypothesis of the vulgar branch of creationists. After a time, Dawkins toned down his militant rhetoric and began to pass himself off as more of an agnostic, claiming simply that God "probably doesn't exist." I would have taken a much more radically atheistic attitude to Dawkins's notion of God than he does: I am convinced that this Enlightenment construct, "God as a natural-science hypothesis," really is just a fiction, that Dawkins's God fortunately does not really "exist." He exists only in the imaginations of fundamentalist believers and fundamentalist atheists. Have the militants of the "new atheism"—who, moreover, have added nothing "new" to the old atheism of Ludwig Feuerbach and the materialists of late modernity, except perhaps militant rhetoric—ever encountered a mature Christian faith and a competent contemporary theology?

Fortunately, a few years later I came across a book by an author who espoused atheism, not agnosticism, but whose thinking and personal approach to religion I could respect. The book is by André Comte-Sponville and is entitled *The Book of Atheist Spirituality*.[4]

André Comte-Sponville had a Catholic upbringing and is aware—and openly admits—that he still retains many of the moral, spiritual, and cultural values he derived from Christianity; he knows and describes without bias the views of his believing friends, whom he respects and values. It was on the threshold of adulthood that he lost his faith in God and his attachment to religion, and although his religious upbringing was not traumatic, he felt this loss of faith as a liberation. He probably experienced something that many people who have outgrown their religion during adolescence have undergone and consigned to their box of childhood memories. Comte-Sponville adds that he knows about people who have undergone a conversion to faith at the same age and who have experienced this conversion as a liberation; this is also the experience of the author of this book.

In his book, Comte-Sponville writes how surprised he was when an old priest thanked him after a lecture on atheism and told him that he agreed with the vast majority of what he had said. Comte-Sponville immediately listed for the priest various articles of faith in which he did not believe, but the priest told him that it was not a matter of importance. As I read that paragraph, I had a wish to tell the author that there is at least one other elderly priest who would have said something similar to him. The differences and similarities between belief and nonbelief are found elsewhere and much deeper than the level of religious opinion.

Comte-Sponville quotes an anecdote about two rabbis in a long night's debate who came to the conclusion that God does not exist. In the morning, one of them saw the other praying; he asked him in astonishment why he was praying, since they had agreed that God did not exist. "What has that to do with it?" the one who was praying asked in amazement in turn. I'm not sure I interpret the story in the same way as Comte-Sponville. I see it as a good example of the important distinction between mere religious beliefs and religious practice, the experience of faith. In an intellectual debate, my religious arguments—my religious beliefs—can totally collapse. The practice of prayer, however, is based on something much deeper than my religious views: faith as basic trust. I don't know why I would stop praying were someone to show me the intellectual inadequacy of my whole theology, of everything I think about God; maybe that would be a reason to pray even more.

It shouldn't be that surprising to learn that quite a few "atheists" pray. I don't just mean prayers in life's emergencies (in liminal life situations, many atheists quickly lose their atheistic convictions and start crying out to God in earnest supplication) or spontaneously sighing in awe and gratitude when confronted by "divine beauty." Many people who, for a variety of reasons, do not understand religious language and do not think in religious terms, nevertheless understand what prayer, meditation, and adoration are—and practice them, sometimes quite spontaneously, though perhaps under a different name. Even many of those who do not subscribe to any religion are not "tone-deaf" with respect to that dimension of spiritual life; they too feel the need to articulate in some way their gratitude for the gift of life that cannot be taken for granted, for the miracle of love and the beauty of the world.

Even the faith of believers whose religious convictions are undergoing crises and passing through the "valley of the shadow" can live on in the experience of prayer. I am not referring to the experience of "answered prayer," such as might be used to overcome doubts, being perceived as saving proof of God's existence. It is unanswered prayer, much more than answered prayer, that is a school of faith for me. It is the experience that God is not an automaton for granting our wishes, that his existence does not consist in "operating" according to our notions. In another wise Jewish anecdote, a rabbi tells a woman who complains that for so many years God has failed to answer her prayers to win the lottery: "But God did answer you! His answer was 'no.'"

Just because God doesn't answer us in the way we would like God to, doesn't mean God doesn't answer at all. It is precisely un-answered prayer that helps us to understand what constitutes true dialogue with God: God's answer is not found on the surface or in the individual things that we choose, wish for, or "order"; God's answer is reality as a whole, the whole of our life. God is "God in all things" and must be continually sought and found, step by step, and then sought again in and as that whole; a whole that both includes and transcends the entire world.

Moreover, Comte-Sponville speaks of this whole with an al-most mystical fascination in the final part of his book, in his proposed spirituality for atheists. Here—as when reading the entire *Book of Atheist Spirituality*—I cannot help wondering what concept of God (and what personal experience) seems to be such an obstacle to our author that it leads him to deny this whole its traditional name: the name God.

Comte-Sponville speaks of the totality of reality as a mystery that can be contemplated without words—and on this we agree. But by resisting so strenuously to refer to this mystery by the word "God" (and claiming that to do so would be to add to this mystery of reality some other, invented mystery), he shows that he already has an idea of the God he does not believe in—and probably he does not believe in that God because it does not correspond to the idea of the God he himself has constructed.

But if we really want to open ourselves up to the absolute mys-tery that we believers call God, we must first put aside ("bracket") all the ideas we have previously formed about God.

The God of my faith is not an objective being, hence no "added mystery." By referring to the mystery of the whole as God, thus analogously as a "person" (in a consciously "anthropomorphic," meta-phorical way), I articulate my experience of prayer: when I listen to the reality of life, I perceive life as a call and I respond to it in prayer. This is certainly not evidence to convince a nonbeliever of God's existence; it is an interpretation of my experience that I have freely chosen. Viktor Frankl admits that sometimes when he prays he wonders if he is only talking to his "higher self," but this doubt does not weaken his faith in the sense of trust; he writes, "If there were to be a God, then he would not take it further amiss if someone mistook him for his own self and renamed him thereupon."[5] I add: Surely God can be humble enough to come to people and speak to them through their higher self.

The kind of prayer that allows faith to live even in the darkness of intellectual uncertainties about the nature of God's existence and sometimes about existence itself is especially contemplative prayer. From a mind that has been overwhelmed by skeptical, even atheistic, views, faith can move to a depth from which the words of the psalm can be uttered with sincerity and fervor against all odds: I love you, my God, my strength! For love has its own special kind of knowledge and certainty, which is why it can live and breathe even in the darkness of uncertainty and doubt. For there is a love that precedes and survives our words, our feelings, and our opinions; it is the human love that is saturated, renewed, and healed by "grace"—the love of God.

In the dialogue between mystical theology and depth psychology, it can be expressed as follows: our beliefs, even our religious beliefs, are constantly revolving around our ego, circulating in that narrow, shallow layer of our psyche that is only conscious and only rational. But the gifts of grace—love, faith, and hope—expressed in prayer, come from that deeper center, from the deep self (*das Selbst*), from that divine spark that, according to the testimony of the mystics, dwells within it. Faith, as John Paul II and Benedict XVI in particular pointed out not long ago, needs a rational dimension; rationality in theology is an important safeguard against both fundamentalism and sentimental fideism. However, the whole of modern culture, including modern theology (especially the aforementioned neo-scholasticism), has overestimated the rational and conscious component of human spiritual life, including the sphere of faith. When considering the human component of faith, today's theology should take note of what contemporary psychology and neurophysiology tell us about the primacy of extrarational elements in the human psyche, in the realms of perception, motivation, decision-making, and action. *Ego cogito* is not as sovereign a master in the house of human life as Descartes and the Enlightenment thought.

Depth psychology once gave me the answer to the agonizing question of why I often get along better with some "nonbelievers" than with some believers. If faith, as a gift from God, permeates all the layers of our psyche, then a substantial part of it lives in that much deeper and more significant part of it that we call the unconscious. Between the conscious and unconscious sides of our religious attitudes there may not be any harmony—and often there is none. This is one reason why we can speak of "the faith of nonbelievers" and "the unbelief of believers." While it is certainly true that "only God sees into the heart," experienced and perceptive observers can sense what is "emanating" from beyond the words of their dialogue partners. There are "believers" whose consciousness and whose utterances are overflowing with religion, but you sense that although it need not be merely hypocritical conscious pretense, it is all superficial and not underwritten by any spiritual life. This is often not only the case of some enthusiastic converts but also of successful religious professionals.

The contradiction between a conscious, verbally expressed, and emotionally experienced religiosity, on the one hand, and something quite different, almost demonic, that slumbers within such a person, on the other hand, is most clearly evident in the case of religious fanatics. They try to remove their doubts by projecting them onto others—and there they try to silence them, preferably by the moral or even physical destruction of real or perceived opponents, heretics, and doubters. We can be cured of bigotry by the seemingly easy but in practice difficult method recommended by Jung: we have to look at those with whom we struggle as in a mirror capable of showing us our own unacknowledged features, our shadow, our other face. The extremist attitude often conceals an unconscious other extreme that instinctively craves compensation.

There are people who claim to be atheists and have a problem with religion in terms of their conscious self. They reject it, finding it alien, unacceptable, and even quite offensive. Yet sometimes— in an unexpected flash, in a moment of truth—they turn out to be strongly attracted to the "sacred." Some resist this unacknowledged attraction—Freud's biographers write of how he resisted the mystical "oceanic feeling" of listening to music, fearing the vertigo that the intense experience of beauty might inflict on his rational, skeptical ego.

If we study carefully the attitudes toward religion of many of its incisive "atheistic" critics, we often discover a certain ambivalence, a "*Hassliebe*"—a love/hate relationship. We sense this especially in the restless, sometimes even passionate atheism of such "wrestlers with God" as Nietzsche. Isn't this attitude closer to God than lukewarm indifference?

Another group are the "anonymous Christians"—people who for some reason reject the faith but of whom one could say what Pastor Oskar Pfister wrote to Freud: "I would say that no better Christian than you has ever lived!"[6] I have also known converts to Christianity whose "conversion" consisted only in the surprising discovery that Christianity, of which they knew almost nothing, was simply a name for what they had long been living "anonymously," for what they believed to be true and right.

To return to Comte-Sponville's book: what I especially appreciate about his "atheism" is that he looks for what needs to be preserved of Christianity after religion has come to an end. It is a stance that brings him in line with a host of humanist atheists from Ludwig Feuerbach to Ernest Bloch, Milan Machovec, Erich Fromm, and Slavoj Žižek. They all argue against a certain type of religion (one that is in danger of degenerating into infantilism, fundamentalism, bigotry, and fanaticism), but at the same time they are aware that Jewish and Christian monotheism contains much that is extremely

valuable, and that it would be foolish, irresponsible, and very dangerous to lose. So far so good—I understand and share this view. Richard Kearney's anatheism or Paul Ricœur's "second naivety," as well
as the appeal made in the present book, are moving in the same
direction: a transition from the remains of morning Christianity to a
more mature afternoon form.

However, there are differing views about what should be abandoned (or what is already dead anyway) and what should be retained.
Comte-Sponville thinks that what must be abandoned is faith (*foi*)
and what must be retained is fidelity (*fidélité*). Both terms are derived
from the Latin *fides* (faith), denoting something very similar, but which
can and ought to be separated. "Of course, faith and fidelity can go
hand in hand—this is what I call piety, which is the legitimate goal of
believers. They can also come separately, however. This is what distinguishes impiety (the absence of faith) from nihilism (the absence
of fidelity). It would be a mistake to confuse the two! When faith is
lost, fidelity remains. When both are lost, only the void remains—or
calamity."[7] Comte-Sponville himself has lost faith (and notes that
faith is weakening in society), but he defends fidelity. Without it, we
descend into barbarism—either godless, which leads to nihilism and
rampant selfishness, or fanatical, which leads to violence.

It seems to me that the difference between my position and
Comte-Sponville's is merely terminological. What I call *faith*, he calls
fidelity (*fidélité*). What he calls faith (*foi*), I call a worldview, a (religious) conviction (belief). Unquestionably, there are religious world-
views that humanity has outgrown, as well as dangerous and destructive religious beliefs and ideologies. These must be separated from
what I call faith and Comte-Sponville calls fidelity.

When Comte-Sponville says he is against "belief in God," I can
still follow him, because he criticizes above all those "objectified"
concepts of God, which I also consider as idols to be abandoned.
When he speaks of those concepts of God that are dear to me such as
God as being itself, God as an unknowable mystery, the God of mysticism and apophatic theology, he is politely dismissive of them: he
does not know why they should be designated by the word God, or
why we should be concerned with the unknowable at all. He writes:

"If God is inconceivable, then nothing justifies our conceiving of him as a Subject, a Person, a Creator, a Protector or Benefactor, the embodiment of Justice or Love. . . . Yet a God without a name would no longer be God. Ineffability is not an argument. Silence is not a religion."[8]

Here I passionately disagree. Perhaps "nothing justifies us" to *think* all this in the sense of *supposing* it, but nothing prevents us from *believing* it: from daring to *trust* it. Here lies the difference between us: for Comte-Sponville, faith is a supposition, an opinion (*belief*), for me it is trust and hope. I believe in the God of the Bible, who is a God without a name, or whose name it is forbidden to pronounce; a God who had a name by which he could be invoked would be only one of the idols or demons. Silence in the face of an elusive mystery may not be "religion" in the pagan sense of the word, but it is an act of faith, hope, and love toward the God of whom the Bible writes and in whom we Christians and Jews believe.

Comte-Sponville claims that he is not only a nonbeliever (a "negative atheist" who does not believe in God), he describes himself as a positive, genuine atheist who believes in the nonexistence of God.[9] Faith, as I understand it, is not a mere belief but an act inseparably linked to hope and love; it also has the passion of desire. To love, I repeat with Augustine, means *volo ut sis*—I want you to be.[10] In a situation in which the existence and nature of God are not evident, we can look into the depths of our hearts and ask whether we *want* God to be or not to be, whether this is our hearts' deep desire.

I cherish this longing of the human heart for absolute love. Comte-Sponville is extremely suspicious of it: he considers it a strong argument against faith; he believes with Freud that desire and wishing breed illusions. But why should thirst call into question the existence of the source? Why should the desire for God be less true than the wish that God did not exist? Comte-Sponville freely chooses a *belief* in God's nonexistence, and he collects arguments against a contrary free choice, and he rejects the desire and hope of faith.

At the same time, however, Comte-Sponville sharply condemns agnosticism for its alleged indifference to the enduring questions that religion and faith raised once and for all, and continue to raise. In this context, he regards his free choice of atheism as much closer to the free choice of faith than the cold "neutrality" of agnostics.[11] (Here again, perhaps mostly terminologically, we differ: alongside "coldly indifferent agnosticism," I have always appreciated the agnosticism of polite, honest, and humble silence at the gate of Mystery, while I have understood atheism as a further step, as an unjustifiably dogmatic negative response, incapable of patience in the face of Mystery.)

As for the *word* "God," I acknowledge, along with Rahner, that it is a word so laden with problematic ideas that it might be useful to dispense with it, at least temporarily. But the ineffable Mystery that apophatic theology arrives at by destroying all positive and ultimately also negative statements about God, I would defend to my last breath. I am convinced—unlike our atheist and, for that matter, unlike Nietzsche—that to ignore or explicitly reject this transcendent dimension would not make our relationship with our earthly life more vibrant, more full, and more authentic but rather the opposite. With another contemporary atheist who is close to Christianity, Slavoj Žižek, I argue that "humanism is not enough";[12] that those for whom "this world" in its present corrupted form is really quite enough are impoverishing and trivializing their perception and experience of this world and this life. I would certainly abandon many "religious notions," but I would never give up hope, including the hope of a life beyond death.

Of the three divine virtues, Comte-Sponville only favors love. In his perceptive exegesis of Paul's "canticle to love" in his first letter to the Corinthians—one of the most powerful passages in his book—he invokes St. Paul's (and also Augustine's and Thomas Aquinas's) assertion that faith and hope are temporary, whereas love alone is eternal. At this point alone, he goes so far with Paul as to admit that love in some sense relativizes even death.

He knows that for Paul, Augustine, and Thomas Aquinas, the extinction of faith and hope and the fulfillment of love does not happen until eternity, but Comte-Sponville turns atheism into a "heaven on earth": already here, in this life, he sees the *kairos* in which faith and hope will prove unnecessary and love will take their place. For him, this world is already that heaven in which, according to the Revelation of John, "there will be no more temple." Comte-Sponville invokes the scholastic theologians, who maintained that Jesus had neither faith nor hope—he did not need them because he was God: he was solely Love. Doesn't our *imitatio Christi* (following Christ) consist in being like Christ—in other words (I am finishing what Comte-Sponville does not fully express, but it follows from the logic of his interpretation) being like God? This is a very loaded question, but as a diligent reader of the book of Genesis, I am rather wary of this apple offered by a sympathetic atheist.

I share with Comte-Sponville, but also with many agnostics, a humble "we don't know" as regards the afterlife, or, more precisely, a critical detachment from our all-too-human notions of heaven. Yet I see in faith and hope that death will not have the last word, that the life of each of us and the history of all humanity will not end as a plunge into the void but that it will undergo some transformation unimaginable to us here and now into something very important; important also for our life here. I see not only love but also hope and faith, that holy restlessness of the heart that has not yet found its rest in God, as an openness to that which transcends, deepens, and expands our life and the world here and now. Hope, too, is transcendental in nature, it is self-transcending—if we want to limit it and squeeze it into the dimensions of this world, if we deny it a completely free space for its full development, we harm not only it but also ourselves and our world. The point is that when we confuse this essentially eschatological virtue with the ideology of expecting "heaven on earth" (whether in the form of communist promises of a classless society or capitalist projects of a society of affluence and unlimited consumerism), we burden our life in this world with unrealistic demands and expectations. By trying to sate our hunger for eternity with the food of our present table, we prepare a cycle of stresses and subsequent frustrations for ourselves. Again, in the light of the costly historical experience of our part of the world, I would issue an urgent warning against all those who promise heaven on earth. I certainly agree that we must not satiate hope with too earthly, all-too-human notions of a heavenly paradise; at this point let us return to "we don't know." But this "we do not know" must leave the door open to hope and longing.

Nor can I follow our author in his rejection of faith. For me—and this is where I fundamentally differ from Comte-Sponville—love, faith, and hope are inseparable. There are times when faith passes through darkness. Thérèse of Lisieux, at the time of her painful death, confessed that her faith became empty and dark, as if it had died, but she added that at such moments she related to God by love, *solely by love*. Doubtless this testimony could be a further argument for Comte-Sponville's concept of love replacing faith in this life, albeit in the case of Thérèse it was a time between life and death. Comte-Sponville, however, rejects the idea of a hidden, silent God. Apparently, he himself "lost faith" at such a moment of God's silence in his own life. But is it possible to lose faith as one does one's keys?

Those who have truly lived by faith and in faith can lose "religious illusions" and ideas (that is, what he calls *foi*). Many a sincere "former believer" may "find faith" again in the course of another life journey—albeit in a very altered form. After all, Comte-Sponville remains faithful to what he calls "faithfulness" (*fidelité*), and I have already hypothesized that his *fidelité* is very close to what I call faith in this book and what I experience and profess as faith in my own life story. I have one strong argument for this assertion of our affinity: the essential ingredient of faith, as I understand it, is spirituality; I have called it the sap and passion of faith, that which nourishes and constantly revives it, that which is the openness through which grace, the divine life itself, can be poured into my personal faith.

Comte-Sponville rejects faith and hope but wants to preserve spirituality; he champions spirituality even for the "godless," for those likeably pious (in his terminology, faithful) atheists—nondogmatic atheists who *know that they don't know* that there is no God, just as they don't know whether there is a God. Their atheism, he honestly admits, is faith, not knowledge; in this it resembles the faith of the nondogmatic believers, which is what I claim to be. We don't "know" either, we have no evidence that God "is," nor do we "know" what it means to "be" in the case of God. If there is a God, then God is indisputably "other" than how things are or how we mortals are. Even our faith is "merely" faith—though I would never associate the word "merely" with this divine virtue.

We both agree that we are all in a Pascal's wager situation; we are both unconvinced by the traditional "evidence for God's existence." Our belief and unbelief are free choices. But this is where we part company: Comte-Sponville dares to bet on atheism, I on faith. We both agree on "we don't know," yet my "we don't know" is quite different from his "we don't know." For both of us, "we don't know" is a defense against fanaticism and fundamentalism as well as against nihilism, against illusory facile "knowing" (where we can't "know") as well as against resignation.

However, I live in a "we don't know" that has the open window of the word "maybe." Thus the fresh air of hope flows freely into my questions and darkness. I repeat: I would never, under any circumstances, close this window. I fear that atheists, by their free choice— that is, their rejection of God, faith, and hope—close their "we don't know" window. I am convinced that the rejection of hope makes the nonbeliever's world poorer and more cramped. I am afraid that, in this closed space, the space for spirituality will soon be gasping for air, that without faith and hope, atheistic spirituality may sooner or later run out of breath.

Comte-Sponville is oddly persistent in his explicit and repeated rejection of hope. He invokes Buddhism, for which hope is a form of desire, a craving that is the expression and cause of unhappiness. He invokes Nietzsche, for whom hope is disloyalty to the earth, to earthly life here and now. My hope, however, is not an escape to an other-world, to *Hinterweltlichkeit*. I am not revoking the "we don't know" that we honestly share in favor of a dishonest contraband of presumed certainties, assertions about when, where, and how my hope will be fulfilled. I really *"don't know"* in what space and time the kingdom Jesus speaks of exists; I just trust his word and pray for its coming. I do not identify this promised kingdom with just an otherworldly afterlife; the Gospel tells us that the kingdom of God "is among us,"[13] that it came with Jesus, and that one enters it when one unites one's life to Christ by faith, love, and hope. I trust Jesus's word that he is the resurrection and the life; I believe that he is the incarnate love of God that is stronger than death. Comte-Sponville also speaks of how life, transformed by love, relativizes death; this atheist does not hesitate to speak of the Absolute. He claims that he only wants to rid this Absolute of its anthropomorphic features—on that point all of us who have been enlightened by mystical apophatic theology applaud him. But I ask again: Why should the Absolute, stripped of its anthropomorphic features, cease to be God?

I confess that my faith and hope do not deprive my love of fidelity to the earth, to today, and to the present, that they do not deprive the world of its beauty, nor life here of its solemnity and responsibility. When, through a humble "perhaps," the Absolute breathes hope into our lives, it strengthens rather than weakens them. When a ray of the sacred shines through our everyday life, it enriches it with beauty, joy, freedom, and depth. In response to Nietzsche, I declare that the God I believe in has already shed his moral skin, does not smell of "moralin," and knows how to dance.[14] Friends of God who have become my friends beyond the bounds of death already "look like ones redeemed" and teach me this dance of freedom.[15] In spite of all my criticisms of the churches, I profess to know Christians who have been tested in the fire of great ordeals; Comte-Sponville names some of them, and adds that because of their testimony he cannot despise even their Christian faith. After all, even Nietzsche declared that a Christianity worthy of respect had already existed in the world in Jesus as a "free spirit," and that it is possible even today.[16]

Ernst Bloch once claimed that only a true Christian can be an atheist and only a true atheist can be a true Christian.[17] I think I now understand what he was trying to say, although I perceive it differently: atheism can be beneficial for believing Christians but dangerous for atheists. Atheism is like fire: it can be a good servant but a bad master. The believing Christian is an "atheist" to many kinds of problematic theism; Christians were considered atheists for several centuries because of their opposition to the state religion of pagan Rome, and even today there are many kinds of theism to which the Christian faith is rightly opposed. When a believer's faith passes through the cleansing fire of atheistic criticism, it can enter the vacated space as a deeper, purer, more mature faith.

Critical atheism is relative with respect to a certain type of theism. But if atheism adopts an absolutist stance and wants to be more than a critique of a certain type of religion, then it becomes a "religion" itself, often a dogmatic and intolerant religion. I have experienced one such atheistic religion up close, and I cannot recommend this paradise to anyone.

I have yet to encounter an atheism that fills the vacant space left by a decadent type of religiosity and theism with something that could be considered more inspiring than mature faith. I would not exchange Christian faith for the deification of man in Feuerbach's humanistic atheism, nor for the Marxist earthly paradise of a classless society, nor for the "anonymously Christian" spirituality of Comte-Sponville, who substitutes the infinite or the Absolute for the word "God." It seems to me that atheistic utopias also need to be thoroughly "demythologized."

In the constricted space of dogmatic religion, where free thought finds it hard to breathe, critical atheism opens a salutary window of skepticism. If atheism, which resists the temptation to become dogmatic, leaves open the window of "perhaps," a window of hope, then the same Spirit that leads into the depths of Mystery, to a treasure inaccessible to all dogmatism and rigidity, can blow through both windows—humble faith and self-critical atheism.

FIFTEEN

The Community of the Way

In the 1920s, the German poet Gertrud von Le Fort wrote a collection of poems, *Hymns to the Church*, imbued with a convert's fascination with her newly discovered spiritual world.[1] Would anyone today dare to publish a book with a similar title?

In one of my books, I compared the Church to Dulcinea of Tobosa. We meet this character in Cervantes's famous novel from a dual perspective. Don Quixote sees her as a noble lady, while his servant Sancho Panza sees her as a scruffy country girl. If approached superficially, the reader immediately identifies with Sancho's realism: the servant sees what is real; the deluded Quixote is mired in his hallucinations. But it was not without good reason that Quixote—God's fool—was called a truly Christian knight by Miguel de Unamuno.[2] His vision of the world really is foolishness in the world of Sancho's down-to-earth realism. Sancho tells what he sees with his eyes and understands with his common sense. Quixote, however, sees in the girl *what she could be*; in his eyes the "eternal femininity," which she possesses, shines through her wretchedness.[3]

The view that the media and the "public" have of the Church and its present unsightly state is the view of Sancho—realistic and demonstrable: this is the Church, discredited by so many scandals and sins. But for me the key to all reflections on the Church is the paradox expressed by the apostle Paul: "But we have this treasure in clay jars."[4] In this book, therefore, I am not only discussing with foolish hope the many aspects of the present crisis of the Church but also searching for the hidden form to which the Church has been called and that, according to our faith, will blossom at the end of the ages—that treasure hidden in the fragile, dusty, and battered clay pots, which is what we who constitute the Church are.

The river of faith has moved away from its former banks; the Church has lost its monopoly on faith. The institutions of the Church no longer have the power to control and discipline faith; to attempt to do so would risk a further loss of influence and moral authority. But the Church, as a community of believers, a community of memory, narrative, and celebration, has an enduring mission to serve the faith, both by its historical experience and, above all, by the power of the Spirit who dwells and works even within "clay jars."

I believe in the Marian character of the Church—the Church is the *christotokos* and the *theotokos*, the mother, giving birth and bearing the incarnate Word of God to the world.[5] But can the Church still fulfill this mission, or has the time come in which faith has grown up and become independent of the mother's womb? The maternal role can take many different forms; the relationship between mother and child changes throughout life. What form can the Church assume today that is beneficial and even necessary for the life of faith? And what form is more likely to stifle faith and keep it childlike? What form of the Church can respond to the needs of faith today and to the present signs of the times?

At present, I see above all four ecclesiological concepts that can and must be built upon, that need to be theologically thought through more deeply and put into practice step by step. First, the concept of the Church as the people of God journeying through history; second, the concept of the Church as a school of Christian wisdom;

third, the concept of the Church as a field hospital; fourth, the idea of the Church as a place of encounter and conversation, a ministry of accompaniment and reconciliation.

The first definition of the Church as the people of God journeying through history is a central element of the ecclesiology of the Second Vatican Council. This image is taken from the Hebrew Bible, where it refers to Israel, the chosen people whose self-understanding was shaped by the experience of the Exodus—the journey from the land of slavery to the promised land of freedom. The Church, in this conception, is part of the river that has its source in Israel; in the words of Paul, it is a branch grafted onto the olive tree of the chosen people.

This picture describes the relationship between the Church and Israel without resorting to the dangerous model of substituting Christianity for the Jewish nation and religion. It had to be made clear that Christianity did not deny Judaism its legitimacy or its right to exist, and that earlier Christian anti-Judaism had tragic consequences, paving the way for neo-pagan anti-Semitism.[6] When, in the early centuries of the Church, the Church decided to accept the Hebrew Bible, Jesus's Bible, as the binding Word of God, it was tantamount to declaring the memory of the people of Israel to be part of the Church's own historical memory. The memory of Israel, the Hebrew Bible, is part of the memory of the Church. Christian writers on post-Auschwitz theology stress that the Church must not be indifferent to the whole history of the Jews, including the tragedy of the Holocaust.

We Christians must never forget that we share common roots with the Jews; if we lost respect for Judaism, we would be denying the Lord and the lineage of Jesus. Also, through the Eucharist, the sign of the new covenant, through the Jewish blood of Jesus, which is shed for all, we are "blood-related" to the people of the original covenant. Jesus's Jewishness and his Jewish faith belong inseparably to his humanity, to his "human nature," that, according to the famous definition of the Council of Chalcedon, is linked "without confusion" and "without separation" to his "divine nature," his unity with the Father.

Perhaps we could say, by analogy, that for us Christians at least, Judaism, the faith of Jesus, and the "religion of Jesus" are linked "without confusion" and "without separation" to our Christianity, to our Christian faith. The latter is both the faith of Jesus and our "faith in Jesus"—namely, the confidence that in Jesus Christ the divine and the human are united ("without confusion" and "without separation"). Hence it can unite even the "circumcised and the uncircumcised": "For he is our peace; in his flesh he has made both groups into one and has broken down the dividing wall, that is, the hostility between us."[7]

This irrevocable interconnection, which is certainly willed by God, presupposes, however, that "nonconfusion"—respect for each other's otherness without trying to replace, appropriate, or colonize each other. After all, what I am saying here about the relationship between Christianity and Judaism applies by analogy to the relationship between traditional Christianity and its unwanted child, modern secularism. Both the relationship between Judaism and Christianity and the relationship between Christianity and secular modernity resemble, in terms of their fatefulness as well as a certain ambivalence and tension, dynamic relationships within families. Shared genes and shared territory offer enormous positive possibilities, but they do not guarantee trouble-free harmony

But let us go back to the definition of the Church as God's people journeying through history. This image represents the Church in motion and in a process of constant change. God shapes the form of the Church in history, is revealed in it, and teaches it through the events of history. God happens in history. This dynamic conception of God in the perspective of process theology is the impetus for a dynamic understanding of the Church. Both the institutional form of the Church and its theological knowledge evolve in the course of history. In relation to no moment of history and no historical form of church and theology can we say with Goethe's Faust, "Stay a while! You are so beautiful!"[8] Throughout its history, the Church has been on a journey, not at a destination. The goal of her history is eschatological; the anticipated encounter with Christ, the "marriage of the Lamb," will occur only beyond the horizon of historical time. If our theology, our constant reflection on faith, were to lose its open and pilgrim character, it would become an ideology, a false consciousness.[9]

One could say of the Church as the journeying people of God what Pope Francis says of people in a general sense: "The concept of 'people' is in fact open-ended. A living and dynamic people, a people with a future, is one constantly open to a new synthesis through its ability to welcome differences. In this way, it does not deny its proper identity but is open to being mobilized, challenged, broadened and enriched by others, and thus to further growth and development."[10]

Also, the main attributes of the Church—unity, holiness, catholicity, and apostolicity—cannot be perfectly fulfilled in history; in their perfect form they are the object of eschatological hope. The history of the Church is a process of maturation, but it is not a one-way progression to higher and better things. It is the intermingling of unity with diversity, concord with strife, holiness with sin, Catholic universality with a narrow and culturally circumscribed "Catholicism," fidelity to apostolic tradition with a maze of heresies and apostasies. We are to open our world, our hearts, our history, and our relationships to the light of the Kingdom of God, to the ultimate triumph of God's will ("as in heaven, so on earth") through prayer and work; yet we must be vigilantly and humbly aware that history is not heaven, that history is not God. On the historical path of the search for God, we cannot escape the constant tension between "already" and "not yet." We cannot forget and deny our experience of the history of the twentieth century—namely, that the ideologies that promised heaven on earth turned the earth into hell.

Church tradition distinguishes three kinds of church—*ecclesia militans*, the earthly Church militant, *ecclesia poenitens*, the Church suffering and penitent with the souls in purgatory, and *ecclesia triumphans*, the Church triumphant of the saints in heaven. To neglect the eschatological distinction, to confuse the earthly Church with the victorious and triumphant heavenly Church, breeds triumphalism. *Ecclesia militans*, the earthly Church, is to struggle first of all with its own temptations, weaknesses, and sins—including the temptations of triumphalism. If it succumbs to the temptation of triumphalism and becomes an institution of militant religion, then it fights first and foremost with others, with those who are different, as well as with those who are bothersome in its own ranks.[11] Triumphalism, a mixture of pride and blindness, is a disease of the Church—Jesus called it the leaven of the Pharisees and Pope Francis has called it clericalism.

The second vision of the Church is a school—a school of life and a school of wisdom. We live at a time when neither traditional religion nor atheism dominates the public space of many European countries, and instead agnosticism, apatheism, and religious illiteracy tend to prevail. Weaker in number, but very vocal, are two minorities, religious fundamentalism and dogmatic atheism. These arrogant possessors of truth resemble each other in many ways; they also share virtually the same primitive conception of God, faith, and religion. They differ only in that one takes this caricature of God seriously and defends it, while the other rejects it without being able to offer a different, deeper relationship to what believers mean by the word "God." Both have made up their minds about God and do not hear or understand the enduring challenge: "*Seek* the Lord!" Faith is a journey, a way of seeking; religious and atheistic dogmatism and fundamentalism are blind alleys or even prisons.

At this time there is an urgent need for Christian communities to be transformed into "schools" along the lines of the original ideal of the medieval universities.[12] Universities were created as communities of teachers and students; they were communities of life, prayer, and learning. The idea behind them was *contemplata aliis tradere*—we can only pass on to others what we ourselves have first meditated on, inwardly digested, and enjoyed. (It is no coincidence that the Latin term for wisdom—*sapientia*—is derived from the verb *sapere*, which also means to savor and enjoy.)

From the very beginning, disputations, sometimes in the form of public intellectual tournaments, were part and parcel of universities; they were governed by the conviction that truth is arrived at through free debate according to logical rules. It is time to renew this culture of dialogue with God and between Christians—linking theology with spirituality, and religious education with the cultivation of the spiritual life—in today's church communities, parishes, religious communities, and movements within the Church.

What should be the main object of study and prayer today? I believe that in the midst of the multitude of topics that need to be studied and reflected upon, as well as meditated upon and discussed, we should never forget the very heart of Christianity: the three "divine virtues" of faith, hope, and love. These are the way God is present in our world. We need to rediscover them: to distinguish faith from religious conviction, hope from optimism, and love from mere emotion. Education for a thoughtful and mature faith has not only an intellectual and moral aspect but also a therapeutic one; such a faith protects against the contagious diseases of intolerance, fundamentalism, and fanaticism.

All the great religious traditions are schools of their own kind; they offer different methods for overcoming selfishness, for refining our instincts (especially the instinct for aggression), and for teaching the art of just and peaceful coexistence in society, but above all, they offer, from the treasure of their traditions, new and old experiences of how we can open ourselves to the mystery we call God. They can certainly inspire each other in many ways.

The third vision of the Church is the analogy often mentioned by Pope Francis: the Church as a field hospital. The pope is referring to the ideal of a Church that does not remain behind the walls of its certainties in splendid isolation from the outside world but rather goes out sacrificially and courageously to places where people are physically, socially, psychologically, and spiritually wounded, trying to dress and heal the wounds.

The field hospital needs the facilities of a proper modern hospital, which has its own research facilities, provides quality diagnostics, and is dedicated to prevention, therapy, and rehabilitation. As a hospital, the Church should keep before its eyes not only the suffering of individuals but also the collective ills of today's societies and civilizations. For too long, the Church has chiefly adopted a moralistic approach to society's ills; its task now is to discover and exercise the therapeutic potential of faith.

The diagnostic function should be performed by the discipline already mentioned, for which I have coined the term "kairology"—the art of reading and interpreting the signs of the times, the theological hermeneutics of events in society and culture. Kairology should pay special attention to times of crisis and changes in cultural paradigms. It should see them as part of "divine pedagogy," as an opportune moment to deepen reflection on faith and to renew the practice of faith. In a sense, kairology develops the method of spiritual discernment that is an important part of the spirituality of St. Ignatius and his disciples; it applies it when contemplating and evaluating the present state of the world and our tasks in it.

The role of prevention is akin to what is sometimes called "pre-evangelization": nurturing the cultural and moral soil in which the seed of faith can be planted in order to take root. The question of why sometimes and in certain places faith is vital and at other times it withers and bears no good fruit is answered by Jesus's parable of the sower mentioned earlier: it depends very much on where the seed falls. The seed of faith needs a favorable environment. This environment is both believers' entire life spans and also the cultural and social context of their life stories. The good, stony, or thorny ground of which the parable speaks can be regarded as both individual human hearts and different cultures and social environments.

Respect for human rights, the struggle for social justice, or the concern for the stability of family life are also part of "pre-evangelization," constituting an intrinsic "earthly side of faith." If the Church did not accept its co-responsibility for the world and strive for the cultivation of society but merely devoted itself to "explicitly religious activities," it would render these activities inauthentic and sterile. The *vita activa* and the *vita contemplativa* belong together; to borrow the language of the Council of Chalcedon's Christological dogma, they belong to each other "without confusion" and "without separation"—to separate one from the other is to damage both.

It is about the prevention of society's spiritual and moral ailments, about strengthening society's immune system and creating a favorable climate for the healthy development of the human person and society, about *integral ecology*. In this field, Christians must work in solidarity with many secular institutions and initiatives; they cannot claim a monopoly on healing the world.

What we might term "rehabilitative" care is primarily the work of believers in societies that have long been wounded by social and political conflicts, or by wars or dictatorial regimes, where the social capital of trust and solidarity has been depleted. Where traumas, unrelieved guilt, and broken relationships between people and human groups persist for a long time, it is up to Christians to apply their experience to the practice of repentance, reconciliation, and forgiveness.[13]

In postcommunist societies, decades after the fall of the Tower of Babel of communism, its uncleaned ruins remain and weeds thrive on them; the hard lessons of recent history are reprehensibly quickly forgotten and many people scurry like rats lured by demagogic political pipers. Undoubtedly, the churches bear their share of the blame here as well, having been too dedicated to their institutional interests in the space afforded by freedom and neglected their therapeutic mission to the whole of society. Churches in postcommunist countries like to blame the "tsunami of liberalism" and unfriendly media for indifference or hostility to religion in its ecclesial form, but the greater blame lies with those Church leaders who have been corrupted by the promises of politicians and their feigned goodwill. Some Church leaders have even stooped to uncritical loyalty toward the establishment and to cowardly silence where it was necessary to call evil "evil" with the prescience of prophets and the courage of true shepherds. The nostalgia of some Church dignitaries for the days when the throne and the altar were united has crippled their ability to understand the new times and their challenges. When Church leaders began to forge an unholy alliance with populist representatives of state power, they gradually began to resemble them. Sometimes it reminded me of the famous scene at the end of Orwell's *Animal Farm*: it was impossible to tell the two sides apart.

It is a pity that the so-called Pact of the Catacombs has so quickly fallen into oblivion; in that pact, at the end of the Second Vatican Council, a group of council fathers undertook to renounce feudal ornaments in their style of life, living, dress, and titularity, and they called on their brethren in episcopal office to follow suit. When Pope Francis decided to live in a modest apartment instead of the Apostolic Palace, he sent an unmistakable signal to the ranks of the Church and to the world around him: the outward style of life and the environment that people choose and create around them also expresses and retroactively influences their thinking and moral attitudes. If the Church wants to help heal the scars of the past and overcome the current pathological phenomena of the society of which it is a part, it cannot do this simply by means of moralizing speeches; it must do so above all by practical example.

The fourth model of the Church, which I believe is necessary for today and especially for the future, is closely related to the last two—the school and the hospital—and also draws on the suggestions of Pope Francis. The Church needs to create spiritual centers, places not only of adoration and contemplation but also of encounter and conversation, where experiences of faith can be shared.

Many Christians are concerned that in a number of countries the network of parishes, which was created several centuries ago in a completely different sociocultural and pastoral context and within the framework of a different theological self-understanding of the Church, is being increasingly torn apart. It is not realistic to expect that this process will stop (such as by importing priests from abroad). Even if the Roman Catholic Church ventures to ordain married men as priests (*viri probati*), give the laity even more scope, and especially use the charism of women in the liturgy, in preaching, and in the leadership of church communities—steps that will probably happen sooner or later—it is not realistic to expect that this will enable the network of territorial pastoral care to be restored to the form it assumed in pre-modern society.

The leadership of the Church ought now to be already considering not only an alternative pastoral ministry in a changed world but also to reform along the same lines the education and training of those whom it elects and equips for ministry in the Church. I am convinced that the major focal points of Christianity in the twilight of its history will not be territorial parishes but rather centers of spirituality and spiritual accompaniment.

A few years ago, Rod Dreher's book *The Benedict Option* attracted a great deal of attention.[14] Its author, a conservative Christian who converted from the Catholic Church to Russian Orthodoxy, recommends that Christians withdraw from contemporary secular society and form communities in the manner of the ancient Benedictine monasteries. Unlike many other conservative Christian writers who spend hundreds of pages indignantly and tearfully voicing a single idea—namely, that yesterday is over and today doesn't resemble it (an undoubtedly true but rather banal observation)—Dreher is not content to simply note this but tries to offer a way out. He calls on Christians to create a parallel polis, quoting Václav Havel and Václav Benda, who once used the term to describe the activities of the Church and political dissent during the time of communist persecution. However, this graphically demonstrates the poverty of traditionalism, which ignores changes of historical context: what was a necessity in the era of a repressive police regime would have devastating consequences today in a free, pluralistic society. If the Catholic Church were to heed this advice, it would turn into a sect with all the concomitants of such a transformation.[15]

Dreher's well-intentioned book, while containing some valuable partial insights and ideas, is truly heretical in its basic message: what it urges is a denial of the very meaning of Catholicism. When the Church was integrating the radical monastic form of Christianity, it was a fundamental choice for the Church's catholicity that it did not require the Church as a whole (the majority of Christians) to adopt this lifestyle. The invitation to escape from the constant need to take decisions in the demanding conditions of freedom into a ghetto—an artificial folk museum of the past—to flee from the God-ordained task of living in the present, is a very alluring temptation, especially today, and it boosts the attractiveness of sects. The tempest of fear endangers the flame of faith—the courage to continually *seek God* anew and more profoundly.

Like any heresy, however, Dreher's *The Benedict Option* contains a part of the truth, and one that has been sadly neglected—namely, that today's Church is in dire need of spiritual centers that will build on the spiritual and cultural mission of the Benedictine monasteries of the early Middle Ages. The Church needs oases of spirituality and those who dedicate their lives to their care. It is a necessary ministry to that majority of Christians who cannot and ought not to isolate themselves from society and its culture, however multifaceted that culture may be, since it tends to express and reflect the horizon of life rather than the steep vertical of radical spirituality. The whole of the Church cannot and should not form an island of counterculture within society.

Of course there are occasions in history when the Church has to retreat into the catacombs, but the inability to emerge in a timely manner from the catacombs into the *areopagus* of contemporary culture and society makes such a Church stale and moldy: barricaded Christians can hardly be the salt and leaven of society. Christians are not to create ghettos, their place is in the midst of the world; they ought not to strive for a parallel society and wage culture wars.

Before they received the name of "Christians" in Antioch, Jesus's disciples were known as "the people of the way." Today, on the threshold of the afternoon of Christianity, the Church must once again become a community of the way, developing the pilgrim character of faith in order to cross this new threshold. But it also needs to build living spiritual centers, hubs from which to draw courage and inspiration for the journey ahead. Christians need to draw on these centers, but they cannot permanently retreat to them or erect "three tents" high above the mundane concerns of life and the world as the apostles on Mount Tabor longed to do.

SIXTEEN

A Community of Listening
and Understanding

According to an old Czech legend, the builder of one of the Gothic churches in Prague ordered the wooden scaffolding to be set alight after the construction was finished. When the fire ignited and the scaffolding tumbled thunderously to the ground, the builder panicked and committed suicide, thinking that his building had collapsed. It seems to me that many Christians who are in a panic at this time of change are succumbing to a similar error. What is collapsing may be only wooden scaffolding; when it burns down, the church building will certainly be scorched by fire, but the essentials, which have long been hidden, are yet to be revealed.

If the Church is to be the Church and not become a self-contained sect, it must undertake a radical shift in its self-conception, in its understanding of its service to God and to people in this world. It needs to reconceive and develop more fully its catholicity and the universality of its mission, to strive to be truly "all things to all people."[1] I repeat: The time has come for the self-transcendence of Christianity.

If the Church wants to go beyond its boundaries and serve all, then this ministry must be linked to respect for the otherness and freedom of those it addresses. It must be free from the intention to squeeze everyone into its ranks and gain control over them, to "colonize them." It must trust in the power of God, taking seriously the fact that the Spirit is at work beyond the visible boundaries of the Church.

Until now, the Church has focused primarily on pastoral care for its faithful and on missions aimed at expanding their ranks. Another area, since the beginnings of Christianity, has been *diakonia*, charity; it is primarily in this field that Christians learned to serve all people in pain and need, thus fulfilling Jesus's call to universal love and to mercy without boundaries and proselytizing intentions. Here Christians have borne and continue to bear witness through deeds without words—through the solidarity of love and by demonstrating close involvement. In the spirit of Jesus's story of the Good Samaritan, they do not ask "who is my neighbor?" (and who is no longer my neighbor) as he was asked by the Pharisee who "wanted to justify himself,"[2] who wanted to justify the narrow limits of his willingness to love and help. They know that they must "make themselves neighbors"—be close to others, especially those in need. This therapeutic closeness and solidarity has taken and continues to take many forms, and it also has a political dimension.

As has already been said, the Church as a hospital must also care for the health of society, for the prevention and diagnosis of diseases that attack entire societies, as well as for subsequent therapy and rehabilitation; it must strive to surmount "social sins" and deviant structures within social systems. For decades, the social teaching of the Church has pointed out that sin is not just a matter for individuals; we are all increasingly entangled in a messy web of economic and political relationships where evil often assumes a suprapersonal and anonymous guise.

One of the many reasons why confessionals and confessional rooms have emptied is that the consciousness of personal responsibility has blurred against the background of what we know about the many biological, psychological, and social factors that strongly influence our actions. We can always hide in a thicket of excuses and justifications. "How can a person be guilty at all. We're all human beings here, one like another," says Josef K. in Kafka's *The Trial*.[3] But the conformity and superficiality of life are also blameworthy, more perhaps than much of what people whisper in the gloom of confessionals. A considerable number of Christians suspect that what separates them from God are far deeper and also subtler realities than those enumerated by the traditional "confessional mirrors," the lists of sins on which those "mortal" sins are marked with an asterisk.

During my forty-three years of priestly ministry, I have heard tens of thousands of confessions. For many years, in addition to the sacrament of penance, I have offered spiritual talks that are longer and more in-depth than the ordinary form of the sacrament allows, and they relate to the broader context of spiritual life. These conversations are sometimes attended by the unbaptized and by many who would or could be described as nonreligious but are nonetheless spiritually grounded or seeking. I have expanded my team of coworkers for this ministry to include laypeople educated in theology and psychotherapy. It is my firm conviction that the ministry of personal spiritual accompaniment will be the crucial pastoral role of the Church in the forthcoming afternoon of Christian history, and the one most needed.

At the same time, it is the ministry in which I have learned the most, in which my theology and spirituality, as well as my understanding of faith and the Church, have undergone a certain transformation. When my bishop, Cardinal Dominic Duka, resolutely refused to speak with victims of sexual abuse by priests (including members of the monastery of which he was superior at the time) and referred them to the police, I engaged in lengthy late-night conversations with many of them, after which I often spent a sleepless night. I didn't learn much more than what has already been published, but I looked these people in the eye and held their hands when they cried. And it was a very different experience from reading the reports of statements made to the police or in court.

I worked for years as a psychotherapist and I know how close and intertwined mental and spiritual pains are, but this was something other than mere psychotherapy; I felt the presence of Christ there with all my heart, on both sides: in the "least of these, the sick, the imprisoned and the persecuted" and also in the ministry of listening, consolation, and reconciliation that I was permitted to provide.

Several of my university colleagues, whom I respect personally and whose piety and goodwill I do not doubt, have endorsed a pharisaical document entitled "The Filial Correction," rebuking Pope Francis for having called in his apostolic exhortation *Amoris Laetitia* for a merciful, individual, and discerning pastoral approach to people in so-called irregular situations, such as homosexuals, and people who are divorced and remarried in a civil ceremony. I was not surprised that the harsh judgments were delivered by people who had never sat in a confessional and listened to these people's stories. Perhaps if I were looking at the world through the lens of neo-Thomist moral textbooks, where individual arguments fit together smoothly and logically like a cold machine but completely bypass the complex realities of life, I would approach people's problems with similarly simple, black-and-white, and uncharitable judgments. I would also probably take offense at a pope who reminds us that the Eucharist is not a reward for model Catholics but a *panis viatorum*, bread for the journey of maturation—nourishment and medicine for the weak and failing.[4]

I have listened to countless stories of women, recklessly abandoned by their husbands, who, years later, having found support for themselves and their children in a new, well-functioning marriage, were, under current Church law, forever banished from Christ's table, from that table to which Jesus, to the indignation of the Pharisees, invited people in "irreligious situations" and did not impose on them any difficult conditions beforehand. He said of them that it was they, because they could appreciate the free gift of unconditional forgiveness and acceptance, who would precede their proud judges and accusers into the kingdom of heaven. Jesus knew that only the experience of unconditional acceptance and pardon could bring about a life transformation, a conversion. Few things were as foreign to Jesus as the legalistic thinking of his greatest opponents among the Pharisees. Those who appeal to Jesus's words about the indissolubility of marriage should realize that Jesus meant by these words to defend wives from the recklessness of men who could easily dismiss them for petty reasons by simply issuing a "certificate of dismissal" and certainly did not intend to place additional burdens on the victims of such behavior—that is, the divorced women.[5]

When a clergyman, in a fiery sermon in a Prague cathedral, warned of global domination by homosexuals and gender theorists who would forcibly remove children from regular families and sell them into slavery, and send devout Catholics to extermination camps, I realized that this bad news of fear is not really my religion—and above all, it is not the *euangelion* (good news), the religion of Jesus. I have listened to dozens of accounts of Christians who discerned their unchosen homosexual orientation and, after coming out, underwent a psychological lynching by their pious milieu, often including their own parents and relatives. Some of them attempted suicide, in despair that they would be rejected by their community. Am I to force these people, when they finally find a partner for life, to commit to lifelong renunciation of the desire for intimacy, or at best "generously" label their love as a "lesser evil" than loneliness or promiscuity?

For too long, the textbooks of Catholic morality obscured people's individual problems for me as well, and today I am ashamed of that. How great is the temptation for us confessors, the bearers of the Church's authority, to become the Pharisees and scribes Jesus so insistently warned against—those who impose heavy burdens on people and do not lift a finger to help them![6] Of course, it is much easier and quicker to judge people arbitrarily by referring to the paragraphs of canon law than it is to do what Pope Francis calls for: to perceive the uniqueness of each person and to help them—taking into account precisely the uniqueness of their life situation and their degree of personal maturity—to find a responsible solution within the real possibilities available to them.[7]

When will there at last be a shift in our Church from "Catholicism without Christianity" and justice without mercy to the "new reading of the Gospel" that Pope Francis urges and teaches?[8]

I often return to a short story that is a kind of mini-gospel in the middle of Matthew's Gospel, the story of the woman who had suffered from a hemorrhage for twelve years, after trying many doctors, and spending her entire fortune on treatment to no avail. This woman was obviously hurt in the very sanctum of her womanhood; she was bearing within her some severe trauma in an intimate region, in her sexuality. According to Jewish law, a bleeding woman is ritually unclean and is not allowed to take part in religious services, and no one is allowed to touch her. Her compulsive desire for human contact led her to do something that violated the prescribed isolation: she touched Jesus.

She touched him stealthily, anonymously, from behind, hidden in the crowd. But Jesus doesn't want her to take her healing that way. He seeks her face—in a way, he "calls her by name," as he called the astonished Zacchaeus; he cancels her anonymity. The woman comes forward—and after years of isolation, she "tells the whole truth" in front of everyone. And in that moment of truth, she is freed from her malady.[9]

But her very touch, that foolhardy gesture of longing and trust, was the manifestation of her faith—the faith that Jesus said healed her. It was an act by which she transgressed the law, for by her touch she made Jesus ritually unclean—a sin according to strict interpretations of the law. And yet Jesus understands what she expressed by this touch, and by his interpretation he lends the action a redemptive meaning. She completed what she had expressed in her body language—which had hitherto manifested itself in blood and pain—by prostrating herself before him and "telling the whole truth."[10]

That is what I experienced in conversations with victims of sexual and psychological abuse in the Church. Their repressed pain, their disillusionment with the Church, and their often unacknowledged grudges against God, which often turned into self-blame or psychosomatic difficulties, needed to be expressed. It required that safe space of unconditional acceptance. That is where the truth is revealed—and it is a very different understanding of the truth from that of the "possessors of the truth." I dream of a church that would create such a safe space—a space of truth that heals and liberates.

I believe the vanguard of this ministry of the Church—the ministry of spiritual accompaniment—is so-called categorial pastoral care: the ministry of chaplains in hospitals, in prisons, in the army, and in education; it can also take the form of spiritual accompaniment of people in all kinds of difficult life situations or supporting those who are engaged in a similarly demanding ministry to others and are at risk of burnout.

The chaplains' ministry is intended for *everyone*, not just the faithful. It differs both from the traditional pastoral ministry of clergy, such as parish priests, who visit their parishioners in hospitals and administer the sacraments, and from mission in the sense of "converting nonbelievers" and winning new members for the Church. It is also different from the work of psychologists and social workers. It is a *spiritual* ministry, a spiritual accompaniment. Spiritual ministry is based on the assumption that the spiritual realm is an anthropological constant, that it is intrinsic to human beings and helps to shape their humanity. The spiritual is concerned with *meaning*, both the "meaning of life" and the meaning of a particular life situation. People need not only to know in theory but also to actually live and experience the fact that their life, with all its joys and pains, has meaning; the need for meaning and awareness of meaningfulness are among people's basic existential needs. However, in demanding life situations the awareness of meaningfulness tends to be shattered and needs to be resurrected.

The worst that threatens us in moments of life's trials and crises, when we experience fear and abandonment, in times of pain, deep sadness, danger, and suffering of all kinds, is what Kierkegaard called "sickness unto death": despair, loss of hope, loss of meaning in life. We need awareness of the meaning of life as much as we need air, food, and drink; we cannot live permanently in inner darkness and disorientation. Since time immemorial, people have demanded that religion and philosophy help them cope with contingency—with "train wrecks"—to help them process and integrate new, disruptive events. They need to be given a name and a place in people's image of the world and their understanding of life.

The ministry of spiritual accompaniment straddles the boundary between the religious and secular spheres: it may draw on the spiritual treasures of religion, but it lives in a nonecclesial, secular space and must express itself in a way that is understandable to that environment. From that point of view, this specific ministry has a similar status and task to that of public theology, which I mentioned in the second chapter of this book. It must transcend the boundaries of the Church's language game.

After special training, which includes some competence in psychotherapy, the churches dispatch their clergy and lay theologians in this ministry also to people who do not identify with churches or with believers. Their job is to listen to them and talk to them, to foster their trust and hope and their own search for meaning; it is not their task to "convert" these people to their faith or to bring them into membership of their churches. Accompanists must have a highly developed capacity for empathy and respect for their clients' values.

There are times when even the nonbeliever asks for prayer and when it is appropriate to use the therapeutic power of religious language, symbols, and rituals, including the sacraments, when ministering to people who are not fully "settled" in the spiritual space of traditional religion. At other times, however, the person accompanying has to forgo all such elements. Chaplains in hospital wards, prison cells, military camps, or university clubs cannot use many of the typical traditional expressions of faith, not only for reasons of political correctness, but primarily because most of their clients would not understand this language. In a dialogue of partnership with those who "believe differently," traditional concepts and symbols of faith must be used very sparingly. In these situations, chaplains rarely speak explicitly about God and Jesus Christ with those who do not belong to their denomination. They find themselves in the realm of a different language game. This does not mean that God is not present, however. Unlike traditional missionary work or traditional therapy, this ministry of closeness has a dialogical, reciprocal character. As Christians, we do not have to consider those "who do not follow in our company"[11] merely as targets for missionary conversion or as potential opponents or enemies. Jesus commanded us to love all people, to become neighbors. One of the faces of love is respect for others' otherness: love is the space of freedom that we open up to others so that they can be truly and fully themselves, without any affectation, and without having to constantly earn our favor. Love is a space of trust, of security, of acceptance; a space enabling our clients to develop what is most precious in themselves, to become themselves. It is only when we have experienced being accepted and loved, just as we are, that we learn to accept and love others.

The royal road of spiritual accompaniment, its alpha and omega, is the cultivation of a contemplative attitude toward the world and one's own life. Spiritual accompaniment can be of assistance to nobody unless it teaches the practice of inner attunement, the art of detaching oneself from life on the surface and "going deeper," of achieving free dispassion and detachment, of perceiving and experiencing one's life from a broader perspective. The mission of the spiritual companion is to say to clients what Jesus said when he first addressed his future disciples: launch out into the deep and wait in silence. But they must also be taught how to do it—to be initiated into the art of contemplation. For only in this way can they find contact with meaning and restore balance and direction in their lives in liminal and crisis situations.

In order to develop a beneficial ministry for their clients and the wider community, accompaniers need to be contemplative—that is, people who meditate regularly. Their task is to teach the art of spiritual discernment, without which people today are utterly at sea in the noisy and overcrowded global marketplace. Spiritual accompaniers do not have to be "spiritual" in the sense of "ordained ministers of the Church" but they must be *spiritual people*—people who do not just live on the surface of life but draw from their inner depths.

With these reflections, we come close to answering the question hidden in the title of this book. What is the task of the afternoon—

the afternoon of individual human lives, the afternoon of human history, the afternoon of Christianity, the afternoon of the history of faith? What was to die in that long historical crisis of certitudes, in that noonday crisis, the glimmerings of which we feel in many crises of our own time? What were we to mature to and what should be the content of that afternoon?

In order to express the experience of the mystics—for they in particular can give us competent guidance in this matter—it is possible to use the language of depth psychology: it is a transition from egocentrism, from the self-centeredness of the "little self" to a new identity, to a deeper, yet also broader, "new self." This transformation—the shift of emphasis from the *ego* to the *self*—is often expressed in spatial metaphors as a journey to the depths, a journey inward. The words "depth" and "inward" here denote the opposite of superficiality and shallowness. "Going into the depths" does not mean turning away from the world of our everyday life and our relationships with others. To the extent to which we bring the center of gravity of our lives to that inner center, we encounter God in a new and fuller way, as well as other people and the whole orchestra of creation. God as the depth of reality is "God in all things."

This transformation of the human individual is also the theme of the mystical paths and the metaphor of the afternoon of life in the writings of C. G. Jung. I have tried to show that this transformation is happening today not only in individual stories (as it has been happening throughout history) but also in the unfolding of our history, including the history of Christianity. The crisis of the churches is *kairos*: a blessed time of transition from the self-centeredness of the churches to a conscious participation in the ongoing story of the Christmas and Easter mysteries, the *incarnatio continua, crucifixio continua, and resurrectio continua.*[12]

The Church must also abandon its fixation on its "little self," its fixation on just its institutional form at a given moment in history, or on its institutional interests. The terms clericalism, fundamentalism, integralism, traditionalism, and triumphalism denote various manifestations of the Church's self-centeredness, its fixation on what is superficial and external. To succumb to nostalgia for an idealized past, for the morning of Christian history, is to be stuck in a too-narrow (and often narrow-minded) form of Christianity and is a sign of immaturity. If the Church is unable to offer a form of Christianity other than that of the morning or, more precisely, a longing for the morning or various attempts to reconstruct or imitate it, it is not surprising that many people believe that the only remaining alternative is to abandon Christianity and the faith.

The assumption still survives in some places that the only alternative to a religion that has lost its vitality and persuasiveness is atheism of one type or another. But Hegel was probably right in regarding atheism as a mere moment of transition in the history of the Spirit. We should not leave the space vacated by a dying religion to dogmatic atheism, nor to religion as an identity-politics ideology, nor to a vague esotericism. It is the place and time for a mature yet humble faith.

What is the future of Christianity? If the mystery of the Incarnation continues in the history of Christianity, then we must be prepared for Christ to continue to enter creatively into the body of our history, into different cultures—and to enter there often with the same inconspicuousness and anonymity as he once did into the stable of Bethlehem. If the drama of the Crucifixion continues in history, then we should learn to accept that many forms of Christianity die painfully, and that this dying includes dark hours of abandonment, even a "descent into hell." If, in the midst of history's changes, our faith is still to be a *Christian* faith, then the sign of its identity is *kenosis*, self-surrender, self-transcendence.

If the mystery of the Resurrection continues in history, then we should be prepared to seek Christ not among the dead, in the empty tomb of the past, but to discover today's Galilee ("the Galilee of the Gentiles"), where we will find him surprisingly transfigured. He will once again walk through the closed doors of our fear, he will show himself by his wounds. I am convinced that this Galilee of today is the world of Nones beyond the visible boundaries of the Church.

If the Church was born out of the event of Pentecost, and this event continues in its history, then it should try to speak in a way that can be understood by people of different cultures, peoples, and languages; it should be constantly learning to understand foreign cultures and different languages of faith; it should teach people to understand each other. It is to speak clearly, but not simplistically; above all, it ought to speak credibly—"heart to heart."[13] It should be a place of encounter and conversation, a source of reconciliation and peace.[14]

Many of our concepts, ideas, and expectations, many forms of our faith, many forms of church and theology must die—they were too small. Our faith must surmount the walls built by our fears and our lack of courage to venture out like Abraham along unknown paths into an unknown future. In our new journeys, we will probably meet those who have their own ideas about the direction and destination, ideas that are surprisingly unfamiliar to us, but even these encounters are a gift to us; we must learn to recognize them as our neighbors and make ourselves their neighbors.

Respect for diversity and acceptance of other people in their distinctiveness, this dimension of love, which is the criterion of its genuineness, is necessary not only in relations between individuals but also in relations between nations, cultures, and religions. The important phrase in the joint statement of Pope Francis and Imam Ahmed el-Tayeb,[15] that *the pluralism and diversity of religions are willed by God in His wisdom*, is the fruit of thousands of years of experience, paid for by countless victims of religious wars. This sentence has aroused resentment in certain religious circles: Isn't it a betrayal of our religion's claim to its own truth?

No: it is the language of a mature, adult faith, devoid of the collective narcissism and self-centeredness of those religious communities unable to acknowledge their status as pilgrims. For Muslims, this means returning to an important and wise passage from the Qur'an, which explicitly states that God desires a diversity of religions and that this diversity is an opportunity to compete in doing good;[16] for Christians, a continuation of Nicholas of Cusa's insight that one single truth is given to us in diversity (*una religio in rituum varietate*).[17] Let us have no fear: the highest form of truth for Christianity is love of God and humankind; wherever it is realized, God, Christ, and the

Christian faith are present. If the Church today can attest to this trust in a God who is greater than all our ideas, definitions, and institutions, something new and significant happens: we enter the afternoon of faith.

Ecumenism is an indispensable form of Christian love. It is one of the most credible and convincing facets of Christianity. If the Catholic Church is to be truly catholic, it must complete the shift that began at the Second Vatican Council: the shift from Catholicism to catholicity. All churches and all Christians that recite the Apostles' or the Niceno-Constantinopolitan Creed thereby proclaim their duty to develop the catholicity of Christianity: that openness of the Church that mirrors the open arms of Jesus on the Cross. No one is outside the love of Christ.

In this book we have examined the various forms that the Christian faith has assumed over the course of history. In particular, we have looked at two versions of Christianity: Christian religion as *religio*, the integrating force of society, specifically the premodern "Christian empire," *Christianitas*, and Christianity as *confessio*, the worldview put forward by the institutional Church or churches. We have also referred to experiments with nonreligious Christianity.

At the end of chapter 5, I suggested an answer to the question as to what form the Christianity of the future might take. The word "religion," *religio*, need not be derived solely from the verb *religare* (to reconnect)—that is, to conceive of religion primarily as an integrating force in society—but can also be derived from the verb *relegere* (to read again). The Church of tomorrow can be a community of a new hermeneutic, of a new and deeper reading and interpretation, both of scripture and tradition (according to the Council of Trent, the two sources of divine revelation) and of the signs of the times. For this, the art of contemplation is needed.

Through contemplation we learn to read and listen anew, more deeply, more carefully. To listen to what is happening in and around us—God can speak to us through both processes.

I think it is very useful for believers of different religions (but also people "without religious affiliation") to read sacred books together and talk about how they understand them.[18] Looking at one's own founding texts through the eyes of others can contribute to a deeper understanding of them and also to better mutual understanding. Facile syncretism or the pursuit of some artificial "religious Esperanto" acceptable to all is a dead end; one must learn to understand and respect others' differences, not to obscure, downplay, or ignore them.

A few years ago, I co-authored a television series that we filmed on several continents: we asked rank-and-file believers of five major world religions what rituals they use to surround the key events and phenomena of life—the birth of a child, initiation into adulthood, marriage, illness and suffering, burial; what the temple, pilgrimage, prayer, and food meant to them; how they understood the role of women; what their relationship was to beauty or violence. In doing so, I realized how important it is not to "speak on behalf of others," not to judge them from the outside, but to *talk to them*, to give them a voice and to listen to them. In our diverse world where ethnicities and cultures intermingle, personal encounters with others are no longer the prerogative of travelers to faraway lands.

An equally important task is to try to understand the signs of the times, to learn the Ignatian art of spiritual discernment. What is it in the events of our time that excites us, fascinates us, irritates us, and frightens us—and why? We need the art of "quietening our hearts," of restraining our immediate gut reactions of enthusiasm or anger, so that we can allow the events of the history of which we are a part to enter the sanctuary of our conscience, where we can reread them and intelligently discern in them the ciphers of God's messages.[19]

When, in much of the world, the network of local parishes collapses like the scaffolding of the church in the legend I quoted at the beginning of this chapter, spiritual strength will have to be derived from centers of communal prayer and meditation, where celebration takes place, as well as reflection and the sharing of faith experiences. Such open centers need to be built now. In them we can learn to distinguish between the secondary support structures that disappear in the course of history and what can be used to build on again.

Perhaps not only the Catholic Church but also other Christian churches and other religions should go through the "synodal process" that Pope Francis has called for within the Catholic Church: a process of listening to each other and finding a way forward together. I believe that this process of "general consultation on the improvement of human affairs," *consultatio catholica de rerum humanarum emendatione*—to borrow the expression of the great seventeenth-century Czech thinker, Jan Amos Comenius—would be an important step toward that universal fraternity of which Pope Francis writes in his encyclical *Fratelli tutti*.

I consider this encyclical to be the most important document of our time, comparable to the importance of the Universal Declaration of Human Rights. If we are looking for spiritual inspiration for transforming the process of globalization into a process of humane communication, then we can find in it inspiration and intuitions that call for further reflection and development.

In the Bible, the first words the Lord says to those he addresses are: Be not afraid! Fear distorts our vision of the world. Many religious professionals have been, and often are, fear merchants; they think that if they properly scare people first, they can better sell them their religious wares. On the threshold of a new chapter in Christian history, let us put aside the religion of fear. Let us no longer buy from the peddlers of cheap certitudes. On the threshold of the future, let us not even be afraid to say "we don't know" with honesty and humility— something that not even faith can deliver us from; faith is the courage to venture with confidence and hope into the cloud of mystery.

In my reflections in this book, I have been thinking about a new reformation that is being increasingly seen as a necessary response to the current state of the Church—and the extent to which the family of believers woven into the entire fabric of human society is related to the transformation of the human family as a whole. I ask myself how we can prevent a new reformation from becoming a painful schism and, above all, from failing to go far enough and disappointing the hopes it raises. The Catholic Reformation of the sixteenth century, which was brought about by mystics such as Teresa of Avila, John of the Cross, and Ignatius of Loyola, as well as by reforming bishops such as Charles Borromeo, may provide some inspiration.

In his *Spiritual Exercises*, Ignatius indicated four stages of *metanoia*.[20] First, *deformata reformare*, to reform what is deformed. Second, *reformata conformare*, one must embark on the path of following Christ, being inspired by the example of Jesus's activity. Third, *conformata confirmare*, to draw strength from the cross of Jesus, to walk through the dark night of suffering. And fourth, *confirmata transformare*, to allow what is consolidated to be transformed, to be illuminated by the light of Jesus's Resurrection, by the presence of the Risen One—to find God in all things. Let us not allow our efforts to reform the Church and society to get bogged down in the first stage, just changing deformed and distorting structures. Real reform must take the form of following Christ: this implies seeking the Risen One afresh over and over again.

This task will not be fulfilled by the traditional forms of pastoral mission to believers, nor by the traditional forms of mission aimed at "converting nonbelievers." A truly new evangelization, worthy of the name, has a difficult task today: to seek the *universal Christ*, whose greatness is often hidden by the limitations of our vision, our too narrow perspectives and intellectual categories.

Seeking the *universal Christ* is both the task and the sign of our times. Teilhard's vision of the universal Christ, present in cosmic evolution, must be complemented by finding the Risen One, present (often anonymously) in the evolution of society. Let us search for him "by his voice" like Mary Magdalene; let us search for him in strangers on the road like the disciples on the road to Emmaus; let us search for him in the wounds of the world like the apostle Thomas; let us search for him wherever he passes through the closed doors of fear; let us search for him where he brings the gift of forgiveness and new beginnings.

We must complete the reformation of the deformed by transforming everything that is consolidated; much in which we have consolidated and fortified ourselves is being shaken. This opens up space for finding the "greater Christ." The ever-greater Christ (*semper maior*) is God, present in all things—in all the events of our lives and our world.

I called this book *The Afternoon of Christianity.* Doesn't the concept of afternoon suggest the proximity of evening, of extinction and death? My answer is: In the biblical concept of time, a new day begins at evening. Let's not miss the moment when the first star appears in the evening sky.

Written between 2015 and 2021 in the United States, the Czech Republic, and Croatia; finished on the shores of the Adriatic Sea on September 7, 2021.

RECOMMENDED READING

PAPAL DOCUMENTS

Pope Francis. *Amoris laetitia* [The Joy of Love]. Post-synodal apostolic exhortation on the pastoral care of families. Vatican City: Libreria Editrice Vaticana, 2016. https://www.vatican.va/content/francesco /en/apost_exhortations/documents/papa-francesco_esortazione -ap_20160319_amoris-laetitia.html.

———. *Evangelii gaudium* [The Joy of the Gospel]. Apostolic exhortation on the proclamation of the Gospel in today's world. Vatican City: Libreria Editrice Vaticana, 2013. https://w2.vatican.va/content/fran cesco/en/apost_exhortations/documents/papa-francesco_esortazi one-ap_20131124_evangelii-gaudium.html.

———. *Fratelli tutti* [All Brothers]. Encyclical letter on fraternity and social friendship. Vatican City: Libreria Editrice Vaticana, 2020. https://www.vatican.va/content/francesco/en/encyclicals/docu ments/papa-francesco_20201003_enciclica-fratelli-tutti.html.

———. *Gaudete et exsultate* [Rejoice and Be Glad]. Apostolic exhortation on the call to holiness in today's world. Vatican City: Libreria Editrice Vaticana, 2018. https://www.vatican.va/content/francesco /en/apost_exhortations/documents/papa-francesco_esortazione -ap_20180319_gaudete-et-exsultate.html.

———. *Laudato si'* [Praise Be to You]. Encyclical letter on care for our common home. Vatican City: Libreria Editrice Vaticana, 2015. https://www.vatican.va/content/francesco/en/encyclicals/docu ments/papa-francesco_20150524_enciclica-laudato-si.html.

Allen, John L. *The Future Church: How the Trends Are Revolutionizing the Catholic Church.* New York: Image, 2009.

Allport, Gordon Willard. *The Individual and His Religion: A Psychological Interpretation.* London: Collier-Macmillan, 1967.

Arendt, Hannah. *Eichmann in Jerusalem: A Report on the Banality of Evil.* New York: Penguin Books, 2006.

Barbieri, William A., ed. *At the Limits of the Secular: Reflections on Faith and Public Life.* Grand Rapids, MI: William B. Eerdmans, 2014.

Baudrillard, Jean. *The Consumer Society: Myths and Structures.* London: Sage, 1998.

Beaudoin, Tom. *Virtual Faith: The Irreverent Spiritual Quest of Generation X.* San Francisco: Jossey-Bass, 1998.

Beck, Ulrich. *A God of One's Own: Religion's Capacity for Peace and Potential for Violence.* Malden, MA: Polity Press, 2010.

———. *Risk Society: Towards a New Modernity.* Translated by Mark Ritter. London: Sage, 1992.

Berger, Peter L. *Altäre der Moderne: Religion in pluralistischen Gesellschaften.* Frankfurt am Main: Campus, 2015.

———, ed. *The Desecularization of the World: Resurgent Religion and World Politics.* Grand Rapids, MI: William B. Eerdmans, 1999.

———. *The Sacred Canopy: Elements of a Sociological Theory of Religion.* New York: Anchor, 1967.

———. *Zur Dialektik von Religion und Gesellschaft: Elemente einer soziologischen Theorie.* Frankfurt am Main: S. Fischer, 1973.

———. *Der Zwang zur Häresie: Religion in der pluralistischen Gesellschaft.* Frankfurt am Main: S. Fischer, 1980.

Berger, Peter L., and Thomas Luckmann. *Die gesellschaftliche Konstruktion der Wirklichkeit: Eine Theorie der Wissenssoziologie.* Frankfurt am Main: S. Fischer, 1969.

Biser, Eugen. *Theologie als Therapie: Zur Wiedergewinnung einer verlorenen Dimension.* Frankfurt am Main: S. Fischer, 1985.

Bloch, Ernst. *Atheismus im Christentum: Zur Religion des Exodus und des Reichs.* Frankfurt am Main: Suhrkamp, 1973.

Bruce, Steve. *God Is Dead: Secularization in the West.* Hoboken, NJ: Wiley-Blackwell, 2002.

Buber, Martin. "Zwei Glaubensweisen." In *Werke: Erster Band: Schriften zur Philosophie.* Kösel-Verlag; Schneider, München, Heidelberg, 1962.

Caputo, John D., ed. *The Religious.* Oxford: Blackwell, 2020.

Casanova, José. "Chancen und Gefahren öffentlicher Religion. Ost- und Westeuropa im Vergleich." In *Das Europa der Religionen: Ein Kontinent zwischen Säkularisierung und Fundamentalismus*, edited by Otto Kallscheuer, 181–210. Frankfurt am Main: Suhrkamp, 1996.

———. "Die Erschließung des Postsäkularen: Drei Bedeutungen von 'säkular' und deren mögliche Transzendenz." In *Postsäkularismus: Zur Diskussion eines umstrittenen Begriffs*, edited by Matthias Lutz-Bachmann, 9–39. Frankfurt am Main: Campus, 2015.

———. *Europas Angst vor der Religion*. Translated by Rolf Schieder. Wiesbaden: Berlin University Press, 2009.

———. *Public Religions in the Modern World*. Chicago: University of Chicago Press, 1994.

Červenková, Denisa. *Etika mezikulturního a mezináboženského dialogu*. Prague: Karolinum, 2018.

———. *Katolický pohled na náboženskou pluralitu*. Prague: Karolinum, 2016.

Comte-Sponville, André. *The Book of Atheist Spirituality*. London: Bantam Books, 2009.

Cox, Harvey. *The Secular City: Secularization and Urbanization in Theological Perspective*. Princeton, NJ: Princeton University Press, 2013.

Davie, Grace. *Religion in Britain since 1945: Believing without Belonging*. Oxford: Blackwell 1994.

———. *Religion in Modern Europe: A Memory Mutates*. Oxford: Oxford University Press, 2000.

Delbrêl, Madeleine. *Auftrag des Christen in einer Welt ohne Gott*. Einsiedeln: Johannes Verlag, 2000.

Derrida, Jacques. *Foi et savoir: suivi de Le Siècle et le Pardon* (Interview with Michel Wieviorka). Paris: Seuil, 2000.

Dobbelaere, Karel. *Secularization: An Analysis at Three Levels*. Brussels: Peter Lang, 2002.

Dreher, Rod. *The Benedict Option*. New York: Sentinel, 2017.

Dworkin, Ronald. *Religion Without God*. Cambridge, MA: Harvard University Press, 2013.

Ebeling, Gerhard. *Das Wesen des christlichen Glaubens*. Tübingen: J. C. B. Mohr, 1959.

Ebertz, Michael N. *Erosion der Gnadenanstalt: Zum Wandel der Sozialgestalt von Kirche*. Frankfurt am Main: Josef Knecht, 1998.

Ebertz, Michael N., Monika Eberhardt, and Anna Lang. *Kirchenaustritt als Prozess: gehen oder bleiben? Eine empirisch gewonnene Typologie*. Berlin: Berlin Münster, 2012.

Foucault, Michel. *Discipline and Punish: The Birth of the Prison*. Translated by Alan Sheridan. New York: Pantheon Books 1977.

Frankl, Viktor E., and Pinchas Lapide. *Gottsuche und Sinnfrage: Ein Gespräch*. Gütersloh, Germany: Gütersloher Verlagshaus, 2011.

Friedman, Richard Elliott. *The Disappearance of God: A Divine Mystery*. Boston: Little, Brown, 1995.

Fuchs, Ottmar. *Die andere Reformation: Ökumenisch für eine solidarische Welt*. Würzburg, Germany: Echter, 2016.

———. *Der zerrissene Gott: Das trinitarische Gottesbild in den Brüchen der Welt*. Ostfildern, Germany: Matthias Grünewald Verlag, 2014.

Fukuyama, Francis. *The End of History and the Last Man*. New York: Free Press, 1992.

Gauchet, Marcel. *La condition historique* (Conversations with François Azouvi and Sylvain Piron). Paris: Gallimard, 2008.

———. *The Disenchantment of the World: A Political History of Religion*. Princeton, NJ: Princeton University Press, 2021.

Girard, René. *Evolution and Conversion: Dialogues on the Origins of Culture*. London: Continuum, 2008.

Graf, Friedrich Wilhelm. *Die Wiederkehr der Götter: Religion in der modernen Kultur*. Munich: Beck, 2004.

Greshake, Gisbert. "Der Wandel der Erlösungsvorstellungen in der Theologiegeschichte." In *Gottes Heil, Glück des Menschen: Theologische Perspektiven*, 50–79. Freiburg: Herder, 1983.

Habermas, Jürgen. *Theorie des kommunikativen Handelns*. Vol. 1, *Handlungsrationalität und gesellschaftliche Rationalisierung*. Frankfurt am Main: Suhrkamp, 1981.

Habermas, Jürgen, and Joseph Ratzinger. *Dialektik der Säkularisierung: Über Vernunft und Religion*. Freiburg: Herder, 2018.

Halbfas, Hubertus. *Glaubensverlust: Warum sich das Christentum neu erfinden muss*. Ostfildern, Germany: Patmos, 2013.

Halík, Tomáš. *Dotkni se ran: spiritualita nelhostejnosti*. Prague: Nakladatelství Lidové noviny, 2008.

———. *I Want You to Be: On the God of Love*. Translated by Gerald Turner. Notre Dame, IN: University of Notre Dame Press, 2016.

———. *Night of the Confessor: Christian Faith in an Age of Uncertainty*. Translated by Gerald Turner. New York: Image Books, 2012.

———. *Patience with God: The Story of Zacchaeus Continuing in Us*. Translated by Gerald Turner. New York: Doubleday, 2009.

Hellemans, Staf, and Peter Jonkers, eds. *Envisioning Futures for the Catholic Church*. Washington, DC: Council for Research in Values and Philosophy, 2018.

Hoff, Gregor Maria. *Ein anderer Atheismus: Spiritualität ohne Gott?* Kevelaer, Germany: Verlagsgemeinschaft topos plus, 2015.

———. *Die prekäre Identität des Christlichen: Die Herausforderung post-Modernen Differenzdenkens für eine theologische Hermeneutik.* Paderborn, Germany: F. Schöningh, 2001.

Horkheimer, Max, and Theodor W. Adorno. *Dialectic of Enlightenment.* Translated by John Cumming. New York: Herder and Herder, 1972.

Hošek, Pavel. *Na cestě k dialogu: křesťanská víra v pluralitě náboženství.* Prague: Návrat domů, 2005.

Huntington, Samuel. *The Clash of Civilizations and the Remaking of World Order.* New York: Simon & Schuster, 2011.

Iannaccone, Laurence. "Religious Market and Economics of Religion." *Social Compass* 39, no. 1 (March 1992): 123–31.

Inglehart, Ronald. *Culture Shift in Advanced Industrial Society.* Princeton, NJ: Princeton University Press, 1990.

Jalics, Franz. *Cesta kontemplace.* Translated by Maria Mlada Ondrášová. Prague: Triton, 2015.

Jaspers, Karl. *The Question of German Guilt.* Translated by E. B. Ashton, with a new introduction by Joseph W. Koterski, S.J. New York: Fordham University Press, 2009.

Jenkins, Philip. *God's Continent: Christianity, Islam, and Europe's Religious Crisis.* Oxford: Oxford University Press, 2007

Joas, Hans. *Braucht der Mensch Religion? Über Erfahrungen der Selbsttranszendenz.* Freiburg: Herder, 2004.

———. *Glaube als Option: Zukunftsmöglichkeiten des Christentums.* Freiburg: Herder, 2012.

———. *Die Macht des Heiligen: Eine Alternative zur Geschichte von der Entzauberung.* Berlin: Suhrkamp, 2017.

Jung, C. G. *Memories, Dreams, Reflections.* New York: Knopf Doubleday, 2011.

Kaufmann, Franz-Xaver. *Kirchenkrise: Wie überlebt das Christentum?* Freiburg: Herder, 2011.

———. *Religion und Modernität: Sozialwissenschaftliche Perspektiven.* Tübingen: Mohr, 1989.

Kearney, Richard. *Anatheism: Returning to God after God.* New York: Columbia University Press, 2010.

———. *The God Who May Be: A Hermeneutics of Religion.* Bloomington: Indiana University Press, 2001.

———. *Strangers, Gods and Monsters: Interpreting Otherness.* London: Routledge, 2003.

Kearney, Richard, and Jens Zimmermann, eds. *Reimagining the Sacred.* New York: Columbia University Press, 2016.

Kehl, Medard. *Wohin geht die Kirche? Eine Zeitdiagnose.* Freiburg: Herder, 1997.

Kerr, Fergus. *Theology after Wittgenstein.* Oxford: Basil Blackwell, 1986.

Kirwan, Michael. *Discovering Girard.* Cambridge, MA: Cowley Publications, 2005.

Knop, Julia, ed. *Die Gottesfrage zwischen Umbruch und Abbruch: Theologie und Pastoral unter säkularen Bedingungen.* Freiburg: Herder, 2019.

———, ed. "Gott—oder nicht. Theologie angesichts des Nicht-Glaubens ihrer Zeit: Ein Paradigmenwechsel." *Theologie der Gegenwart* 60 (2017): 141–54.

Krause, Boris. *Religion und die Vielfalt der Moderne: Erkundungen im Zeichen neuer Sichtbarkeit von Kontingenz.* Paderborn, Germany: Schöninngh, 2012.

Küng, Hans. *Why Priests?* Glasgow: Collins, 1971.

Lash, Nicholas. *The Beginning and the End of Religion.* Cambridge: Cambridge University Press, 1996.

———. *Easter in Ordinary: Reflections on Human Experience and the Knowledge of God.* Notre Dame, IN: University of Notre Dame Press, 1988.

———. *Holiness, Speech and Silence: Reflections on the Question of God.* Aldershot, UK: Ashgate, 2004.

Lotz, Johannes Baptist. *In jedem Menschen steckt ein Atheist.* Frankfurt am Main: Knecht, 1981.

Luckmann, Thomas. *The Invisible Religion: The Problem of Religion in Modern Society.* New York: Macmillan, 1967.

Luhmann, Niklas. *Die Funktion der Religion.* Frankfurt am Main: Suhrkamp, 1972.

———. *Die Religion der Gesellschaft.* Frankfurt am Main: Suhrkamp, 2000.

Marion, Jean-Luc. *God Without Being: Hors-Texte.* Chicago: University of Chicago Press, 1991.

———. *The Idol and Distance: Five Studies.* New York: Fordham University Press, 2001.

McLuhan, Marshall. *Understanding Media: The Extensions of Man.* New York: McGraw-Hill, 1964.

Metz, Johann Baptist. *Glaube in Geschichte und Gesellschaft: Studien zu einer praktischen Fundamentaltheologie.* Mainz, Germany: Matthias Grünewald Verlag, 1991.

————. *Mystik der offenen Augen: Wenn Spiritualität aufbricht.* Freiburg: Herder, 2011.

Micklethwait, John, and Adrian Wooldridge. *God Is Back: How the Global Revival of Faith Is Changing the World.* New York: Penguin, 2009.

Nagel, Thomas. *Der Blick von nirgendwo.* Frankfurt am Main: Suhrkamp, 1992.

Nancy, Jean-Luc. *Adoration: The Deconstruction of Christianity II.* New York: Fordham University Press, 2012.

Neubauer, Zdeněk. *O počátku, cestě a znamení časů: úvahy o vědě a vědění.* Prague: Malvern, 2007.

Nietzsche, Friedrich. *The Anti-Christ.* New York: Cosimo, 2005.

————. *The Gay Science: With a Prelude in German Rhymes and an Appendix of Songs.* Edited by Bernard Williams. Translated by Josefine Nauckhoff. Poems translated by Adrian Del Caro. Cambridge: Cambridge University Press, 2001.

————. *Thus Spoke Zarathustra: A Book for Everyone and No One.* Harmondsworth, UK: Penguin, 1961.

Ondrášek, Ľubomír Martin. *Úvahy verejného teológa o viere, spoločnosti a politike.* Trnava, Slovakia: Dobrá kniha, 2021.

Patočka, Jan. *Evropa a doba poevropská.* Edited by Ivan Chvatík and Pavel Kouba. Prague: Lidové noviny, 1992.

————. *Heretical Essays in the Philosophy of History.* Translated by Erazim Kohák. Edited by James Dodd. Chicago: Open Court, 1996.

Petráček, Tomáš. *Bible a moderní kritika: česká a světová progresivní exegeze ve víru (anti-) modernistické krize.* Prague: Vyšehrad, 2011.

————. *Církev, tradice, reforma: odkaz Druhého vatikánského koncilu.* Prague: Vyšehrad, 2011.

Pollack, Detlef. "Religion und Moderne: Versuch einer Bestimmung ihres Verhältnisses." In *Gottesrede in postsäkularer Kultur,* edited by Peter Walter, 19–52. Freiburg: Herder, 2007.

————. *Rückkehr des Religiösen? Studien zum religiösen Wandel in Deutschland und Europa II.* Tübingen: Mohr Siebeck, 2009.

————. *Säkularisierung—ein moderner Mythos? Studien zum religiösen Wandel in Deutschland.* Tübingen: Mohr Siebeck, 2003.

————. "Was ist Religion? Probleme der Definition." *Zeitschrift für Religionswissenschaft* 3, no. 2 (1995): 163–90.

Pompe, Hans-Hermann, and Daniel Hörsch, eds. *Indifferent? Ich bin normal: Indifferenz als Irritation für kirchliches Denken und Handeln.* Leipzig: Evangelische Verlagsanstalt, 2017.

Rahner, Karl. *Alltägliche Dinge*. Einsiedeln, Switzerland: Benziger, 1969.

———. "Zur Frage der Dogmenentwicklung." In *Schriften zur Theologie I*, 49–90. Einsiedeln, Switzerland: Benziger, 1954.

Rahner, Karl, and Heinrich Fries, eds. *Theologie in Freiheit und Verantwortung*. Munich: Kösel, 1981.

Ratzinger, Joseph Cardinal, with Vittorio Messori. *Ratzinger Report: An Exclusive Interview on the State of the Church*. San Francisco: Ignatius Press, 1985.

Rideau, Emile. *Thought of Teilhard de Chardin*. New York: Harper & Row, 1965.

Rizzuto, Ana-Maria. *The Birth of the Living God: A Psychoanalytic Study*. Chicago: University of Chicago Press, 1979.

Rorty, Richard, and Gianni Vattimo. *The Future of Religion*. New York: Columbia University Press, 2005.

Roy, Olivier. *La Sainte Ignorance: Le temps de la Religion Sans Culture*. Paris: Seuil, 2014.

Ruhstorfer, Karlheinz. *Glaube im Aufbruch: Katholische Perspektiven*. Paderborn: F. Schöningh, 2013.

Ruster, Thomas. *Der verwechselbare Gott: Theologie nach der Entflechtung von Christentum und Religion*. Freiburg: Herder, 2001.

Schellenbaum, Peter. *Stichwort: Gottesbild*. Stuttgart: Kreuz Verlag, 1981.

Schillebeeckx, Edward. *Church: The Human Story of God*. New York: Crossroad, 1990.

Scholl, Norbert. *Religiös ohne Gott: Warum wir heute anders glauben*. Darmstadt: Lambert Schneider, 2010.

Shanks, Andrew. *God and Modernity: A New and Better Way to Do Theology*. London: Routledge, 2000.

Shortt, Rupert. *God Is No Thing: Coherent Christianity*. London: C. Hurst, 2016.

Sloterdijk, Peter. *Nach Gott*. Berlin: Suhrkamp, 2017.

Smith, Wilfred Cantwell. *Patterns of Faith around the World*. Oxford: Oneworld Publications, 1998.

Sölle, Dorothee. *Atheistisch an Gott glauben: Beiträge zur Theologie*. Olten, Switzerland: Walter, 1968.

———. *Christ the Representative: An Essay in Theology after the 'Death of God.'* London: SCM Press, 1967.

Taylor, Charles. *A Catholic Modernity? Charles Taylor's Marianist Award Lecture*. With responses by William M. Shea, Rosemary Luling Haughton, George Marsden, and Jean Bethke Elshtain. Edited by James L. Heft. Oxford: Oxford University Press, 1999.

———. *The Ethics of Authenticity*. Cambridge, MA: Harvard University Press, 2018.

———. *The Explanation of Behaviour*. London: Routledge & Kegan Paul, 1964.

———. "Ein Ort für die Transzendenz?" *Information Philosophie* 2 (2003): 7–16.

———. *A Secular Age*. Cambridge, MA: Belknap Press of Harvard University Press, 2007.

———. *Sources of the Self: The Making of the Modern Identity*. Cambridge, MA: Harvard University Press, 1989.

———. *Varieties of Religion Today: William James Revisited*. Cambridge, MA: Harvard University Press, 2002.

Teilhard de Chardin, Pierre. *The Human Phenomenon*. Translated by Sarah Appleton-Weber. Eastbourne, UK: Sussex Academic Press, 1999.

Tiefensee, Eberhard. "Anerkennung der Alterität: Ökumene mit den Religionslosen." Special issue, *Herder Korrespondenz*, no. 1 (2010): 39–43.

———. "Der homo areligiosus und die Entkonfessionalisierung in der ehemaligen DDR." In *Bildung als Mission? Kirchliche Bildungsarbeit im Kontext einer konfessionslosen Gesellschaft*, edited by Matthias Hahn, 15–30. Jena, Germany: Garamond, 2014.

———. "Theologie im Kontext religiöser Indifferenz." In *Die Gottesfrage zwischen Umbruch und Abbruch: Theologie und Pastoral unter säkularen Bedingungen*, edited by Julia Knop, 130–44. Freiburg: Herder, 2019.

Tillich, Paul. *The Courage to Be*. New Haven, CT: Yale University Press, 2008.

Traer, Robert. *Faith, Belief, and Religion*. Aurora, CO: Davies Group, 2001.

Vattimo, Gianni. *After Christianity*. New York: Columbia University Press, 2002.

Volf, Miroslav. *Exclusion and Embrace: A Theological Exploration of Identity, Otherness, and Reconciliation*. Nashville: Abingdon, 1996.

Wolf, Hubert. *Krypta: Unterdrückte Traditionen der Kirchengeschichte*. Bonn: Budeszentrale für polit Bildung, 2015.

Žižek, Slavoj. *The Fragile Absolute:; Or, Why Is the Christian Legacy Worth Fighting For?* London: Verso, 2001.

———. *The Puppet and the Dwarf: The Perverse Core of Christianity*. Cambridge, MA: MIT Press, 2003.

———. *Das Reale Christentum*. Frankfurt am Main: Suhrkamp, 2006.

Zulehner, Paul M. *Ein Obdach der Seele*. Düsseldorf: Patmos, 1997.

NOTES

Preface

1. Pope Francis, "Address of the Holy Father" (pastoral visit of His Holiness Pope Francis to Prato and Florence, meeting with the participants in the Fifth Convention of the Italian Church, Cathedral of Santa Maria del Fiore, Florence, November 10, 2015), available via www.vatican.va.

ONE.   Faith in Motion

1. Luke 5.

2. The term "Axial Age" was coined by Karl Jaspers; he was referring to the period between the eighth century BC and the second century BC when a number of religions that are still alive today emerged independently of each other, and the older ones were transformed with an emphasis on transcendence and ethics. See Karl Jaspers, *Vom Ursprung und Ziel der Geschichte* (Munich: R. Piper, 1949).

3. In a certain sense it is also present in secular humanism, that unwanted child of traditional Christianity, and probably also in various forms of contemporary nontraditional spiritualities; in these, however, faith is often confused with gnosis, a spiritual orientation that has been its competitor for centuries.

4. See Isaiah 1:17; Psalms 82:3; James 1:27.

5. Hebrews 11:8.

6. Martin Buber, "Zwei Glaubensweisen," in *Schriften zur Philosophie*, 1: 651–782, München—Heidelberg 2011, particularly 654.

7. This perception of Christ is based on John's Revelation, the theology of the ancient church fathers, the spirituality of the Christian East, and the medieval Franciscan tradition, and it is revived in Teilhard de Chardin's understanding of

Christ as the Omega Point of cosmic development and in the spirituality of the cosmic Christ developed today especially by the American Franciscan Richard Rohr. See Pierre Teilhard de Chardin, *The Divine Milieu: An Essay on the Interior Life* (New York: Harper & Row, 1965); Richard Rohr, *The Universal Christ: How a Forgotten Reality Can Change Everything We See, Hope for, and Believe* (New York: Convergent, 2021).

8. Galatians 3:28.

9. James 2:18.

10. Matthew 25:31–46.

11. Theophilus of Antioch, *To Autolycus*, book I, chapter 2.

Two.   Faith as Experience of Mystery

1. The founder of depth psychology, Carl Gustav Jung, whose work is one of the inspirations for this book, carved on the door of his house the phrase: "Vocatus atque non vocatus, Deus aderit" (God, invoked or not invoked, named or unnamed, is present). Faith has its manifest and latent forms; it lives in human consciousness and unconsciousness. The manifest and the hidden, the conscious and the unconscious, the explicit and the implicit ("anonymous") forms of belief (and unbelief) can sometimes be in tension; hence, in some cases, we can speak of "the belief of unbelievers" and "the unbelief of believers."

2. This motif pervades almost all of Kierkegaard's writings on faith. See, e.g., Søren Kierkegaard, *Fear and Trembling* (Cambridge: Cambridge University Press, 2006).

3. *The Cloud of Unknowing* is the title of an English medieval mystical text by an unknown author.

4. Hebrews 11:8.

5. 2 Timothy 1:12.

6. Acts 17:22–23.

7. Traditional Thomist theology teaches that God respects the limits of human knowledge of God, but there is a relationship of similarity, an analogy, between human concepts and God's mysterious essence. The Fourth Lateran Council adds that the dissimilarity in this relationship infinitely exceeds the similarity.

8. Matthew 17:1–8.

9. The term "peak experience" for transformative mystical experiences is used by existential psychology, especially by Abraham H. Maslow. See Maslow, *Religions, Values, and Peak-Experiences* (New York: Viking Press, 1976).

10. 1 Corinthians 13:12.

11. See Nicholas of Cusa, "De non-aliud," trans. Jan Sokol, in Pavel Floss, *Mikuláš Kusánský: Život a dílo* (Prague: Vyšehrad, 1977), 281–85.

12. Philippians 2:6–11.

13. Matthew 7:21.

14. Acts 17:28.

THREE. Reading the Signs of the Times

1. I have subsequently discovered that this term was already used in the 1980s by the Viennese pastoral theologian Paul Zulehner (Paul Michael Zulehner, *Pastoraltheologie*, vol. 1, *Fundamentalpastoral* (Düsseldorf: Patmos, 1989).

2. Ecclesiastes 3:1–8.

3. Luke 12:54–56.

4. Arguably, we could identify Peter L. Berger as one of the pioneers of this socio-theology, as he gave his most important works on contemporary changes in religion the form of essays in which sociological analyses are interspersed with theological reflections. I have in mind in particular the loose trilogy: *A Rumor of Angels: Modern Society and the Rediscovery of the Supernatural* (Garden City, NY: Doubleday, 1969); *The Heretical Imperative: Contemporary Possibilities of Religious Affirmation* (Garden City, NY: Anchor, 1979); *A Far Glory: The Quest for Faith in an Age of Credulity* (New York: Doubleday, 1992).

5. Michel de Certeau, *Note sur l'expérience religieuse* (Paris, 1956).

6. E.g., Tomáš Halík, *Stromu zbývá naděje: Krize jako šance* (Prague: Nakladatelství Lidové noviny, 2009), 200. I also return to this idea in chapter 14 of this book.

7. Suffice it to recall Dietrich Bonhoeffer and Alfred Delp, who were involved in the anti-Nazi resistance, as well as Martin Luther King, Bishops Desmond Tutu and Oscar Romero, Józef Tischner, the theologian of the Polish Solidarity movement, and the Czech dissidents of the communist era, Josef Zvěřina and Jakub S. Trojan.

8. Colossians 2:9.

9. Hebrews 12:2.

10. I accept the concept of culture in John Paul II's encyclical *Centesimus annus*: "Man is understood in a more complete way when he is situated within the sphere of culture through his language, history, and the position he takes towards the fundamental events of life, such as birth, love, work and death. At the heart of every culture lies the attitude man takes to the greatest mystery: the mystery of God" (para. 24).

11. The concept of "Ultimate Concern" is particularly used by Paul Tillich.

12. The term "depth theology" was coined especially by the Jewish philosopher of religion Abraham Heschel. He used it to denote a kind of pretheological common ground of religion to which one must return in interreligious dialogue.

He compared theology and depth theology in a manner reminiscent of our distinction between the act of faith (*fides qua*) and the content or object of faith (*fides quae*): "Theology is like sculpture, depth theology is like music. Theology is in the books, depth theology is in the hearts. The former is doctrine, the latter an event. Theologies divide us; depth theology unites us." Abraham Heschel, *Insecurity of Freedom: Essays on Human Existence* (New York: Schocken Books, 1972), 119. My understanding and use of this term differs, as it implies, on the one hand, a consideration of the unconscious dimension of individual religiosity (i.e., also a constant dialogue with the work of C. G. Jung), and on the other, an affinity with Tillich's understanding of God as the ground of being.

13. "Sis tu tuus et ego ero tuus," from chapter 7 of Nicholas of Cusa's *De visione dei*, in Jasper Hopkins, *Nicholas of Cusa's Dialectical Mysticism: Text, Translation, and Interpretive Study of "De visione dei"* (Minneapolis: Arthur J. Banning Press, 1988).

14. From the Chalcedon Formula, available at http://anglicansonline.org /basics/chalcedon.html.

15. Northrup Frye, *The Double Vision: Language and Meaning in Religion* (Toronto: University of Toronto Press, 1991), 43.

FOUR. A Thousand Years Like a Day

1. The concept of persona (*prosópon*) is taken from the theatre of antiquity: the actor who played different roles always put on a different mask to distinguish the identities of each person.

2. Psalm 91:5.

3. 2 Peter 3:8.

4. The best known of the "revisionists"—the original proponents and later vigorous critics of the theology of secularization—is the eminent American sociologist Peter L. Berger.

5. See Nietzsche, *The Gay Science*.

FIVE. Religious or Nonreligious Christianity?

1. See Eric J. Sharpe, *Understanding Religion* (London: Duckworth, 1997), 40.

2. See Matthew 15:24 and Matthew 28:17–20.

3. See 1 Corinthians 13:8–10.

4. See Galatians 3:28.

5. See Galatians 2:6–10.

6. See Denisa Červenková, *Jak se křesťanství stalo náboženstvím* (Prague: Karolinum, 2012), 25.

7. See Mark 1:21–28.

8. In the first millennium in particular, there was considerable plurality in liturgy, spirituality, and theological emphases in Christianity; only after the break with Byzantine Christianity did the Latin Church become significantly "Romanized."

9. See Charles Taylor, *A Catholic Modernity? Charles Taylor's Marianist Award Lecture*, ed. James L. Heft (Oxford: Oxford University Press, 1999).

10. See Marcel Gauchet, *The Disenchantment of the World: A Political History of Religion* (Princeton, NJ: Princeton University Press, 2021).

11. I draw a distinction between *secularization* (a sociocultural process), *secularism* (an ideological interpretation of secularization), and the *secular age* (a particular historical period). More on this at the beginning of chapter 7 of this book.

12. On the pseudo-religious role of capitalism, see, for example, Thomas Ruster, *Der verwechselbare Gott: Theologie nach der Entflechtung von Christentum und Religion* (Freiburg: Herder, 2000).

13. Ulrich Beck, *A God of One's Own : Religion's Capacity for Peace and Potential for Violence* (Malden, MA: Polity, 2010).

14. See Émile Durkheim, *The Elementary Forms of Religious Life*, trans. Carol Cosman (Oxford: Oxford University Press, 2008), 46.

15. These letters of Bonhoeffer were published posthumously in the book Dietrich Bonhoeffer, *Widerstand und Ergebung* (Gütersloh, Germany: Gütersloher Verlagshaus, 2019).

16. Similar Eckhartian themes are later echoed in the existentialist theology of Paul Tillich, in his belief in a "God above the god of theism." Paul Tillich, *The Courage to Be* (New Haven, CT: Yale University Press, 1952).

17. I am thinking in particular of Antonín Mandl (1917–1972), Josef Zvěřina (1913–1990), and Ota Mádr (1917–2011).

Six.   Darkness at Noon

1. Arthur Koestler, *Darkness at Noon* (London: J. Cape, 1940).

2. Tomáš Halík, *Čas prázdných kostelů* (Prague: NLN, s.r.o., 2020).

3. Père Alain Clément Amiézi, "En Afrique, on produit des baptisés et non des chrétiens, on leur donne les sacrements, sans évangéliser," interview by Guy Aimé Eblotié, *LaCroix Africa*, January 9, 2019, https://africa.la-croix.com/pere-alain-clement-amiezi%E2%80%89-en-afrique-on-produit-des-baptises-et-non-des-chretiens-on-leur-donne-les-sacrements-sans-evangeliser.

4. Eugen Drewermann, *Kleriker: Psychogramm eines Ideals* (Freiburg im Breisgau: Walter-Verlag, 1989); Frédéric Martel, *In the Closet of the Vatican: Power, Homosexuality, Hypocrisy* (London: Bloomsbury Continuum, 2019).

5. Matthew 23:27.

6. Karl Jaspers, *The Question of German Guilt*, trans. E. B. Ashton, with a new introduction by Joseph W. Koterski, S.J. (New York: Fordham University Press, 2009).

7. Something else that makes traditionalist seminaries attractive to certain types of candidates nowadays is that they often become a refuge for people who lack the ability and courage to live and serve the Church in this day and age and in contemporary society; they tend to seek a protected monument of the past. Unfortunately, the Catholic Church has so far failed to sufficiently reform the way priests are trained.

8. Dorothee Sölle made a distinction between a representative and a substitute. The representative temporarily assumes the role of the one represented, but points to them. The substitute tries to make the one substituted redundant. See Dorothee Sölle, *Christ the Representative: An Essay in Theology After the 'Death of God'* (London: SCM Press, 1967).

9. Jean-Luc Marion, *L'idole et la distance* (Paris: Bernard Grasset, 1989).

10. The words used in many European languages to refer to priests (Priester, prêtre, prete, etc.) are derived from the Greek *presbyter* (elder), recalling the New Testament origin of this ministry (quite different from the priest-sacrificers in Judaism and pagan religions).

11. Charles Taylor, *A Secular Age* (Cambridge, MA: Belknap Press of Harvard University Press, 2007).

12. See 1 Corinthians 13:1.

13. In Beck, *A God of One's Own*, 88: "in a country-wide opinion poll on the religious beliefs of Catholics and Protestants in Switzerland, only 2 per cent of the respondents agreed with the statement that 'All religion should be respected but only mine is true.' . . . According to an opinion poll in France in 1998, 6 per cent of all 18- to 29-year-olds regard their religion as the only true one."

14. Isaiah 1:5–6.

15. Romans 8:9.

16. Tomáš Halík, "Pseudonáboženství F: příklad náboženské patologie," *Christnet*, November 12, 2020, https://www.christnet.eu/clanky/6471/pseudo nabozenstvi_f_priklad_nabozenske_patologie.url.

17. *Mysterium tremendum et fascinans* (the mystery that shakes and attracts) was how Rudolf Otto, the phenomenologist of religion, characterized the sacred (numinous), which he considered to be the essential dimension of religion. See Rudolf Otto, *The Idea of the Holy: An Inquiry into the Non-Rational Factor in the Idea of the Divine and Its Relation to the Rational* (Eugene, OR: Wipf and Stock, 2021).

18. See, for example, Tomáš Halík, *Patience with God: The Story of Zacchaeus Continuing in Us*, trans. Gerald Turner (New York: Doubleday, 2009); Tomáš Halík, *Touch the Wounds: On Suffering, Trust, and Transformation*, trans. Gerald Turner (Notre Dame, IN: University of Notre Dame Press, 2023).

19. The mystery of lawlessness (2 Thessalonians 2:7).

20. I have in mind authors such as Paul Ricœur, Jean-Luc Marion, Jean-Luc Nancy, Michel Henry, the Irish philosopher William Desmond, and in America, John D. Caputo, Merold Westphal, and especially the one closest to me, Richard Kearney, an Irishman who has worked in the United States for many years.

21. Richard Kearney, *The God Who May Be: A Hermeneutics of Religion* (Bloomington, IN: Indiana University Press, 2001).

22. St. John of the Cross, *Dark Night of the Soul*, trans. E. Allison Peers, from the critical edition of P. Silverio de Santa Teresa, C.D. (Mineola, NY: Dover Publications, 2003).

23. Jan Patočka, "Wars of the Twentieth Century and the Twentieth Century as War," in Jan Patočka, *Heretical Essays in the Philosophy of History*, trans. Erazim Kohák, ed. James Dodd (Chicago: Open Court, 1996), 119–38.

24. See Hans Jonas, "The Concept of God after Auschwitz: A Jewish Voice," *Journal of Religion* 67, no. 1 (January 1987): 1–13.

SEVEN. Is God Coming Back?

1. Nature in the Bible is not divine in character and is not "full of gods and demons" but is God's creation, entrusted to the care of humankind. Nor are political rulers gods or sons of God—Moses refuses to obey the pharaoh and Nathan strongly criticizes King David.

2. I refer in particular to the book by John Micklethwait and Adrian Wooldridge, *God is Back: How the Global Revival of Faith is Changing the World* (New York: Penguin, 2009).

3. Ferdinand Tönnies, *1880–1935: Gemeinschaft und Gesellschaft*, ed. Bettina Clausen and Dieter Haselbach, vol. 2 of *Ferdinand Tönnies Gesamtausgabe TG* (Berlin: Walter de Gruyter, 2019).

4. One remembers the iconic example of the condemnation of Galileo and his rehabilitation by John Paul II, or the disparity between Pope Pius IX's *Syllabus of Modern Errors* (*Syllabus errorum modernorum*) and the documents of the Second Vatican Council, especially *Gaudium et spes, Nostra aetate*, and *Dignitatis humanae*.

5. Much of the credit must go to the American Jesuit John Courtney Murray and to the French philosopher Jacques Maritain, who spent many years at American universities.

6. See Hans Blumenberg, *Die Legitimität der Neuzeit* (Freiburg am Main: Suhrkamp Verlag, 1966).

7. See, for instance, Karl Gabriel, *Christentum zwischen Tradition und Postmoderne* (Freiburg im Breisgau: Herder, 1992).

8. See Joseph Cardinal Ratzinger with Vittorio Messori, *Ratzinger Report: An Exclusive Interview on the State of the Church* (San Francisco: Ignatius Press, 1985).

9. 1 Thessalonians 5:2.

10. See Luke 17:23.

EIGHT. The Heirs of Modern Religion

1. See Beck, *A God of One's Own*, 87.

2. One example is the pseudonym Madonna, used by a pop singer who certainly does not symbolize traditional Marian attributes.

3. I myself have witnessed on more than one occasion how some of the films and theatrical works to which conservative Christians have reacted indignantly— for example, *The Last Temptation of Christ*, or *Jesus Christ Superstar*—have roused young people from their apathy and sparked their interest in religion, even inspiring them to convert to Christianity. Jesus's parable of the wheat and the tares should caution Church leaders against efforts to censor the arts.

4. Gilles Kepel, *The Revenge of God: The Resurgence of Islam, Christianity, and Judaism in the Modern World* (University Park, PA: Pennsylvania State University Press, 1994).

5. See Gordon Willard Allport, *The Individual and His Religion: A Psychological Interpretation* (London: Collier-Macmillan, 1967).

6. See C. Daniel Batson and Patricia A. Schoenrade, "Measuring Religion as Quest: 1) Validity Concerns," *Journal for the Scientific Study of Religion* 30, no. 4 (December 1991): 416–29.

7. This is pointed out by the American theologian Massimo Faggioli, among others. See Massimo Faggioli, "A Wake-Up Call to Liberal Theologians: Academic Theology Needs the Church," *Commonweal* 145, no. 9 (May 18, 2018), https://www.commonwealmagazine.org/wake-call-liberal-theologians.

8. This is certainly also because believers in the Czech Republic do not pay any church tax.

9. Just a formal attachment to the Church, more out of a habitual attachment to a family or cultural tradition, not backed by a personal experience of faith.

10. Revelation 3:20.

11. Robert Traer, *Faith, Belief, and Religion* (Aurora, CO: Davies Group, 2001).

12. See Taylor, *A Catholic Modernity?*; Taylor, *A Secular Age*.

13. See Hans Küng, *Wozu Priester? Eine Hilfe* (Zürich: Benziger Verlag, 1971).

14. The term "third ecumenism" was coined by the Erfurt theologian and philosopher Eberhard Tiefensee. See the interview with Eberhard Tiefensee by Felizia Merten in "Kirche hat eine Stellvertreterfunktion," *Herder Korrespondenz*, no. 12 (2016): 17–21.

NINE. From Global Village to *Civitas Oecumenica*

1. See Jan Patočka, *Evropa a doba poevropská*, ed. Ivan Chvatík and Pavel Kouba (Prague: Lidové noviny, 1992).

2. I used this term in my book *Night of the Confessor: Christian Faith in an Age of Uncertainty* (New York: Image Books, 2012). Milan Petrusek included it among contemporary sociological diagnoses. See Milan Petrusek, *Společnosti pozdní doby* (Prague: Slon, 2006), 303–4.

3. Marshall McLuhan, *Understanding Media: The Extensions of Man* (Corte Madera, CA: Gingko Press, 2003).

4. See Martin Heidegger, ". . . dichterisch wohnet der Mensch . . . ," in *Vorträge und Aufsätze (1936–1953)*, ed. Friedrich-Wilhelm von Herrmann, vol. 7 of Martin Heidegger, *Gesamtausgabe* (Frankfurt am Main: Vittorio Klostermann, 2000).

5. Samuel P. Huntington, *The Clash of Civilizations and the Remaking of World Order* (New York: Simon & Schuster, 1996), 184.

6. This includes fantasies about the "Illuminati," or the demonization of personalities such as George Soros or Bill Gates, thus supplanting or complementing the earlier fear of worldwide conspiracies of "Jews and Freemasons." An extreme form is the paranoid delusion known as QAnon, a conspiracy theory that originated in October 2017 and was supported by President Trump and his followers.

7. Pierre Teilhard de Chardin, *The Phenomenon of Man* (New York: Harper & Row, 1965), 265.

8. "When everything is subjected to him, then the Son himself will [also] be subjected to the one who subjected everything to him, so that God may be all in all." 1 Corinthians 15:28.

9. Augustine, *De civitate Dei*, IV, 4.

TEN.   A Third Enlightenment

1. See Pope Francis's address to the representatives of the national conven-
tion of the Italian Catholic Church laying out his vision for "a new humanism in
Christ Jesus." Pope Francis, "Address of the Holy Father" (pastoral visit of His Ho-
liness Pope Francis to Prato and Florence, meeting with the participants in the Fifth
Convention of the Italian Church, Cathedral of Santa Maria del Fiore, Florence,
November 10, 2015), available via www.vatican.va.

2. Romans 12:2.

3. See Revelation 2:11.

4. Where I use the term "Enlightenment" in this book without qualification,
I am referring to the first Enlightenment of the seventeenth and eighteenth centuries.

5. See for instance Max Horkheimer and Theodor W. Adorno, *Dialectic of
Enlightenment*, trans. John Cumming (New York: Herder and Herder, 1972); Zyg-
munt Bauman, *Modernity and the Holocaust* (Ithaca, NY: Cornell University Press,
1989); Hannah Arendt, *Eichmann in Jerusalem: A Report on the Banality of Evil*
(New York: Penguin Books, 2006); Michel Foucault, *Discipline and Punish: The
Birth of the Prison*, trans. Alan Sheridan (New York: Pantheon Books, 1977).

6. From chthonic: of or related to the underworld.

7. These themes were already present in the Second Enlightenment of the
1960s.

8. At the time of writing this book, it is not yet clear whether the forced re-
location to the internet of interpersonal communication in the professional, educational, and ecclesiastical spheres as a result of the coronavirus pandemic will lead
people to become more accustomed to the new kind of communication or, on the
contrary, whether they will realize the indispensability of face-to-face encounters.

ELEVEN.   The Identity of Christianity

1. Mark 11:22 (Wycliffe Bible).

2. Hebrews 12:2

3. 2 Timothy 2:13.

4. Jan Zahradníček, *Znamení moci*, in Jan Zahradníček, *Dílo II*, ed. Mojmír
Trávníček and Radovan Zejda (Prague: Československý Spisovatel, 1992), 274.

5. Friedrich Nietzsche, *Thus Spoke Zarathustra*, trans. with an introduction
by R. J. Hollingdale (London: Penguin Books, 1978).

6. John 20:28.

7. See Halík, *Touch the Wounds*.

8. See 1 John 4:20.

9. See Matthew 25:31–46.

10. See Matthew 7:21.
11. See John 10:7–10.
12. Philippians 2:6–11.
13. John 10:7–10.
14. See James 2:17–18.
15. See Mark 9:38–40.
16. See John 1:10.
17. John 10:30.
18. See Galatians 2:20.
19. See Richard Rohr, *The Universal Christ*, 45.
20. See John 3:1–21.
21. See Mark 1:27.
22. See Romans 6:3–11.
23. See Acts 10:41.

TWELVE.   God Near and Far

1. The concept of religion as collective memory has been particularly developed by the French sociologist Danièle Hervieu-Léger. See Hervieu-Léger, *Religion as a Chain of Memory* (Cambridge: Polity Press, 2000).

2. See David M. Knight, "Should Protestants Receive Communion at Mass? Theologian Takes a Critical Look at the Catholic Church's Communion Line Policies," *La Croix International*, July 23, 2020, https://international.la-croix.com /news/religion/should-protestants-receive-communion-at-mass/12797.

3. See Vladimír Boublík, *Teologie mimokřesťanských náboženství* (Kostelní Vydří, Czech Republic: Karmelitánské nakladatelství, 2000).

4. See *Lumen Gentium*, chap. 16; *Gaudium et Spes*, chap. 22.

5. The American Jesuit Leonard Feeney, originally a student chaplain at Harvard, was excommunicated in 1953 for this statement and for disobedience to Church authorities. This was preceded by an opinion of the Holy Office dated August 8, 1949.

6. See Mark 3:28–29.

7. Timothy Ware, *The Orthodox Church* (London: Penguin Books, 1997), 308.

8. See 1 Corinthians 13:8–13.

9. See St. Augustine, Sermon 117.3.5 (Concerning John 1.1–3), available at https://catholiclibrary.org/library/view?docId=Fathers-OR/PL.038.html.

10. More on this in Tomáš Halík, *I Want You to Be: On the God of Love,* trans. Gerald Turner (Notre Dame, IN: University of Notre Dame Press, 2016).

11. See Matthew 5:43–48.

12. See James 2:17.

13. In Catholic sacramental theology, this is expressed by linking the *opus operatum* with the *opus operantis*, the "objective" and "subjective" elements in the administration and reception of the sacraments.

14. Grace Davie, *Religion in Modern Europe: A Memory Mutates* (Oxford: Oxford University Press, 2000).

15. Sociology uses this term to refer to those who recognize religion as part of culture but lack faith as a personal religious experience—a personal relationship with God.

16. Ana-Maria Rizzuto, *The Birth of the Living God: A Psychoanalytic Study* (Chicago: University of Chicago Press, 1979).

17. Jeremiah 23:23.

18. Hebrews 1:1–2.

19. Christianity rejects pantheism, the identification of God with the world, but in the Bible we find important passages that are close to "panentheism," according to which God includes and simultaneously transcends everything created.

20. See 1 John 4:16.

21. See, for instance, 1 John 4:8.

22. Mark 11:22.

23. *Neque enim quaero intelligere ut credam, sed credo ut intelligam* (I do not seek understanding in order to believe, but I believe in order to understand)—with this sentence in his *Proslogion*, Anselm of Canterbury supplements St. Augustine's statement *crede ut intelligas* (believe, so that you may understand—from his commentary on the Gospel of John). Augustine's idea of faith seeking understanding comes from the Latin translation of Isaiah 7:9, which reads *nisi credideritis non intelligetis* (unless you believe, you will not understand). See his Sermon 43, available at https://catholiclibrary.org/library/view?docId=Fathers-EN/Augustine.Sermons NT.en.html.

24. See Matthew 17:20.

25. See Halík, *Night of the Confessor*.

26. See 1 Corinthians 1:25–29.

27. John 12:24.

28. 1 Kings 19:12.

29. C. G. Jung, *Memories, Dreams, Reflections*, recorded and edited by Aniela Jaffé, trans. Richard and Clara Winston (London: Fontana, 1983).

30. Colossians 1:24.

31. The declaration *Dominus Iesus*, issued by the Congregation for the Doctrine of the Faith in August 2000 and approved by Pope John Paul II, even seeks to

preserve the term "Church" only for the Roman Catholic Church; other Christian communities are said to be "churches" in a different sense than the Church of Rome.

32. Matthew 13:52.

33. 1 John 3:20.

34. David Steindl-Rast calls the heart the organ for the perception of meaning. See Steindl-Rast, *The Way of Silence: Engaging the Sacred in Daily Life* (Cincinnati: Franciscan Media, 2016), 19.

35. See Mark 10:17–22.

THIRTEEN.   Spirituality as the Passion of Faith

1. See John 3:3–6.

2. Boaz Huss, "Spiritual, but Not Religious, but Not Secular: Spirituality and Its New Cultural Formations" (paper read at the European University at Saint Petersburg, November 17, 2018).

3. For more information, see https://www.templeton.org/grant/faith-and -beliefs-of-nonbelievers.

4. André Comte-Sponville has written explicitly about this; see *The Book of Atheist Spirituality* (London: Bantam, 2009).

5. One of them, for example, was the Hussite movement in Bohemia.

6. James 2:14–26.

7. Traditionally, these centers of renewal were located rather on the periphery—for example, the Hiberno-Scottish mission. Under the pontificate of Pope Francis, significant reform impulses have come directly from the See of St. Peter, making it a remarkable sign of the times.

8. I have in mind, for example, the spirituality of the Little Brothers and Little Sisters of Jesus (especially in the books of Carlo Carretto) or the Jerusalem Charismatic Community.

9. Toward the end of his life, Thomas Merton enriched his monastic spirituality with other elements, including interfaith dialogue with Buddhism and Hinduism and left-wing political involvement in the spirit of liberation theology.

10. Ulrich Beck speaks similarly of this danger: "No doubt, the pragmatic stripping away of dogma gives rise to feelings of ambivalence. After all, it opens the floodgates to every trivialization of belief: every wellness hotel decorates its premises with pearls of wisdom from Buddhist scriptures. Religious illiteracy spreads like a plague and atheists cannot even remember which God they *no longer* believe in"; Beck, *A God of One's Own*, 86; emphasis in original.

11. *"Parum est voluntate, etiam voluptate traheris"* (St. Augustine, *Tractates on the Gospel of John* 26, 4–6).

FOURTEEN. The Faith of Nonbelievers and a Window of Hope

1. See Gerhard Ebeling, *Das Wesen des christlichen Glaubens* (Tübingen: J. C. B. Mohr, 1963).

2. Zdeněk Neubauer, *O počátku, cestě a znamení časů* (Prague: Malvern, 2007), 214.

3. Johannes B. Lotz, *In jedem Menschen steckt ein Atheist* (Frankfurt am Main: Knecht, 1981).

4. Comte-Sponville, *Book of Atheist Spirituality*.

5. Viktor E. Frankl and Pinchas Lapide, *Gottsuche und Sinnfrage: Ein Gespräch* (Gütersloh, Germany: Gütersloher Verlagshaus, 2011), 97.

6. See Pfister to Freud, Zürich, October 29, 1918, in *Psychoanalysis and Faith: The Letters of Sigmund Freud and Oskar Pfister*, ed. Heinrich Meng and Ernst L. Freud, trans. Eric Mosbacher (New York: Basic Books, 1963), 63.

7. Comte-Sponville, *Book of Atheist Spirituality*, 22.

8. Comte-Sponville, *Book of Atheist Spirituality*, 22.

9. Comte-Sponville, *Book of Atheist Spirituality*, 22.

10. For more see Halík, *I Want You to Be*.

11. Comte-Sponville, *Book of Atheist Spirituality*.

12. Slavoj Žižek, "Humanism Is Not Enough: Interview with Slavoj Žižek," by Michael Hauser, Prague, November 2007, *International Journal of Žižek Studies* 3, no. 3 (2009), https://zizekstudies.org/index.php/IJZS/article/view/202/202.

13. Luke 17:20–21.

14. Nietzsche mentions that even after the "death of God" we may see God again "when he has shed his moral skin." He called heteronomous morality "moralin," a neologism and allusion to the word "naphthalene." He claimed that he could only believe in a God "who could dance." See Friedrich Nietzsche, *The Anti-Christ* (New York: Tribeca Books, 2010). For more detail, see Halík, *I Want You to Be*.

15. Nietzsche said to Christians: "They would have to sing better songs to make me believe in their Redeemer: his disciples would have to look more redeemed"; Nietzsche, *Thus Spake Zarathustra*, 116.

16. Nietzsche, *Anti-Christ*.

17. See Ernst Bloch, *Atheismus im Christentum: Zur Religion des Exodus und des Reichs* (Frankfurt am Main: Suhrkamp, 1973).

FIFTEEN. The Community of the Way

1. Gertrud von Le Fort, *Hymnen an die Kirche* (Munich: Kösel, 1924).

2. Miguel de Unamuno, *Tragic Sense of Life* (Hamburg: Tradition Classics, 2012).

3. Halík, *Patience with God*, 68–88.

4. 2 Corinthians 4:7.

5. The ancient ecclesiastical dispute as to whether Mary was entitled only to the title *christotokos* (mother or bearer of Christ) or also *theotokos* (Mother of God) was decided in 431 by the Council of Ephesus against Nestorius in favor of the legitimacy of the title *theotokos*.

6. The apostle Paul is clear about Israel's being the chosen people. "For God's gifts and his calling are irrevocable" (Romans 11:29); that statement in particular is the basis for the Second Vatican Council's rejection of the notion that the Church supplants Israel.

7. See Ephesians 2:14–16.

8. Johann Wolfgang von Goethe, *Faust* (Prague: SNKLHU, 1955), 91.

9. The notion of ideology as false consciousness was one of those ideas where Marx was not wrong.

10. Pope Francis, *Fratelli tutti*, para. 160.

11. See Halík, *Stromu zbývá naděje*, 200.

12. Nicholas Lash offers a similar picture of the Church in Lash, *Holiness, Speech and Silence: Reflections on the Question of God* (Aldershot, UK: Ashgate, 2004), 5.

13. A positive example is the work of Christian communities in South Africa after the fall of apartheid and in many other countries where it was necessary to "heal the scars of the past."

14. Rod Dreher, *The Benedict Option* (New York: Sentinel, 2017).

15. Dreher explicitly calls on Christians to "build a Christian way of life that stands as an island of sanctity and stability amid the high tide of liquid modernity" (Dreher, *Benedict Option*, 54). But not even Benedictine monasteries were closed islands in the middle of a hostile world.

Sixteen.   A Community of Listening and Understanding

1. See 1 Corinthians 9:22.

2. See Luke 10:25–29.

3. Franz Kafka, *The Trial* (London: Arcturus, 2019), 192.

4. See Pope Francis, *Evangelii gaudium*, para. 47.

5. Those who claim that Jesus's statements in the Gospels concerning divorce cannot be altered or mitigated in any way, nor exceptions made, should know that the New Testament itself does so, when Matthew's Gospel makes an exception "except in the case of unchastity" (Matthew 5:32), thus correcting the earlier uncompromising statements in the Gospels of Mark and Luke (Mark 10:2–12 and Luke 16:18), which recognize no exception.

6. See Luke 11:42–46.

7. See Pope Francis, *Amoris laetitia*, paras. 300, 303, 312.

8. In the Epistle of James, we read: "So speak and so act as those who are to be judged by the law of liberty. For judgment will be without mercy to anyone who has shown no mercy; mercy triumphs over judgment" (James 2:12–13).

9. Mark 5:25–34.

10. See also Halík, *Patience with God*, 170–72.

11. See Luke 9:49.

12. Continuing incarnation, continuing crucifixion, and continuing resurrection.

13. "Heart speaks to heart" (*Cor ad cor loquitur*) was Cardinal Newman's heraldic motto.

14. This is one of the main messages of Pope Francis's encyclical *Fratelli tutti*.

15. Verbatim: "The pluralism and the diversity of religions, colour, sex, race and language are willed by God in His wisdom, through which He created human beings." Pope Francis and the Grand Imam of Al-Azhar, Ahmed el-Tayeb, *Document on Human Fraternity for World Peace and Living Together* (Abu Dhabi, February 4, 2019), https://www.vaticannews.va/en/pope/news/2019-02/pope-francis-uae-declaration-with-al-azhar-grand-imam.html.

16. It is the Surah of the Spread Table (Surah 5:48); where the owners of the scriptures (Jews and Christians) are told: "If God had pleased He could surely have made you one people (professing one faith). But He wished to try and test you by that which He gave you. So try to excel in good deeds. To Him will you all return in the end, when He will tell you of what you were at variance."

17. One religion in a diversity of rites, see Nicholas of Cusa, *De pace fidei* I, para. 6, https://urts99.uni-trier.de/cusanus/content/werke.php.

18. One such attempt was a dialogue about the Gospels with the Tibetan Dalai Lama. See Bstan-'dzin-rgya-mtsho (current Dalai Lama), *The Good Heart: A Buddhist Perspective on the Teachings of Jesus* (Somerville, MA: Wisdom Publications, 2016).

19. It is worth recalling that the word "intelligence" is related *to inter-legere*: to read between the lines.

20. These were Ignatius's designations for the tasks of the four weeks of his Spiritual Exercises: *deformata reformare*, to reform (to correct) what is deformed, degenerate; *reformata conformare*, to conform what has been corrected (to conform to the life and actions of Christ); *conformata confirmare*, to reinforce what has been conformed by meditating on the Passion of Christ; and finally *confirmata transformare*, to transform what has been conformed by meditating on the Resurrection of Jesus and on the love of God "present in all things."

TOMÁŠ HALÍK is a Czech Roman Catholic priest, philosopher, theologian, and scholar. He is a professor of sociology at Charles University in Prague, pastor of the Academic Parish of St. Salvator Church in Prague, president of the Czech Christian Academy, and a winner of the Templeton Prize. He is the author of many books, including *Touch the Wounds, From the Underground Church to Freedom*, and *I Want You to Be*. His books have been published in twenty languages and received many awards, including the Foreword Reviews' INDIES Book of the Year Awards in Philosophy and in Religion.

GERALD TURNER has translated numerous authors from Czechoslovakia, including Václav Havel, Ivan Klíma, and Ludvík Vaculík, among others. He received the US PEN Translation Award in 2004.